Natural Language Proc
and Computational Linguistics

A practical guide to text analysis with Python, Gensim,
spaCy, and Keras

Bhargav Srinivasa-Desikan

BIRMINGHAM - MUMBAI

Natural Language Processing and Computational Linguistics

Acquisition Editors: Frank Pohlmann, Suresh Jain
Project Editor: Suzanne Coutinho
Content Development Editor: Alex Sorentinho
Technical Editor: Gaurav Gavas
Proofreader: Tom Jacob
Indexer: Tejal Daruwale Soni
Graphics: Tom Scaria
Production Coordinator: Sandip Tadge

First published: June 2018

Production reference: 1280618

Published by Packt Publishing Ltd.
Livery Place
35 Livery Street
Birmingham
B3 2PB, UK.

ISBN 978-1-78883-853-5

www.packtpub.com

`mapt.io`

Mapt is an online digital library that gives you full access to over 5,000 books and videos, as well as industry leading tools to help you plan your personal development and advance your career. For more information, please visit our website.

Why subscribe?

- Spend less time learning and more time coding with practical eBooks and Videos from over 4,000 industry professionals

- Improve your learning with Skill Plans built especially for you

- Get a free eBook or video every month

- Mapt is fully searchable

- Copy and paste, print, and bookmark content

PacktPub.com

Did you know that Packt offers eBook versions of every book published, with PDF and ePub files available? You can upgrade to the eBook version at `www.PacktPub.com` and as a print book customer, you are entitled to a discount on the eBook copy. Get in touch with us at `service@packtpub.com` for more details.

At `www.PacktPub.com`, you can also read a collection of free technical articles, sign up for a range of free newsletters, and receive exclusive discounts and offers on Packt books and eBooks.

Contributors

About the author

Bhargav Srinivasa-Desikan is a research engineer working for INRIA in Lille, France. He is part of the MODAL (Models of Data Analysis and Learning) team, and he works on metric learning, predictor aggregation, and data visualization. He is a regular contributor to the Python open source community, and he completed Google Summer of Code in 2016 with Gensim where he implemented Dynamic Topic Models. Bhargav is a regular speaker at PyCons and PyDatas across Europe and Asia, and conducts tutorials on text analysis using Python. He is the maintainer of the Python machine learning package pycobra, and has published in the Journal of Machine Learning Research.

I would like to thank the Python community for all their help, and for building such incredible packages for text analysis. I would also like to thank Lev Konstantinovskiy for introducing me to the world of open source scientific computing and Dr. Benjamin Guedj for always helping me with writing technical articles and material. I would also like to thank my parents, brother and friends for their constant support throughout the process of writing the book.

About the reviewers

Brian Sacash is a data scientist and Python developer in the Washington, DC area. He helps various organizations discover the best ways to extract value from data. His interests are in the areas of Natural Language Processing, Machine Learning, Big Data, and Statistical Methods. Brian holds a Master of Science in Quantitative Analysis from the University of Cincinnati and a Bachelor of Science in Physics from the Ohio Northern University.

Reddy Anil Kumar is a data scientist working at Imaginea technologies Inc. He has over 4 years of experience in the field of data science which includes 2 years of freelance experience. He is experienced in implementing Artificial Intelligence solutions in various domains using Machine Learning / Deep Learning, Natural Language Processing, and Big Data Analytics. In his free time, he loves to participate in data science competitions and he is also a Kaggle expert.

Packt is searching for authors like you

If you're interested in becoming an author for Packt, please visit `authors.packtpub.com` and apply today. We have worked with thousands of developers and tech professionals, just like you, to help them share their insight with the global tech community. You can make a general application, apply for a specific hot topic that we are recruiting an author for, or submit your own idea.

Table of Contents

Preface

Modern text analysis is now very accessible using Python and open source tools, so discover how you can now perform modern text analysis in this era of textual data.

This book shows you how to use natural language processing, and computational linguistics algorithms, to make inferences and gain insights about data you have. These algorithms are based on statistical machine learning and artificial intelligence techniques. The tools to work with these algorithms are available to you right now - with Python, and tools like Gensim and spaCy.

You'll start by learning about data cleaning, and then how to perform computational linguistics from first concepts. You're then ready to explore the more sophisticated areas of statistical NLP and deep learning using Python, using realistic language and text samples. You'll learn to tag, parse, and model text using the best tools. You'll gain hands-on knowledge of the best frameworks to use, and you'll know when to choose a tool like Gensim for topic models, and when to work with Keras for deep learning.

This book balances theory and practical hands-on examples, so you can learn about and conduct your own natural language processing projects and computational linguistics. You'll discover the rich ecosystem of Python tools you have available to conduct NLP - and enter the interesting world of modern text analysis.

Who this book is for

Fluency in Python is assumed, but the book attempts to be accessible to even Python beginners. Basic statistics is helpful. Given that this book introduces Natural Language Processing from first principles, it helps, although it is not a requirement, to be familiar with basic linguistics.

What this book covers

Chapter 1, *What is Text Analysis?* There is no time like now to do text analysis - we have an abundance of easily available data, powerful and free open source tools to conduct our analysis and research on Machine Learning, Computational Linguistics, and computing with text is progressing at a pace we have not seen before. In this chapter, we will go into details about what exactly text analysis is, and the motivations for studying and understanding text analysis.

Chapter 2, *Python Tips for Text Analysis.* We mentioned in *Chapter 1, What is Text Analysis*, that we will be using Python throughout the book because it is an easy-to-use and powerful language. In this chapter, we will substantiate these claims, while also providing a *revision* course in basic Python for text analysis. Why is this important? While we expect readers of the book to have a background in Python and high-school math, it is still possible that it's been a while since you've written Python code - and even if you have, Python code you write during text analysis and string manipulation is quite different from, say, building a website using the web framework Django.

Chapter 3, *spaCy's Language Models.* While we introduced text analysis in the previous chapter, we did not discuss any of the technical details behind building a text analysis pipeline. In this chapter, we will introduce you to spaCy's Language Model - these will serve as the first step in text analysis, and are the first building block in our pipelines. Also, we will introduce the reader to spaCy and how we can use spaCy to help us in our text analysis tasks, as well as talk about some of it's more powerful functionalities, such as POS-tagging and NER-tagging. We will finish up with an example of how we can preprocess data quickly and efficiently using spaCy.

Chapter 4, *Gensim – Vectorizing Text and Transformations and n-grams.* While we have worked with raw textual data so far, any Machine Learning or information retrieval related algorithm will not accept data like this - which is why we use mathematical constructs called Vectors to help let the algorithms make sense of the text. We will introduce gensim as the tool to conduct this transformation, as well as scikit-learn, which will be used before we plug in the text to any sort of further analysis. A huge part of preprocessing is carried on over when we start our vectorization - bi-grams, tri-grams, and n-grams, as well using term frequencies to get rid of some words which we deem to not be useful.

Chapter 5, *POS-Tagging and Its Applications.* Chapters 1 and 2 introduced text analysis and Python, and chapters 3 and 4 helped us set-up our code for more advanced text analysis. This chapter discusses the first of such advanced techniques - part of speech tagging, popularly called POS-tagging. We will study what parts of speech exist, how to identify them in our documents, and what possible uses these POS-tags have.

Chapter 6, *NER-Tagging and Its Applications.* In the previous chapter, we saw how we can use spaCy's language pipeline - POS-tagging is a very powerful tool, and we will now explore itsanother interesting usage, NER-tagging. We will discuss what exactly this is from a both linguistic and text analysis point of view, as well as detailing examples of its usage, and how to train our own NER-tagger with spaCy.

Chapter 7, *Dependency Parsing*. We saw in Chapters 5 and 6 how spaCy's language pipeline performs a variety of complex Computational Linguistics algorithms, such as POS-tagging and NER-tagging. This isn't all spaCy packs though, and in this chapter we will explore the power of dependency parsing and how it can be used in a variety of contexts and applications. We will have a look at the theory of dependency parsing before moving on to using it with spaCy, as well as training our own dependency parsers.

Chapter 8, *Topic Models*. Until now, we dealt with Computational Linguistics algorithms and spaCy, and understood how to use these computational linguistic algorithms to annotate our data, as well as understand sentence structure. While these algorithms helped us understand the finer details of our text, we still didn't get a big picture of our data - what kind of words appear more often than others in our corpus? Can we group our data or find underlying themes? We will be attempting to answer these questions and more in this chapter.

Chapter 9, *Advanced Topic Modeling*. We saw in the previous chapter the power of topic modeling, and how intuitive a way it can be to understand our data, as well as explore it. In this chapter, we will further explore the utility of these topic models, and also on how to create more useful topic models which better encapsulate the topics that may be present in a corpus. Since topic modeling is a way to understand the documents of a corpus, it also means that we can analyze documents in ways we have not done before.

Chapter 10, *Clustering and Classifying Text*. In the previous chapter we studied topic models and how they can help us in organizing and better understanding our documents and its sub-structure. We will now move on to our next set of Machine Learning algorithms, and for two particular tasks - clustering and classification. We will learn what is the intuitive reasoning of these two tasks, as well as how to perform these tasks using the popular Python Machine Learning library, scikit-learn.

Chapter 11, *Similarity Queries and Summarization*. Once we have begun to represent text documents in the form of vector representations, it is possible to start finding the similarity or distance between documents - and that is exactly what we will learn about in this chapter. We are now aware of a variety of different vector representations, from standard bag-of-words or TF-IDF to topic model representations of text documents. We will also learn about a very useful feature implemented in gensim and how to use it - summarization and keyword extraction.

Chapter 12, *Word2Vec, Doc2Vec and Gensim*. We previously talked about vectors a lot throughout the book - they are used to understand and represent our textual data in a mathematical form, and the basis of all the Machine Learning methods we use rely on these representations. We will be taking this one step further, and *use* Machine Learning techniques to generate vector representations of words which better encapsulate the meaning of a word. This technique is generally referred to as *word embeddings*, and Word2Vec and Doc2Vec are two popular variations of these.

Chapter 13, *Deep Learning for Text*. Until now, we have explored the usage of Machine Learning for text in a variety of contexts - topic modelling, clustering, classification, text summarisation, and even our POS-taggers and NER-taggers were trained using Machine Learning. In this chapter, we will begin to explore one of the most cutting-edge forms of Machine Learning - Deep Learning. Deep Learning is a form of ML where we use biologically inspired structures to generate algorithms and architectures to perform various tasks on text. Some of these tasks are text generation, classification, and word embeddings. In this chapter, we will discuss some of the underpinnings of Deep Learning as well as how to implement our own Deep Learning models for text.

Chapter 14, *Keras and spaCy for Deep Learning*. In the previous chapter, we introduced Deep Learning techniques for text, and to get a taste of using Neural Networks, we attempted to generate text using an RNN. In this chapter, we will take a closer look at Deep Learning for text, and in particular, how to set up a Keras model which can perform classification, as well as how to incorporate Deep Learning into spaCy pipelines.

Chapter 15, *Sentiment Analysis and ChatBots*. By now, we are equipped with the skills needed to get started on text analysis projects, and to also take a shot at more complicated, meatier projects. Two common text analysis projects which encapsulate a lot of the concepts we have explored throughout the book are sentiment analysis and chatbots. In fact, we've already touched upon all the methods we will be using for these projects, and this chapter will serve as a guide to how one can put up such an application on their own. In this chapter, we will not be providing the code to build a chatbot or sentiment analysis pipeline from the first step to the last, but will rather introduce the reader to a variety of techniques that will help when setting up such a project.

To get the most out of this book

Follow the listed steps and commands to prepare the system environment:

1. Python:

   a. Most, if not all, OS come installed with Python. It is already available on Windows, Ubuntu 14.04 onwards, and macOS

   b. If not, please follow the official wiki documentation: `https://wiki.python.org/moin/BeginnersGuide/Download`

 This is a good time to start migrating all of the code to Python 3.6 (`http://python3statement.org/`). By 2020, a lot of scientific computing packages (such as NumPy) will be dropping support for python 2.

2. spaCy:

   ```
   pip install spacy
   ```

3. Gensim:

   ```
   pip install gensim
   ```

4. Keras:

   ```
   pip install keras
   ```

5. scikit-learn:

   ```
   pip install scikit-learn
   ```

Download the example code files

You can download the example code files for this book from your account at `www.packtpub.com`. If you purchased this book elsewhere, you can visit `www.packtpub.com/support` and register to have the files emailed directly to you.

You can download the code files by following these steps:

1. Log in or register at `www.packtpub.com`.
2. Select the **SUPPORT** tab.
3. Click on **Code Downloads & Errata**.
4. Enter the name of the book in the **Search** box and follow the onscreen instructions.

Once the file is downloaded, please make sure that you unzip or extract the folder using the latest version of:

- WinRAR/7-Zip for Windows
- Zipeg/iZip/UnRarX for Mac
- 7-Zip/PeaZip for Linux

The code bundle for the book is also hosted on GitHub at `https://github.com/PacktPublishing/Natural-Language-Processing-and-Computational-Linguistics`. The code and the PDF version of all Jupyter notebooks is hosted at `https://github.com/PacktPublishing/Natural-Language-Processing-and-Computational-Linguistics/tree/master/notebooks`. In case there's an update to the code, it will be updated on the existing GitHub repository.

We also have other code bundles from our rich catalog of books and videos available at `https://github.com/PacktPublishing/`. Check them out!

Download the color images

We also provide a PDF file that has color images of the screenshots/diagrams used in this book. You can download it here: `https://www.packtpub.com/sites/default/files/downloads/NaturalLanguageProcessingandComputationalLinguistics_ColorImages.pdf`.

Conventions used

There are a number of text conventions used throughout this book.

`CodeInText`: Indicates code words in text, database table names, folder names, filenames, file extensions, pathnames, dummy URLs, user input, and Twitter handles. Here is an example: "Mount the downloaded `WebStorm-10*.dmg` disk image file as another disk in your system."

A block of code is set as follows:

```
print('Build model...')
model = Sequential()
model.add(Embedding(max_features, 128))
model.add(LSTM(128, dropout=0.2, recurrent_dropout=0.2))
model.add(Dense(1, activation='sigmoid'))
```

When we wish to draw your attention to a particular part of a code block, the relevant lines or items are set in bold:

```
print('Loading data...')
(x_train, y_train), (x_test, y_test) =
imdb.load_data(num_words=max_features)
print(len(x_train), 'train sequences')
print(len(x_test), 'test sequences')
```

Any command-line input or output is written as follows:

```
virtualenv env
source env/bin/activate

pip install spacy
```

Bold: Indicates a new term, an important word, or words that you see onscreen. For example, words in menus or dialog boxes appear in the text like this. Here is an example: "Select **System info** from the **Administration** panel."

Warnings or important notes appear like this.

Tips and tricks appear like this.

Get in touch

Feedback from our readers is always welcome.

General feedback: Email feedback@packtpub.com and mention the book title in the subject of your message. If you have questions about any aspect of this book, please email us at questions@packtpub.com.

Errata: Although we have taken every care to ensure the accuracy of our content, mistakes do happen. If you have found a mistake in this book, we would be grateful if you would report this to us. Please visit www.packtpub.com/submit-errata, selecting your book, clicking on the Errata Submission Form link, and entering the details.

Piracy: If you come across any illegal copies of our works in any form on the Internet, we would be grateful if you would provide us with the location address or website name. Please contact us at copyright@packtpub.com with a link to the material.

If you are interested in becoming an author: If there is a topic that you have expertise in and you are interested in either writing or contributing to a book, please visit authors.packtpub.com.

Reviews

Please leave a review. Once you have read and used this book, why not leave a review on the site that you purchased it from? Potential readers can then see and use your unbiased opinion to make purchase decisions, we at Packt can understand what you think about our products, and our authors can see your feedback on their book. Thank you!

For more information about Packt, please visit packtpub.com.

1
What is Text Analysis?

There is no time like now to do text analysis – we have an abundance of easily available data, powerful and free open source tools to conduct our analysis, and research on machine learning, computational linguistics and computing with text is progressing at a pace we have not seen before.

In this chapter, we will go into details about what exactly text analysis is and look at the motivations for studying and understanding text analysis. Following are the topics we will cover in this chapter:

- What is text analysis?
- Where's the data at?
- Garbage in, garbage out
- Why should YOU be interested?
- References

A note about the references: they will appear throughout the PDF version of the book as links, and if it is an academic reference it will link to the PDF of the reference or the journal page. All of these links and references are then displayed as the final section of the chapter, so offline readers can also visit the websites or research papers.

What is text analysis?

If there's one medium of media which we are exposed to every single day, it's text. Whether it's our morning paper or the messages we receive, it's likely you receive your information in the form of text.

Let's put things into a little more perspective – consider the amount of text data handled by companies such as Google (1+ trillion queries per year), Twitter (1.6 billion queries per day), and WhatsApp (30+ billion messages per day). That's an incredible resource, and the sheer ubiquitous nature of the text is enough reason for us to take it seriously. Textual data also has huge business value, and companies can use this data to help profile customers and understand customer trends. This can either be used to offer a more personalized experience for users or as information for targeted marketing. Facebook, for example, uses textual data heavily, and one of the algorithms we will learn later in this book was developed at Facebook's AI research team.

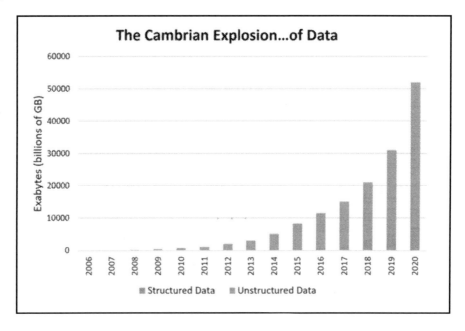

Fig 1.1 Rate of data growth from 2006 – 2018 with predicted rates of data in 2019 and 2020. Source: Patrick Cheeseman, https://www.eetimes.com/author.asp?section_id=36&doc_id=1330462

Text analysis can be understood as the technique of gleaning useful information from text. This can be done through various techniques, and we use **Natural Language Processing (NLP)**, **Computational Linguistics (CL)**, and numerical tools to get this information. These numerical tools are machine learning algorithms or information retrieval algorithms. We'll briefly, informally explain these terms as they will be coming up throughout the book.

Natural language processing (NLP) refers to the use of a computer to process natural language. For example, removing all occurrences of the word *thereby* from a body of text is one such example, albeit a basic example.

Computational linguistics (CL), as the name suggests, is the study of linguistics from a computational perspective. This means using computers and algorithms to perform linguistics tasks such as marking your text as a part of speech (such as noun or verb), instead of performing this task manually.

Machine Learning (ML) is the field of study where we use statistical algorithms to teach machines to perform a particular task. This *learning* occurs with data, and our task is often to predict a new value based on previously observed data.

Information Retrieval (IR) is the task of looking up or retrieving information based on a query by the user. The algorithms that aid in performing this task are called information retrieval algorithms, and we will be encountering them throughout the book.

Text analysis itself has been around for a long time – one of the first definitions of **Business Intelligence (BI)** itself, in an October 1958 IBM Journal article by H. P. Luhn, *A Business Intelligence System* [1], describes a system that will do the following:

> *"...utilize data-processing machines for auto-abstracting and auto-encoding of documents and for creating interest profiles for each of the 'action points' in an organization. Both incoming and internally generated documents are automatically abstracted, characterized by a word pattern, and sent automatically to appropriate action points."*

It's interesting to see talk about documents, instead of numbers – to think that the first ideas of business *intelligence* were understanding text and documents is again a testament to text analysis throughout the ages. But even outside the realm of text analysis for business, using computers to better understand text and language has been around since the beginning of ideas of artificial intelligence. The 1999 review on text analysis by John Hutchins, *Retrospect and prospect in computer-based translation* [2], talks about efforts to do machine translation as early as the 1950s by the United States military, in order to translate Russian scientific journals into English.

Efforts to make an intelligent machine started with text as well – the ELIZA program developed in 1966 at MIT by Joseph Weizenbaum is one example. Even though the program had no real understanding of language, by basic pattern matching it could attempt to hold a conversation. These are just some of the earliest attempts to analyze text – computers (and human beings!) have come a long way since, and we now have incredible tools at our disposal.

Machine translation itself has come a long way, and we can now use our smartphones to effectively translate between languages, and with cutting-edge techniques such as Google's **Neural Machine Translation**, the gap between academia and industry is reducing – allowing us to actually experience the magic of natural language processing first hand.

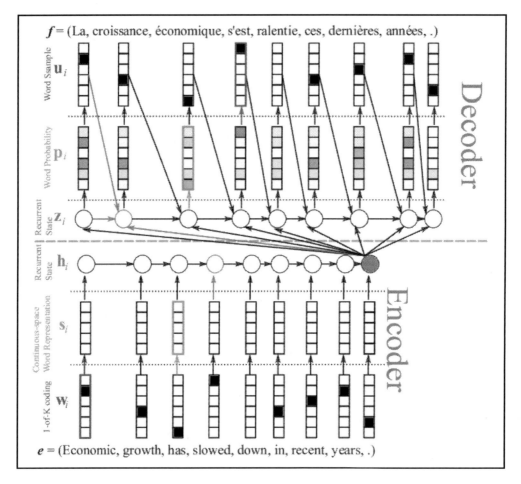

Fig 1.2 An example of a Neural Translation model, working on French to English

Advances in this subject have helped advance the way we approach speech as well – closed captioning in videos, and personal assistants such as Apple's Siri or Amazon's Alexa are greatly benefited by superior text processing. Understanding structure in conversations and extracting information were key problems in early NLP, and the fruits of the research done are being very apparent in the 21st century.

Search engines such as Google or Bing! also stand on the shoulders of the research done in NLP and CL and affect our lives in an unprecedented way. Information retrieval (IR) builds on statistical approaches in text processing and allows us to classify, cluster, and retrieve documents. Methods such as topic modeling can help us identify key topics in large, unstructured bodies of text. Identifying these topics goes beyond searching for keywords, and we use statistical models to further understand the underlying nature of bodies of text. Without the power of computers, we could not perform this kind of large-scale statistical analysis on the text. We will be exploring topic modeling in detail later on in the book.

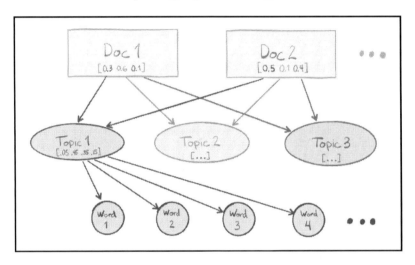

Fig 1.2 Techniques such as topic modeling use probabilistic modeling methods to identify key topics from the text. We will be studying this in detail later in the book

Going one step ahead of just being able to experience the wonders of modern computing on our mobile phones, recent developments in both Python and NLP means that we can now *develop* such systems on our own!

Not only has there been an evolution in the techniques used in NLP and text analysis, it has become very accessible to us – open source packages are becoming state-of-the-art, performing as well as commercial tools. An example of a commercial tool would be Microsoft's **Text Analysis API** (https://azure.microsoft.com/en-us/services/cognitive-services/text-analytics/).

MATLAB is another example of a popular commercial tool used for scientific computing. While historically such commercial tools performed better than free, open source software, an increase in people contributing to open source libraries, as well as funding from industry has helped the open source community immensely. Now, the tables appear to have turned and many software giants use open source packages for their internal systems – such as Google using TensorFlow and Apple using scikit-learn! Tensor flow and scikit-learn are two open source Python machine learning packages.

It can be argued that the sheer number of packages offered by the python ecosystem means it leads the pack when it comes to doing text analysis, and we will focus our efforts here. A very strong and active open source community adds to the appeal.

Throughout the course of the book, we will discuss modern natural language processing and computational linguistics techniques and the best open source tools available to us which we can use to apply these techniques.

Where's the data at?

While it is important to be aware of the techniques and the tools involved in NLP and CL, it is, of course, pointless without any data. Luckily for us, we have access to an abundance of data if we look in the right places. The easiest way to find textual data to work on is to look for a *corpus*.

A text corpus is a large and structured set of texts and is a great way to start off with text analysis. Examples of such corpora that are free are the Open American National Corpus [5] or the British National Corpus [6]. Wikipedia has a useful list of the largest corpuses available in its article on text corpuses [7]. These are not limited to the English language, and there also exist various corpuses in European and Asian languages, and there are constant efforts worldwide to create corpuses for majority of languages. Universities research labs are another valuable source for obtaining corpuses – indeed, one of the most iconic English language corpuses, the **Brown Corpus**, was put together at Brown University.

Different corpuses tend to have varying levels of information present, usually dependent on the primary purpose for that corpora – for example, corpora whose primary function is to aid during translation would have the same sentence present in multiple languages. Another way corpora have extra information is through annotation. Examples of annotation in text usually include **Part-Of-Speech (POS)** tagging or **Named-Entity-Recognition (NER)**. POS-tagging refers to marking each word in a sentence with its part of speech (Noun, verb, adverb, and so on), and a corpus annotated for NER would have all named entities recognized, such as places, people, and times. We'll be further going into details of both POS-tagging and NER later on in the book, in Chapter 5, *POS-Tagging and its Applications* and Chapter 6, *NER-Tagging and its Applications*.

Based on the structure and varying levels of information present in the corpora, it would have a different purpose. Some corpora are also built to evaluate clustering or classification tasks, where rather than annotation being important, the label or class would be. This means that some corpora are designed to aid with machine learning tasks such as cluster or classification by providing text with labels tagged by humans. Clustering refers to the task of grouping similar objects together, and classification is the process of deciding which pre-defined class an identifying what exactly your dataset is going to be used for is a crucial part of text analysis and an important first step.

Apart from downloading datasets or scraping data off the internet, there are still some rich sources for gathering our textual data – in particular, literature. One example of this is the research done at the University of Pennsylvania, where Alejandro Ribeiro, Santiago Segarra, Mark Eisen, and Gabriel Egan discovered possible collaborators of Shakespeare, a literary history problem that stumbled many researchers [14]. They approached the problem by identifying literary styles – an upcoming field of study in computational linguistics called **style analysis**.

The increased use of computational tools to perform research in the humanities has also led to the growth of **Digital Humanities** labs in universities, where traditional research approaches are either aided or overtaken by computer science, and in particular machine learning (and by extension), natural language processing. Speeches of politicians, or proceedings in parliament, for example, are another example of a data source used often in this community. TheyWorkForYou [17] is A UK parliament tracking system, which gets speeches and uploads them and is an example of the many sites available doing this kind of work.

Project Gutenberg is likely the best resource to download books and contains over 50,000 free eBooks and many literary classics. Personal PDFs and eBooks also remain a resource, but again, it is important to know the legal nature of your text before analyzing it. Downloading a pirated copy of, say, Harry Potter off the internet and publishing text analysis results might not be the best idea if you cannot explain where you got the text from! Similarly, text analysis on private text messages might not only annoy your friends but also could be infringing on privacy laws.

Dataset Name ⬍	Brief description ⬍	Preprocessing ⬍	Instances ⬍	Format ⬍	Default Task ⬍	Created (updated) ⬍	Reference ⬍	Creator ⬍
Amazon reviews	US product reviews from Amazon.com.	None.	~ 82M	Text	Classification, sentiment analysis	2015	[131]	McAuley et al.
OpinRank Review Dataset	Reviews of cars and hotels from Edmunds.com and TripAdvisor respectively.	None.	42,230 / ~259,000 respectively	Text	Sentiment analysis, clustering	2011	[132][133]	K. Ganesan et al.
MovieLens	22,000,000 ratings and 580,000 tags applied to 33,000 movies by 240,000 users.	None.	~ 22M	Text	Regression, clustering, classification	2016	[134]	GroupLens Research
Yahoo! Music User Ratings of Musical Artists	Over 10M ratings of artists by Yahoo users.	None described.	~ 10M	Text	Clustering, regression	2004	[135][136]	Yahoo!
Car Evaluation Data Set	Car properties and their overall acceptability.	Six categorical features given.	1728	Text	Classification	1997	[137][138]	M. Bohanec
YouTube Comedy Slam Preference Dataset	User vote data for pairs of videos shown on YouTube. Users voted on funnier videos.	Video metadata given.	1,138,562	Text	Classification	2012	[139][140]	Google
Skytrax User Reviews Dataset	User reviews of airlines, airports, seats, and lounges from Skytrax.	Ratings are fine-grain and include many aspects of airport experience.	41396	Text	Classification, regression	2015	[141]	Q. Nguyen
Teaching Assistant Evaluation Dataset	Teaching assistant reviews.	Features of each instance such as class, class size, and instructor are given.	151	Text	Classification	1997	[142][143]	W. Loh et al.

Fig 1.3 An example of a text dataset list – here, it is of reviews datasets found on

So where else apart from downloading a structured data-set straight off the internet, do we get our textual data? Well, the internet, of course. Even if it isn't labelled, the sheer amount of text on the internet means that we can access large parts of it – the [7] is one such example, and the media dump of all the content on Wikipedia, after unzipping, is about 58 GB (as of April 2018) – more than enough text to play around with. The popular news aggregation website `reddit.com` [9] allows for easy web-scraping and is another great resource for text analysis.

Python again remains a great choice to use for any such web-scraping, and libraries such as `BeautifulSoup` [10], `urllib` [11] and `scrapy` [12] are designed particularly for this. It is important to remain careful about the legal side of things here, and make sure to check the terms and conditions of the website where you are scraping the data from – a number of websites will not allow you to use the information on the website for commercial purposes.

Twitter is another website that is fast becoming a very important part of text analysis – you even have academia taking this resource very seriously (*What is Twitter, a social network or a news media?* [13] has over 5000 citations!), with multiple papers being written on text analysis of tweets, and even full-fledged tools [15] to do sentiment analysis have been built! The Twitter-streaming API allows us to easily mine for textual data from Twitter as well, and the Python interface [16] is straightforward. Most world leaders are users of Twitter, as well as celebrities and major news corporations – there is a lot of interesting insights Twitter can offer us.

Twitter and tweets [edit]

Dataset Name ⬦	Brief description ⬦	Preprocessing ⬦	Instances ⬦	Format ⬦	Default Task ⬦	Created (updated) ⬦	Reference ⬦	Creator ⬦
Sentiment140	Tweet data from 2009 including original text, time stamp, user and sentiment.	Classified using distant supervision from presence of emoticon in tweet.	1,578,627	Tweets, comma, separated values	Sentiment analysis	2009	[161][162]	A. Go et al.
ASU Twitter Dataset	Twitter network data, not actual tweets. Shows connections between a large number of users.	None.	11,316,811 users, 85,331,846 connections	Text	Clustering, graph analysis	2009	[163][164]	R. Zafarani et al.
SNAP Social Circles: Twitter Database	Large twitter network data.	Node features, circles, and ego networks.	1,768,149	Text	Clustering, graph analysis	2012	[165][166]	J. McAuley et al.
Twitter Dataset for Arabic Sentiment Analysis	Arabic tweets.	Samples hand-labeled as positive or negative.	2000	Text	Classification	2014	[167][168]	N. Abdulla
Buzz in Social Media Dataset	Data from Twitter and Tom's Hardware. This dataset focuses on specific buzz topics being discussed on those sites.	Data is windowed so that the user can attempt to predict the events leading up to social media buzz.	140,000	Text	Regression, Classification	2013	[169][170]	F. Kawala et al.
Paraphrase and Semantic Similarity in Twitter (PIT)	This dataset focuses on whether tweets have (almost) same meaning/information or not. Manually labeled.	tokenization, part-of-speech and named entity tagging	18,762	Text	Regression, Classification	2015	[171][172]	Xu et al.

Fig 1.4 An example of the rich text resource Twitter has become, with multiple structured datasets available [7]. These datasets, all mined from Twitter, have particular tasks, which can be used for and fall under the category of labeled datasets which we discussed before.

Other examples of textual information you can get off the internet include research articles, medical reports, restaurant reviews (the Yelp! dataset comes to mind), and other social media websites. Sentiment analysis is usually the prime objective in these cases. As the name suggests, sentiment analysis refers to the task of identifying sentiment in text. These sentiments can be basic, such as positive or negative sentiment, but we could have more complex sentiment analysis tasks where we analyze whether a sentence contains happy, sad, or angry sentiments.

It's clear that if we look hard enough, it's more than easy to find data to play around with. But let's take a small step back from downloading data off the internet – where else can we try and find information?

Right in our hands, as it may seem – we send and receive text messages and emails every day, and we can use this text for text analysis. Most text messaging applications have interfaces to download chats. WhatsApp, for example, will mail the data to you [18], with both media and text. Most mail clients have the same option, and the advantage in both these cases is that this kind of data is often well organized, allowing for easy cleaning and pre-processing before we dive into the data.

One aspect we've ignored so far whilst talking about data is the noise which is often in the text – in tweets, for example, short forms and emoticons which are often used, and in some cases, we have multi-lingual data where a simple analysis might fail. This brings us to arguably the most important aspect of text analysis – pre-processing.

Garbage in, garbage out

Garbage in, garbage out (or **GIGO**) is an adage of computer science which is even more important when dealing with machine learning and possibly even more so when dealing with textual data. Garbage in, garbage out means that if we have poorly formatted data, it is likely we will have poor results.

Fig 1.5 XKCD hits the hammer on the nail once again (https://xkcd.com/1838/)

While more data usually leads to a better prediction, it isn't always the same case with text analysis, where more data can result in nonsense results or results which we don't always want. An intuitive example: the part of speech, articles, such as the words *a*, or *the* tend to appear a lot in text, but not adding any information to the text, and is usually limited to grammar or structure.

Words such as these which don't provide useful information are called **stop words**, and these words are often removed from the text before applying text analysis techniques on them. Similarly, sometimes we remove words with very high frequency in the body of text, and words which only appear once or twice – it is highly likely these words will not be useful to our analysis. That being said, this depends heavily on the kind of task being performed - if, for example, we would want to replicate human writing styles, stop words are important because humans many such words when writing. An example of how stop words can also include useful information is in this article, *Pastiche detection based on stopword rankings. Exposing impersonators of a Romanian writer* [20], is a study identified a certain author using frequency of stop words.

Let's consider another example where we might be dealing with *useless* data – if searching for influential words or topics in the text, would it make sense to have both the words *reading* and *read* in the results? Here, shortening the word *reading* to *read* would not lead to any loss of information. But on a similar note, it would make sense to have the words *information* and *inform* exist separately in the same body of text, because they could mean different things based on the context. We would then need techniques to shorten words appropriately. Lemmatizing and stemming are two methods we use to tackle this problem and remain two of the core concepts in natural language processing. We will be exploring these two techniques in more detail in `Chapter 3`, *spaCy's Language models*.

Even after basic text-processing, our data is still a collection of words. Since machines do not inherently understand the concepts tied to words, we can instead use numbers that represent individual words. The next important step in text analysis is converting words into numbers, whether it is **bag-of-words (BOW)**, or **term frequency-inverse document frequency (TF-IDF)**, which are different ways to count the number of words in each document or sentence. There are also more advanced techniques to represent words such as Word2Vec and GloVe.

We will go into these details and techniques in more detail in the chapter on pre-processing techniques – it is especially important to understand the motivation behind these techniques, and that a computer's output is only as good as the input you feed it.

Why should you do text analysis?

We've talked about what text analysis is, where we can find the data, and some of the things to keep in mind before diving into text analysis. But after all, what motivation do you, the reader, have to actually go about doing text analysis?

For starters, it's the sheer abundance of easily available data that we can use. In the big data age, there really is no excuse to not have a look at what all our data really means. In fact, apart from the massive data sets, we can download off the internet, we also have access to *small data* – text messages, emails, a collection of poems are such examples. You could even do a meta-analysis and run an analysis on this very book! Textual data is even easier to get a hold-off, but far more importantly - it's easy to interpret and understand the results of the analysis. Numbers might not always make sense and are not always appealing to look at - but words are easier for us human beings to appreciate.

Text analysis remains exciting also because we can use data which directly involves the user- our own text conversations, our favorite childhood book, or tweets by our favorite celebrity. The personal nature of text data always adds an extra bit of motivation, and it also likely means we are aware of the nature of the data, and what *kind* of results to expect.

NLP techniques can also help us construct tools that can assist personal businesses or enterprises – chatbots, for example, are becoming increasingly common in major websites, and with the right approach, it is possible to have a personal chat-bot. This is largely due to a sub-field of machine learning, called **Deep Learning**, where we use algorithms and structures that are inspired by the structure of the human brain. These algorithms and structures are also referred to as neural networks. Advances in deep learning have introduced to powerful neural networks such as **Recurrent Neural Networks** (**RNN**s) and **Convolutional Neural Networks** (**CNN**s). Now, even with minimal knowledge of the mathematical functioning of these algorithms, high-level APIs are allowing us to use these tools. Integrating this into our daily life is no longer reserved for computer science researchers or full-time engineers – with the right collection of data and open source packages, this is well within our capabilities.

Open source packages have become industry standard – Google has released and maintains **TensorFlow** [21], and packages such as **scikit-learn** [22] are used by Apple and Spotify, and **spaCy** [23], which we will extensively discuss throughout this book – is used by Quora, a popular question-answer website.

We are no longer limited by either data or the tools – the only two things we would need to do text analysis.

The programming language python will be our friend throughout the book, and all the tools we will use will all be free open-source software. While we move towards open science, we also move towards open source code, and this will remain a key philosophy throughout the book. In the world of research, open source code means academic results are reproducible and available to all those interested. Python remains an easy-to-use and powerful language and serves as a great way to enter the world of natural language processing.

One could argue that the last thing needed was the knowledge of how to apply these tools and to wrangle with the data – but that is precisely the purpose of the book and, hoping to let the reader build their own natural language processing pipelines and models at the end of the journey.

Summary

We've had a look at the incredible power of text analysis, and the kind of things we can do with it – as well as the kind of tools we would be using to take advantage of this. Data has become increasingly easy for us to access, and with the growth of social media, we have continuous access to both new data, as well as standardized annotated datasets.

This book will aim at walking the reader through the tools and knowledge required to conduct textual analysis on their own personal data or own standardized datasets. We will discuss methods to access and clean data to make it ready for pre-processing, as well as how to explore and organize our textual data. Classification and clustering are two other commonly conducted text processing tasks, and we will figure out how to perform this as well, before finishing up with how to use deep learning for text.

In the next chapter, we will introduce how and why Python is the right choice for our purposes, as well as discuss some python tricks and tips to help us with text analysis.

References

[1] A business intelligence system – H. P. Lunn, October 1958
(https://dl.acm.org/citation.cfm?id=1662381)

[2] Retrospect and prospect in computer-based translation – John Hutchins, September 1999
(http://www.mt-archive.info/90/MTS-1999-Hutchins.pdf)

[3] Introduction to Neural Machine Translation with GPUs:
https://devblogs.nvidia.com/parallelforall/introduction-neural-machine-translation-gpus-part-2/

[4] Text Mining :
https://en.wikipedia.org/wiki/Text_mining

[5] Open American National Corpus:
http://www.anc.org

[6] British National Corpus:
http://www.natcorp.ox.ac.uk

[7] List of Text Corpora:
https://en.wikipedia.org/wiki/List_of_text_corpora

[8] Wikipedia Dataset:

https://en.wikipedia.org/wiki/Wikipedia:Database_download

[9] Reddit, news aggregation website:
https://www.reddit.com

[10] Beautiful Soup:
https://www.crummy.com/software/BeautifulSoup/bs4/doc/

[11] UrlLib:
https://docs.python.org/2/library/urllib.html

[12] Scrapy:
https://scrapy.org

[13] What is Twitter, a social network or a news media?:
https://dl.acm.org/citation.cfm?id=1772751

[14] Shakespeare and his co-authors:
https://www.upenn.edu/spotlights/shakespeare-and-his-co-authors-told-penn-engineers

[15] Tweet Sentiment Visualization:
https://www.csc2.ncsu.edu/faculty/healey/tweet_viz/tweet_app/

[16] Tweepy, twitter API:
http://www.tweepy.org

[17] TheyWorkForYou:
https://www.theyworkforyou.com

[18] Mailing WhatsApp chat history:
https://faq.whatsapp.com/en/android/23756533/

[19] Project Gutenburg:
https://www.gutenberg.org

[20] Pastiche detection based on stopword rankings. Exposing impersonators of a Romanian writer:
http://www.aclweb.org/anthology/W12-0411

[21] TensorFlow:
https://www.tensorflow.org

[22] Scikit-learn:
http://scikit-learn.org/stable/

[23] spaCy: https://spacy.io

2
Python Tips for Text Analysis

We mentioned in Chapter 1, *What is Text Analysis*, that we will be using Python throughout the book because it is an easy-to-use and powerful language. In this chapter, we will substantiate these claims, while also providing a *revision* course in basic Python for text analysis.

Why is this important? While we expect readers of the book to have a background in Python and high-school level math, it is still possible that it's been a while since you've written Python code – and even if you have, the Python code you write during text analysis and string manipulation is quite different from, say, building a website using the web framework Django. Following are the topics we will cover in this chapter:

- Why Python?
- Text manipulation in Python

Why Python?

In Python, we represent text in the form of string [1], which are objects of the str [2] class. They are an immutable sequence of Unicode code points or characters. It is important to make a careful distinction here, though; in Python 3, all strings are by default Unicode, but in Python 2, the str class is limited to ASCII code, and there is a Unicode class to deal with Unicodes.

Unicode is merely an encoding language or a way we handle text. For example, the Unicode value for the letter Z is U+005A. There are many encoding types, and historically in Python, developers were expected to deal with different encodings on their own, with all the low-level action happening in bytes. In fact, the shift in the way Python handles Unicode has led to a lot of discussions [3], criticism [4], and praise [5] within the community. It also remains an important point of contention when we are porting code from Python 2 and Python 3.

We said earlier on that the low-level action was going on in bytes - what does this mean? Bytes are numbers, and these numbers are used to represent different characters or symbols. This is what Unicode or ASCII is - different ways to represent characters. In Python 2, strings are stored as bytes, and in Python 3 by default, it is stored as a Unicode code point.

We will not be going deep into the technicalities of how text is encoded and the problems we encounter when dealing with these encodings but can give the following advice in general when dealing with text and Python - use Python 3 and use Unicode! The reason is mainly that we want to stop using Python 2; it is going to be phased out [6] by the scientific computing community, and there makes no sense in still using Python 2 applications and code. Since Python 3 supports Unicode as well, we will be supporting the use of Unicode for all text as well. This would mean remembering to include *u* before our string starts, which ensures that it is a Unicode string.

While most of the text analysis that we will be doing throughout this book will not feature extensive *string* manipulation, it is still something we should be comfortable doing, and often we will have *troublesome* words in our dataset, where we would need to clean things up before starting any kind of text analysis. It may also be important to make our final *pretty*, and for these kind of tasks, it is worth knowing how to be able to manipulate strings.

The other useful Python knowledge that will help us in text analysis is basic data structures and how to use them - lists remain one of the most used data structures during text analysis and knowing how a dictionary works is also important to us.

The purpose of this chapter is to illustrate some of the functions we can perform with strings, and how we use strings in lists and dictionaries.

But we still haven't explained *why* we decided Python as the language of our choice - there are a number of text analysis packages in Java as well, and Perl is another programming language with a reputation for being good with text. But what sets Python apart is the community and open source libraries we have access to.

You would have had a taste of this in the previous chapter as well - we talked about Google using TensorFlow and Apple using SciKit-learn, for example. The open source code is reaching the same standards and efficiency as industry code - one of the libraries we will focus on throughout this book, spaCy, is an example of this. Collecting data is also largely done with Python, using libraries such as tweepy (Twitter), urllib (accessing web pages), and beautiful soup (extracting HTML from web pages). More people using a certain ecosystem means it will grow (the Stack Overflow blog post does a good write up regarding this [6]), and this means that both researchers and industry are increasingly using it, which means it is a good time to jump on the bandwagon!

Apart from the external support Python receives from the wide variety of libraries (and in particular, NLP libraries), there are other reasons why Python is an attractive language to use. One of these is Python's predominant use as a scripting language. A scripting language is one where the ability to run scripts is supported; programs that are written for a run-time environment that usually automate tasks. For example, if you write up a few lines of code to quickly reply to Facebook birthday wishes, and this is done every year - it is an example of a script. There is no hard and fast rule to what you call a scripting language, but its rather a way we colloquially discuss programming languages.

Python is a very useful scripting language because of how quickly we can code up a script to manipulate text files - it is easily readable, fast enough for file sizes that are not massive, and is an interpreted language [7], meaning we don't need to compile our code before running it. It is dynamically typed [8], meaning we don't need to define data types while writing code.

But more than the technical reasons of why Python is superior, we are more interested in Python because of its ease-of-use. It is flexible, readable, and with a high level of abstraction, allowing us to be more productive. We can focus more on the *problem,* rather than on programming technicalities and code errors. This is not to suggest we won't have code errors when coding in Python; just that they tend to be more solvable and provide more information than just, for example - SEGMENTATION FAULT.

We will now illustrate basic Python commands for string manipulation and text analysis. For users who are already familiar with the basics of Python and text, you are welcome to not run all the code in this chapter, but a quick glance through the code will serve as a useful reminder!

Text manipulation in Python

We mentioned earlier in the chapter that the way we represent text in Python is through strings. So how do we specify that an object is a string?

```
word = "Bonjour World!"
```

Now the `word` variable contains the text, `Bonjour World!`. Note how we used double quotes around the text that we intend to use - while single quotes also work; if we also wish to use a single quote *in* our string, we would need to use double quotes. Printing our word is straightforward, where all we need to do is use the print function. Remember to use parentheses if we are coding in Python 3!

```
print(word)
Bonjour World!
```

We don't have to use variables to be able to print string though - we can also just do:

```
print("Bonjour World!")
Bonjour World!
```

Be careful not to enclose your variable in quotations though! Consider this example:

```
print("word")
word
```

This will just print the word out.

We mentioned before in the chapter that a string is a sequence of characters; how do we then access the first character of a string?

```
print(word[0])
B
```

We can similarly access subsequent indices. What about finding the length of a string?

```
print(len(word))
14
```

Let us now quickly run through more String functions, such as finding characters, counting characters, and changing the case of letters in a word.

```
word.count("o")
3
```

There are three o letter, so the output is 3.

```
word.find("j")
3
```

The index of the j character in the string is the three.

```
word.index("World")
8
```

This helps us find where the World string starts.

```
word.upper()
'BONJOUR WORLD!'
```

The upper method converts all characters to uppercase.

```
word.lower()
'bonjour world!'
```

The lower method converts all characters to lowercase.

```
word.title()
'Bonjour World!'
```

The title method capitalizes the first letter of every word.

```
word.capitalize()
'Bonjour world!
```

The capitalize method only capitalizes the first letter.

```
word.swapcase()
'bONJOUR wORLD!'
```

The swapcase method, as the name suggests, changes the cases of each letter.

Pythonic strings can also be manipulated by arithmetic operators:

Adding the Fromage word (which means cheese, in French) to our word string can be done by simply adding Fromage to the end of it!

```
print(word + " Fromage!")
'Bonjour World! Fromage!'
```

Similarly, we can also multiply words the same way:

```
print("hello " * 5)
hello hello hello hello hello
```

String functions can also help us easily reverse a string or add an extra whitespace between every character.

```
print( ''.join(reversed(word)))
!dlroW ruojnoB
```

Reversed returns a generator - which we then join using the `join` function. We can similarly use `join` to add an extra whitespace.

```
print( " ".join(word))
B o n j o u r   W o r l d !
```

We may also often find the need to check different properties of our strings. This can be done with the following methods:

```
word.isalnum()
```

Checks if all char are alphanumeric.

```
word.isalpha()
```

Checks if all char in the string are alphabetic.

```
word.isdigit()
```

Checks if string contains digits.

```
word.istitle()
```

Checks if string contains title words.

```
word.isupper()
```

Checks if the string is in upper case.

```
word.islower()
```

Checks if string is in lower case.

```
word.isspace()
```

Checks if string contains spaces.

```
word.endswith('f')
```

Checks if string ends with a f character.

```
word.startswith('H')
```

Checks if string starts with H.

It is also possible to replace characters in strings, as well as slice them up; in fact, slicing strings for sub-strings is a very useful and fundamental part of playing with strings.

```
word.replace("World", "Pizza")
'Bonjour Pizza!'
```

The straightforward replace function makes our world into pizza!

Slicing is the process of getting a portion of your string. The syntax is as follows:

```
New_string = old_string[startloc:endloc]
```

If, for example, we only want the second part of our sentence and we are aware it is from the 8th to the 16th character, we can try this:

```
word[8:16]
'World!'
```

And if we only wish for the first word, we can use this:

```
word[:7]
'Bonjour'
```

Leaving the part before the semi-colon blank means the index starts from zero.

Summary

With the knowledge of the functions and strategies we have discussed, our text analysis can be aided; it is often when we are doing large scale text analysis that a small error can lead to completely nonsense results (remember garbage in, garbage out from `Chapter 1`, *What is Text Analysis?*).

We finish this *mini-chapter* with a few useful links on basic text manipulation:

1. **Printing and Manipulating Text** [9]: Basic manipulation and printing of text, recommended if interested in how to display text in different ways.
2. **Manipulating Strings** [10]: Basic String functions as well as exercises, useful for the further practice of string manipulation.
3. **Manipulating Strings in Python** [11]: Similar to the two-preceding links includes a section on escape sequences as well.
4. **Text Processing in Python (book)** [12]: Unlike the other links, this is a whole book. It covers the very fundamentals of text and string manipulation in Python and includes useful material on some uncovered topics such as regular expressions.
5. **An Introduction to Text Analysis in Python** [13]: This provides great further reading if you want to get a more general view of the relationship between Python and text analysis. Recommended if you're a beginner and you need more foundation to this chapter.

Understanding how strings behave in Python and being able to quickly perform basic operations on them will come in handy multiple times throughout the book - after all, no house can be built to last long without a strong foundation!

References

[1] Strings:
https://docs.Python.org/3/library/string.html

[2] str:
https://docs.Python.org/3.4/library/stdtypes.html#str

[3] Strings, Bytes, and Unicode in Python 2 and 3:
https://timothybramlett.com/Strings_Bytes_and_Unicode_in_Python_2_and_3.html

[4] More About Unicode in Python 2 and 3:
http://lucumr.pocoo.org/2014/1/5/unicode-in-2-and-3/

[5] Python 3 and ASCII Compatible Binary Protocols:
https://Python-notes.curiousefficiency.org/en/latest/Python3/binary_protocols.html

[6] The Incredible Growth of Python:
https://stackoverflow.blog/2017/09/06/incredible-growth-Python/

[7] Interpreted Language:
https://en.wikipedia.org/wiki/Interpreted_language

[8] Dynamically Typed:
https://en.wikipedia.org/wiki/Type_system#Combining_static_and_dynamic_type_checking

[9] Printing and Manipulating Text:
https://Pythonforbiologists.com/printing-and-manipulating-text/

[10] Manipulating Strings:
https://automatetheboringstuff.com/chapter6/

[11] Manipulating Strings in Python:
https://programminghistorian.org/lessons/manipulating-strings-in-Python

[12] Text Processing in Python:
http://gnosis.cx/TPiP/

[13] An Introduction to Text Analysis in Python:
http://nealcaren.web.unc.edu/an-introduction-to-text-analysis-with-Python-part-1/

3
spaCy's Language Models

While we introduced text analysis in `Chapter 1`, *What is Text Analysis?*, we did not discuss any of the technical details behind building a text analysis pipeline. In this chapter, we will introduce you to spaCy's language model – these will serve as the first step in text analysis and are the first building block in our pipelines. In this chapter, we will introduce the reader to spaCy and how we can use spaCy to help us in our text analysis tasks, as well as talk about some of its more powerful functionalities, such as **Part of Speech**-tagging and **Named Entity Recognition**-tagging. We will finish up with an example of how we can preprocess data quickly and efficiently using the natural language processing Python library, spaCy.

We will cover the following topics in this chapter:

- spaCy
- Installation
- Tokenizing Text
- Summary
- References

spaCy

Having discussed some of the basics of text analysis, let's dive head first into our first Python package we'll be learning to use - **spaCy** [1].

spaCy describes itself as **Industrial Strength Natural Language Processing** – and it most certainly does its best to live up to this promise. Focused on getting things done rather than a more academic approach, spaCy ships with only one part-of-speech tagging algorithm and only one named-entity-recognizer (per language). What this also means is that the package is not bloated with unnecessary features.

We previously mentioned academic approach – what does this mean? A large number of the open-source packages in the natural language processing and machine learning are usually created or maintained by researchers and those working in academia. While they do end up *working* – the aim of the projects is not to provide state-of-the-art implementations of algorithms. **NLTK** [2] is one such example, where the primary focus of the library is to give students and researchers a toolkit to play around with. spaCy, on the other hand, can be used pretty satisfactorily in production code – this means that you can expect it to perform on real-world data, and with the right amount of foresight, it can also be scalable.

The blog post [3] by Matt Honnibal, creator and maintainer of spaCy, goes into some more detail about the problems being faced in open source NLP libraries, and the philosophy of spaCy. The crux of the problems is still lack of curation and maintenance in some libraries (such as **Pattern** [4], which only very recently attempted to move to Python 3), and in the case of NLTK, outdated techniques or serving simply as a **Wrapper** [5] tool, providing bindings which let you use other POS-taggers or parsers.

However, with all this being said it is still worthwhile to explore what NLTK has to offer – it still serves as a fairly handy tool to studying traditional NLP techniques as well as providing a variety of corpuses (such as brown corpus [6]). This `link` [7] is part of the NLTK Book and serves as a way to get started with exploring a few of these corpuses. We will not be going into the inner workings of NLTK, and a prerequisite knowledge of NLTK is not required to make the most of your NLP projects.

Throughout this book, we will be using spaCy (v2.0) for our text preprocessing and computational linguistics purposes. Following are the features of spaCy:

1. Non-destructive tokenization
2. Support for 21+ natural languages
3. 6 statistical models for 5 languages
4. Pre-trained word vectors
5. Easy deep learning integration
6. Part-of-speech tagging
7. Named entity recognition
8. Labeled dependency parsing
9. Syntax-driven sentence segmentation
10. Built-in visualizers for syntax and NER
11. Convenient string-to-hash mapping
12. Export to numpy data arrays

13. Efficient binary serialization
14. Easy model packaging and deployment
15. State-of-the-art speed
16. Robust, rigorously evaluated accuracy

The following is a table that has features of spaCy as mentioned on their `website`:

Feature comparison

Here's a quick comparison of the functionalities offered by spaCy, SyntaxNet, NLTK and CoreNLP.

	SPACY	SYNTAXNET	NLTK	CORENLP
Programming language	Python	C++	Python	Java
Neural network models	●	●	●	●
Integrated word vectors	●	●	●	●
Multi-language support	●	●	●	●
Tokenization	●	●	●	●
Part-of-speech tagging	●	●	●	●
Sentence segmentation	●	●	●	●
Dependency parsing	●	●	●	●
Entity recognition	●	●	●	●
Coreference resolution	●	●	●	●

Fig 3.1 Feature comparison from the Facts & Figures page

Installation

Let's get started with setting up and installing spaCy. spaCy is compatible with 64-bit CPython [8] 2.6+/3.3+ and runs on Unix/Linux, macOS/OS X, and Windows. CPython is a reference implementation of Python written in C – we don't need to know the details behind it, and if you have a stable installation of Python running, it is likely your CPython modules are just fine as well. The latest spaCy releases are available over **Pip** [9] (source packages only) and **Conda** [10]. Pip and conda are two Python package distributors. Installation requires a working build environment. We will be using Python 3, though the examples are all valid for Python 2 as well.

Pip remains the most straightforward choice, but for users with anaconda installed, they will be using conda instead.

```
pip install -U spacy
```

 When using `pip`, it is generally recommended that you install packages in a `virtualenv` tool to avoid modifying system state.

Since we will be downloading a number of Python packages throughout the book, it makes sense to understand exactly how virtual environments in Python work – this `post` [11] serves as a good resource to learn the same.

```
virtualenv env
source env/bin/activate

pip install spacy
```

Hopefully, by now you should have spaCy up and running –

```
import spacy
```

Into your Python, the Terminal should let you verify the spaCy installation.

Troubleshooting

Now, it may be the case that some issues would have popped up during the installation process; this might be because of CPython installation complications. If you are running a Mac system, you may need to run this command:

```
xcode-select -install
```

This installs Mac command-line developer tools.

Most of the common installation problems that may occur are well documented in both Stack Overflow and the spaCy GitHub page.

The following two links are useful in troubleshooting:

- Can't Pip Install (Mac) [12]
- Failed building wheel for spacy (Windows) [13]

In general, if you are using a virtual environment with the correct Xcode (for Mac users) and Python dependencies, there should not be unsolvable installation problems.

While we are discussing spaCy, it is important to know what other tools are available for similar tasks and how spaCy compares to these – the Facts & Figures [14] page on the spaCy page goes into the numbers behind spaCy's performance.

Let's move on to our first usage of spaCy – language models.

Language models

One of spaCy's most interesting features is its language models [15]. A language model is a statistical model that lets us perform the NLP tasks we want to, such as POS-tagging and NER-tagging. These language models do not come packaged with spaCy, but need to be downloaded – we'll get into details of exactly *how* we can download these models later on in the chapter.

Different languages have different models to perform these tasks, and there are also different models for the same language – the difference between these models is mostly statistical, and you can use different models based on your use case. A different model would just be trained on a different dataset. It is still the same underlying algorithm. The spaCy documentation on their models gives us some more insight into how they work.

As of now, there are models available for English, German, French, Spanish, Portuguese, Italian, and Dutch, and this number is expected to grow. For more information about the models, such as naming conventions or versioning, you can visit the model overview page [16]. We will be focusing more on using these models, before briefly going over how to create our own pipelines and models.

Installing language models

As of v1.7.0, models for spaCy can be installed as Python packages. This means that they're a component of your application, just like any other module. Models can be installed from a download URL or a local directory, manually or via pip.

The easiest way to download and use these models is using spaCy's `download` command.

```
# out-of-the-box: download best-matching default model
spacy download en # english model
spacy download de # german model
spacy download es # spanish model
spacy download fr # french model
spacy download xx # multi-language model

# download best-matching version of specific model for your spaCy
installation
spacy download en_core_web_sm

# download exact model version (doesn't create shortcut link)
spacy download en_core_web_sm-2.0.0 --direct
```

What the `download` command does is to use pip to install the model, place it in your `site-packages` folder, and create a shortcut link that allows you to easily load it later.

For example, if we want to use the English language model, we start by running these commands in Terminal:

```
pip install spacy

spacy download en
```

Next we run the following commands in our Python shell:

```
import spacy

nlp = spacy.load('en')
```

We now have the English language model loaded, and we can use it to process our text through the pipeline, like this:

```
doc = nlp(u'This is a sentence.')
```

Strings are Unicode by default in Python 3, however, in Python 2, we need to enclose strings using `u'`. We will discuss more of the nature of the `doc` object, as well as exactly what goes on in the pipeline in the upcoming section.

It's also possible to download the models via `pip` – to download a model directly using `pip`, simply point `pip install` to the URL or local path of the archive file. To find the direct link to a model, head over to the model releases [17] and find the archive links.

> Some of these models can be quite large, and the full English model is over 1 GB.

```
# with external URL
pip install
https://github.com/explosion/spacy-models/releases/download/en_core_web_md-
1.2.0/en_core_web_md-1.2.0.tar.gz

# with local file
pip install /Users/you/en_core_web_md-1.2.0.tar.gz
```

By default, this will install the model into your `site-packages` directory. You can then use `spacy.load()` to load it via its package name, create a shortcut link to assign it a custom name or import it explicitly as a module.

Once we've downloaded a model through pip or via spaCy's downloader, we can call the `load()` method, as follows:

```
import en_core_web_md

nlp = en_core_web_md.load()

doc = nlp(u'This is a sentence.')
```

The model usage page [15] of spaCy has details on how to manually download models, using custom shortcut links, and other information which might be useful – we will be covering some of these topics further in the book (In Chapter 5, *POS-Tagging and its Applications*, Chapter 6, *NER-Tagging and its Applications*, and Chapter 7, *Dependency Parsing*, on POS-tagging, NER-tagging, and dependency parsing), but it is worth having a quick glance at how we can organize these models.

Installation – how and why?

How you choose to load your models is a matter of personal preference and the type of project you are working on. For example, with larger code bases, native imports are usually recommended, as this will make it easier to integrate models with your existing build process, continuous integration workflow, and testing framework. You can also add the model in your `requirements.txt` file like any other library or module being used in your project. Note that a requirements file is a standard feature in most Python projects. The documentation page [18] explains it in more detail. It'll also prevent you from ever trying to load a model that is not installed, as your code will raise an `ImportError` error immediately, instead of failing later when `spacy.load()` is called.

Apart from the languages we previously spoke about, spaCy has started tokenization work on Italian, Portuguese, Dutch, Swedish, Finnish, Norwegian, Danish, Hungarian, Polish, Hebrew, Bengali, Hindi, Indonesian, Thai, Chinese (Mandarin), and Japanese. Again, since spaCy is open source, you can contribute to the ongoing efforts.

Now that we know exactly how to get the models on our systems, let's start asking more questions about these models – how does it perform the POS-tagging or NER-tagging? What kind of object is returned when we pass Unicode (Unicode is an industry standard for consistent encoding) through the pipeline? How do we use that object to do our preprocessing? We'll attempt to answer these in the coming section, while also discussing the other possibilities spaCy has to offer with regard to its models, such as training our own models or adding new languages to spaCy.

Basic preprocessing with language models

In `Chapter 1`, *What is Text Analysis?*, we mentioned the importance of preprocessing – after all, garbage in, garbage out, right? But we didn't go into many details about *how* we clean up our dirty data. Luckily for us, this is a well-researched problem in natural language processing, and there are many different preprocessing techniques, pipelines, and ideas for us to use when we want to clean up.

Technically, we don't need a package to specifically help us with preprocessing – simple string manipulation with Python can do the trick, albeit with a lot more effort. We'll use spaCy to help us with preprocessing, though in theory, even NLTK, for example, can be used. So why even bother with using spaCy? It's because along with basic preprocessing, it achieves a lot more in just one processing step – something we will see very soon in this chapter.

In particular, we will be using spaCy's language model to help us with the preprocessing. Before we get into the exact preprocessing steps, let's first understand what happens when running this:

```
doc = nlp(u'This is a sentence.')
```

When you call `nlp` on Unicode text, spaCy first tokenizes the text to produce a **Doc** object. **Doc** is then processed in several different steps, what we also refer to as our *pipeline*.

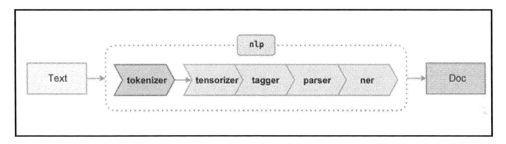

Fig 3.2 The default pipeline

Tokenizing text

You can see that the first step in this pipeline is tokenizing – what exactly is this?

Tokenization is the task of splitting a text into meaningful segments, called tokens. These segments could be words, punctuation, numbers, or other special characters that are the building blocks of a sentence. In spaCy, the input to the tokenizer is a Unicode text, and the output is a `Doc` object [19].

Different languages will have different tokenization rules. Let's look at an example of how tokenization might work in English. For the sentence – *Let us go to the park.*, it's quite straightforward, and would be broken up as follows, with the appropriate numerical indices:

0	1	2	3	4	5	6
Let	us	go	to	the	park	.

This looks awfully like the result when we just run `text.split(' ')` – when does tokenizing involve more effort?

If the previous sentence was *Let's go to the park.* instead, the tokenizer would have to be smart enough to split *Let's* into *Let* and *'s*. This means that there are some special rules to follow. spaCy's English language tokenizer checks the following after splitting a sentence up:

Does the substring match a tokenizer exception rule? For example, *don't* does not contain whitespace, but should be split into two tokens, *do* and *n't*, while *U.K.* should always remain one token.

Can a prefix, suffix or infix be split off? For example, punctuation such as commas, periods, hyphens, or quotes.

Unlike the other parts of the pipeline, we don't need a statistical model to perform tokenization. Global and language-specific tokenizer data is supplied via the language data in the `spacy/lang` [20] folder, which is simply a directory that contains model specific data. The tokenizer exceptions define special cases such as "don't" in English, which needs to be split into two tokens: `{ORTH: "do"}` and `{ORTH: "n't", LEMMA: "not"}`. The prefixes, suffixes, and infixes mostly define punctuation rules – for example, when to split off periods (at the end of a sentence), and when to leave token containing periods untouched (abbreviations such as *N.Y.*). Here, ORTH refers to the textual content, and LEMMA, the word with no inflectional suffix.

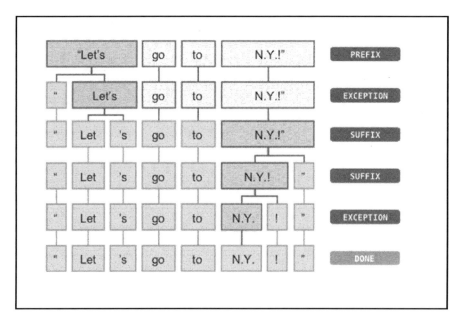

Fig 3.3 An example of spaCy's tokenizing for the sentence "Let's go to N.Y!"

We can add our own special cases to the tokenizer, as well as customize the spaCy's tokenizer class. If we construct our own tokenizer, we can add it is as simple as this:

```
nlp = spacy.load('en')
```

The details for creating our own tokenizer is in the Linguistic Features [21] section of spaCy's documentation, though we will into the details of training and creating our own models in Chapter 5, *POS-Tagging and its Applications*, Chapter 6, *NER-Tagging and its Applications*, and Chapter 7, *Dependency Parsing*.

So, once we pass our sentence to the nlp pipeline, the first step was tokenization – once this is done, we are now dealing with Doc objects, which are comprised of tokens – which we described before as the basic parts of our sentence. Once we have our tokens in the doc, each token is then worked on by the other components of the pipeline.

Part-of-speech (POS) – tagging

The second component of the default pipeline we described before was the **tensorizer**.

A tensorizer encodes the internal representation of the doc as an array of floats. This is a necessary step because spaCy's models are neural network models, and only *speak* tensors – every Doc object is expected to be tenzorised. We as users do not need to concern ourselves with this. After this step, we start with our first annotation – part of speech tagging.

In the first chapter, we briefly mentioned POS-tagging as marking each token of the sentence with its appropriate part of speech, such as noun, verb, and so on. spaCy uses a statistical model to perform its POS-tagging. To get the annotation from a token, we simply look up the pos_ attribute on the token.

Consider this example:

```
doc = nlp(u'John and I went to the park'')

for token in doc:
  print((token.text, token.pos_))
```

This will give us the following output:

```
(u'John', u'PROPN')
(u'and', u'CCONJ')
(u'I', u'PRON')
(u'went', u'VERB')
(u'to', u'ADP')
(u'the', u'DET')
(u'park', u'NOUN')
(u'.', u'PUNCT')
('John', 'PROPN')
('and', 'CCONJ')
('I', 'PRON')
('went', 'VERB')
('to', 'ADP')
('the', 'DET')
('park', 'NOUN')
('.', 'PUNCT')
```

We'll go into more details about POS-tagging and train our own POS-tagger in Chapter 4, *Gensim – Vectorizing text and transformations and n-grams*. As of now, it is enough to know what exactly POS-tagging is, and that we can use it to clean our text if we wish to remove a particular part of speech, for example.

The next part of our pipeline is the parser, which performs dependency parsing. While parsing refers to any kind of analysis of a string of symbols to understand relationships between the symbols, dependency parsing refers to the understanding of dependencies between these symbols. For example, in the English language, this could be for describing the relations between individual tokens, such as subject or object. spaCy has a rich API for navigating parse trees. Since parsing isn't really used in preprocessing, we will skip going into details, and save it for the coming chapters.

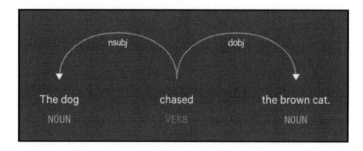

Fig 3.4 An example of dependency parsing

Named entity recognition

We now have the last part of our pipeline, where we perform named entity recognition. A named entity is a *real-world object* that is assigned a name – for example, a person, a country, a product, or organization. spaCy can recognize various types of named entities in a document, by asking the model for a prediction. We have to remember that since models are statistical and depend on the examples they were trained on, they don't always work perfectly and might need some tuning later, depending on your use case – we have a chapter saved up just to better understand named entity recognition and how to train our own models.

Named entities are available as the `ents` property of a Doc:

```
doc = nlp(u'Microsoft has offices all over Europe.')

for ent in doc.ents:
    print(ent.text, ent.start_char, ent.end_char, ent.label_)

(u'Microsoft', 0, 9, u'ORG')
(u'Europe', 31, 37, u'LOC')
```

spaCy has the following built-in entity types:

- PERSON: People, including fictional ones
- NORP: Nationalities or religious or political groups
- FACILITY: Buildings, airports, highways, bridges, and so on
- ORG: Companies, agencies, institutions, and so on
- GPE: Countries, cities, and states
- LOC: Non GPE locations, mountain ranges, and bodies of water
- PRODUCT: Objects, vehicles, foods, and so on (not services)
- EVENT: Named hurricanes, battles, wars, sports events, and so on
- WORK_OF_ART: Titles of books, songs, and so on
- LAW: Named documents made into laws
- LANGUAGE: Any named language

Rule-based matching

- ORTH: The exact verbatim text of a token
- LOWER, UPPER: The lowercase and uppercase form of the token
- IS_ALPHA: Token text consists of alphanumeric chars
- IS_ASCII: Token text consists of ASCII characters
- IS_DIGIT: Token text consists of digits
- IS_LOWER, IS_UPPER, IS_TITLE: Token text is in lowercase, uppercase, and title
- IS_PUNCT, IS_SPACE, IS_STOP: Token is punctuation, whitespace, and a stop word
- LIKE_NUM, LIKE_URL, LIKE_EMAIL: Token text resembles a number, URL, and email
- POS, TAG: The token's simple and extended POS tag
- DEP, LEMMA, SHAPE: The token's dependency label, lemma, and shape

SpaCy's default pipeline also performs rule-based matching. This further annotates tokens with more information and is valuable during preprocessing. The following token attributes are available:

As with the previous components of the pipeline, we can add our own rules. For now, though, this much information is enough for us to use in preprocessing.

Now that we know *how* spaCy processes our text when we pass it through the pipeline, we can discuss common preprocessing techniques.

Preprocessing

The wonderful thing about preprocessing text is that it almost feels intuitive – we get rid of any information which we think won't be used in our final output and keep what we feel is important. Here, our information is words – and some words do not always provide useful insights. In the text mining and natural language processing community, these words are called **stop words** [22].

Stop words are words that are filtered out of our text before we run any text mining or NLP algorithms on it. Again, we would like to draw attention to the fact this is not in every case – if we intend to find stylistic similarities or understand how writers use stop words, we would obviously need to stop words!

There is no universal stop words list for each language, and it largely depends on the use case and what kind of results we expect to be seeing. Usually, it is a list of the most common words in the language, such as *of, the, want, to,* and *have.*

With spaCy, stop words are very easy to identify – each token has an IS_STOP attribute, which lets us know if the word is a stop word or not. The list of all the stop words for each language can be found in the spacy/lang [20] folder.

We can also add our own stop words to the list of stop words. For example:

```
my_stop_words = [u'say', u'be', u'said', u'says', u'saying', 'field']
for stopword in my_stop_words:
  lexeme = nlp.vocab[stopword]
  lexeme.is_stop = True
```

We can also add words using this:

```
from spacy.lang.en.stop_words import STOP_WORDS

print(STOP_WORDS) # <- Spacy's default stop words

STOP_WORDS.add("your_additional_stop_word_here")
```

When cleaning our text, we can simply choose not to add stopwords to our corpus.

You might have noticed in the preceding example how the words say, saying, and says all pretty much provide the same information to us – grammatical differences aside, it won't hurt our results to only see one representation of these words.

There are two popular techniques to achieve this, stemming and lemmatization. Stemming usually involves chopping off the end of the word, following some basic rules. For example, the words say, saying, and says would all become say. Stemming is contextless and does not rely on part of speech, for example, to make its decisions. Lemmatization, on the other hand, conducts morphological analysis to find the root word.

The Stanford NLP book [23] page on this provides a nice explanation describing both and their differences. As far as we are concerned, we need not worry where we get our root words, just that we are getting them. In spaCy, the lemmatized form of a word is accessed with the .lemma_ attribute.

Now, with what we know, we can do some basic preprocessing. Let's clean up this sentence: the horse galloped down the field and past the 2 rivers.. We would like to get rid of stop words, numbers, and convert our string into a list so that we can use it later.

```
doc = nlp(u'the horse galloped down the field and past the river.')
sentence = []
for w in doc:
  # if it's not a stop word or punctuation mark, add it to our article!
  if w.text != 'n' and not w.is_stop and not w.is_punct and not w.like_num:
    # we add the lematized version of the word
    sentence.append(w.lemma_)
print(sentence)
```

By using the `.is_stop`, `is_punct`, and `w.like_num` attributes, we could remove the parts of the sentence we did not need. Make sure to note that we appended to the sentence the lemmatized form of the word which we accessed through `w.lemma_`.

This is what our output will look like after the preprocessing:

```
[u'horse', u'gallop', u'past', u'river']
```

We can further remove or not remove words based on our use-case. In our example, it is deemed that numbers are not important information, but in some cases, it might be. For example, it might be that we want to remove all verbs from a sentence – in which case we can, by simply checking the POS tag of that particular token.

Note that we had added *field* to our stop-words earlier – it's because of this we don't have a field in our final sentence.

spaCy's pipeline annotates text in such a way that we can very easily use that information to process our text. The handy thing is that we can further use that information later on in our text-processing, and not just in pre-processing. It makes sense to start any of our NLP tasks by running it through a spaCy pipeline, custom or otherwise, just for the large amount of information and annotation we will get, in almost just five lines of code.

Summary

spaCy offers us an easy way to annotate your text data very easily, and with the language model, we annotate your text data with a *lot* of information – not just tokenizing and whether it is a stop word or not, but also the part of speech, named entity tag, and so on – we can also train these annotating models on our own, giving a lot of power to the language model and processing pipeline! Downloading the models and using virtual environments are also an important part of this process. We will now move on to using our cleaned data in a way that machines can understand us – with vectors, and what kind of Python libraries we would need for the same.

References

[1] spaCy:
https://spacy.io

[2] NLTK:
http://www.nltk.org

[3] Dead Code should be buried:
https://explosion.ai/blog/dead-code-should-be-buried

[4] Pattern:
https://www.clips.uantwerpen.be/pattern

[5] Wrapper Function:
https://en.wikipedia.org/wiki/Wrapper_function

[6] Brown Corpus:
https://en.wikipedia.org/wiki/Brown_Corpus

[7] NLTK Corpus:
http://www.nltk.org/book/ch02.html

[8] CPython:
https://en.wikipedia.org/wiki/CPython

[9] PyPi:
https://pypi.python.org/pypi

[10] Conda:
https://conda.io/docs/

[11] Virtual Environments:
http://docs.python-guide.org/en/latest/dev/virtualenvs/

[12] Can't Pip Install:
https://github.com/explosion/spaCy/issues/269

[13] Failed building wheel for spacy:
https://stackoverflow.com/questions/43370851/failed-building-wheel-for-spacy

[14] spaCy Facts & Figures:
https://alpha.spacy.io/usage/facts-figures

[15] spaCy Language Models:
https://alpha.spacy.io/usage/models#languages

[16] spaCy Models overview:
https://alpha.spacy.io/models/

[17] spaCy Models releases:
https://github.com/explosion/spacy-models/releases

[18] Requirements File:
https://pip.readthedocs.io/en/1.1/requirements.html

[19] spaCy Doc object:
https://spacy.io/api/doc

[20] spaCy Language Directory:
https://github.com/explosion/spaCy/tree/develop/spacy/lang

[21] spaCy linguistic features:
https://alpha.spacy.io/usage/linguistic-features#section-tokenization

[22] Stop Words:
https://en.wikipedia.org/wiki/Stop_words

[23] Lemmatization and Stemming:
https://nlp.stanford.edu/IR-book/html/htmledition/stemming-and-lemmatization-1.html

4

Gensim – Vectorizing Text and Transformations and n-grams

- Introducing Gensim
- Vectors and why we need them
- Vector transformations in Gensim
- n-grams and some more preprocessing
- Summary

Introducing Gensim

So far, we haven't spoken much about finding hidden information - more about how to get our textual data in shape. We will be taking a brief departure from spaCy to discuss vector spaces and the open source Python package Gensim - this is because some of these concepts will be useful in the upcoming chapters and we would like to lay the foundation before moving on. However, we'll only be touching the surface of Gensim's capabilities. This chapter will introduce you to the data structures largely used in text analysis involving machine learning techniques - **vectors** [1].

This means that we are still in the domain of preprocessing and getting our data ready for further machine learning analysis. It may seem like overkill, focusing so much on just setting up our text/data, but like we've said before - garbage in, garbage out. While the previous chapter mostly involved text cleaning, we will be discussing converting our textual representations to numerical representations in this chapter, in particular, moving from strings to vectors.

When we talk about representations and transformations in this chapter, we will be exploring different kinds of ways of representing our strings as vectors, such as bag-of-words, **TF-IDF (term frequency-inverse document frequency)**, **LSI (latent semantic indexing)**, and the more recently popular word2vec. We will explain these methods soon on in *Vectors and why we need them* section and the rest in Chapter 8, *Topic Models* (**Topic Modelling** with Gensim) and Chapter 12, *Word2Vec, Doc2Vec and Gensim*, and gensim includes methods to do all of the above. The transformed vectors can be plugged into scikit-learn machine learning methods just as easily. Gensim started off as a modest project by Radim Rehurek and was largely the discussion of his Ph.D. thesis [17], *Scalability of Semantic Analysis in Natural Language Processing* [2]. It included novel implementations of **Latent Dirichlet allocation** [3] (**LDA**) and **Latent Semantic Analysis** [4] among its primary algorithms, as well as TF-IDF and **Random projection** [5] implementations. It has since grown to be one of the largest NLP/Information Retreival Python libraries, and is both memory-efficient and scalable, as opposed to the previous largely academic code available for semantic modelling (for example, the *Stanford Topic Modelling Toolkit* [6]).

Gensim manages to be scalable because it uses Python's in-built generators and iterators for streamed data-processing, so the data-set is never actually completely loaded in the RAM. Most IR algorithms involve matrix decompositions - which involve matrix multiplications. This is performed by numpy, which is further built on FORTRAN/C, which is highly optimized for mathematical operations. Since all the heavy lifting is passed on to these low-level BLAS libraries, Gensim offers the ease-of-use of Python with the power of C.

The primary features of Gensim are its memory-independent nature, multicore implementations of latent semantic analysis, latent Dirichlet allocation, random projections, **hierarchical Dirichlet process** (**HDP**), and **word2vec deep learning**, as well as the ability to use LSA and LDA on a cluster of computers. It also seamlessly plugs into the Python scientific computing ecosystem and can be extended with other vector space algorithms. Gensim's directory of Jupyter notebooks [7] serves as an important documentation source, with its tutorials covering most of that Gensim has to offer. Jupyter notebooks are a useful way to run code on a live server - the documentation page [8] is worth having a look at!

The tutorials page can help you with getting started with using Gensim, but the coming sections will also describe how to get started with using Gensim, and about how important a role vectors will play in the rest of our time exploring machine learning and text processing.

Vectors and why we need them

We're now moving toward the machine learning part of text analysis - this means that we will now start playing a little less with words and a little more with numbers. Even when we used spaCy, the POS-tagging and NER-tagging, for example, was done through statistical models - but the inner workings were largely hidden for us - we passed over Unicode text and after some magic, we have annotated text.

For Gensim however, we're expected to pass vectors as inputs to the IR algorithms (such as LDA or LSI), largely because what's going on under the hood is mathematical operations involving matrices. This means that we have to represent what was previously a string as a vector - and these kind of representations or models are called **Vector Space Models** [9].

From a mathematical perspective, a vector is a geometric object that has magnitude and direction. We don't need to pay as much attention to this, and rather think of vectors as a way of projecting words onto a mathematical space while preserving the information provided by these words.

Machine learning algorithms use these vectors to make predictions. We can understand machine learning as a suite of statistical algorithms and the study of these algorithms. The purpose of these algorithms is to learn from the provided data by decreasing the error of their predictions. As such, this is a wide field - we will be explaining particular machine learning algorithms as and then they come up.

Let's meanwhile discuss a couple of forms of these representations.

Bag-of-words

The **bag-of-words** model is arguably the most straightforward form of representing a sentence as a vector. Let's start with an example:

```
S1:"The dog sat by the mat."
S2:"The cat loves the dog."
```

If we follow the same preprocessing steps we did in the *Basic Preprocessing with language models* section, from Chapter 3, *spaCy's Language Models*, we will end up with the following sentences:

```
S1:"dog sat mat."
S2:"cat love dog."
```

As Python lists, these will now look like this:

```
S1:['dog', 'sat', 'mat']
S2:['cat', 'love', 'dog']
```

If we want to represent this as a vector, we would need to first construct our vocabulary, which would be the unique words found in the sentences. Our vocabulary vector is now as follows:

```
Vocab = ['dog', 'sat', 'mat', 'love', 'cat']
```

This means that our representation of our sentences will also be vectors with a length of 5 - we can also say that our vectors will have 5 dimensions. We can also think of mapping of each word in our vocabulary to a number (or index), in which case we can also refer to our vocabulary as a dictionary.

The bag-of-words model involves using word frequencies to construct our vectors. What will our sentences now look like?

```
S1:[1, 1, 1, 0, 0]
S2:[1, 0, 0, 1, 1]
```

It's easy enough to understand - there is 1 occurrence of dog, the first word in the vocabulary, and 0 occurrences of love in the first sentence, so the appropriate indexes are given the value based on the word frequency. If the first sentence has 2 occurrences of the word dog, it would be represented as:

```
S1: [2, 1, 1, 0, 0]
```

This is just an example of the idea behind a bag of words representation - the way Gensim approaches bag of words is slightly different, and we will see this in the coming section. One important feature of the bag-of-words model which we must remember is that it is an order less document representation - only the counts of the words matter. We can see that in our example above as well, where by looking at the resulting sentence vectors we do not know which words came first. This leads to a loss in spatial information, and by extension, semantic information. However, in a lot of information retrieval algorithms, the order of the words is not important, and just the occurrences of the words are enough for us to start with.

An example where the bag of words model can be used is in spam filtering - emails that are marked as spam are likely to contain spam-related words, such as *buy, money,* and *stock.* By converting the text in emails into a bag of words models, we can use **Bayesian probability** [10] to determine if it is more likely for a mail to be in the spam folder or not. This works because like we discussed before, in this case, the order of the words is not important - just whether they exist in the mail or not.

TF-IDF

TF-IDF is short for term frequency-inverse document frequency. Largely used in search engines to find relevant documents based on a query, it is a rather intuitive approach to converting our sentences into vectors.

As the name suggests, TF-IDF tries to encode two different kinds of information - term frequency and inverse document frequency. **Term frequency (TF)** is the number of times a word appears in a document.

IDF helps us understand the importance of a word in a document. By calculating the logarithmically scaled inverse fraction of the documents that contain the word (obtained by dividing the total number of documents by the number of documents containing the term) and then taking the logarithm of that quotient, we can have a measure of how common or rare the word is among all documents.

In case the preceding explanation wasn't very clear, expressing them as formulas will help!

TF(t) = (number of times term t appears in a document) / (total number of terms in the document)

IDF(t) = log_e (total number of documents / number of documents with term t in it)

TF-IDF is simply the product of these two factors - TF and IDF. Together it encapsulates more information into the vector representation, instead of just using the count of the words like in the bag-of-words vector representation. TF-IDF makes rare words more prominent and ignores common words such as *is, of,* and *that,* which may appear a lot of times, but have little importance.

For more information on how TF-IDF works, especially with the mathematical nature of TF-IDF and solved examples, the Wikipedia page [11] on TF-IDF is a good resource.

Other representations

It's possible to extend these representations - indeed, topic models, which we will explore later, are one such example. Word vectors are also an interesting representation of words, where we train a shallow neural network (a neural network with 1 or 2 layers) to describe words as vectors, where each feature is a semantic decoding of the word. We will be spending an entire chapter discussing word vectors, in particular, Word2Vec. To get a taste of what word vectors do, this blog post, *The amazing power of word vectors* [12], is a good start.

Vector transformations in Gensim

Now that we know what vector transformations are, let's get used to creating them, and using them. We will be performing these transformations with Gensim, but even scikit-learn can be used. We'll also have a look at scikit-learn's approach later on.

Let's create our corpus now. We discussed earlier that a corpus is a collection of documents. In our examples, each document would just be one sentence, but this is obviously not the case in most real-world examples we will be dealing with. We should also note that once we are done with preprocessing, we get rid of all punctuation marks - as for as our vector representation is concerned, each document is just one *sentence*.

Of course, before we start, be sure to install Gensim. Like spaCy, pip or conda is the best way to do this based on your working environment.

```
from gensim import corpora

documents = [u"Football club Arsenal defeat local rivals this weekend.",
u"Weekend football frenzy takes over London.", u"Bank open for takeover
bids after losing millions.", u"London football clubs bid to move to
Wembley stadium.", u"Arsenal bid 50 million pounds for striker Kane.",
u"Financial troubles result in loss of millions for bank.", u"Western bank
files for bankruptcy after financial losses.", u"London football club is
taken over by oil millionaire from Russia.", u"Banking on finances not
working for Russia."]
```

Just a note - we make sure that all the strings are Unicode strings so that we can use spaCy for preprocessing.

```
import spacy
nlp = spacy.load("en")
texts = []
for document in documents:
```

```
        text = []
        doc = nlp(document)
        for w in doc:
            if not w.is_stop and not w.is_punct and not w.like_num:
                text.append(w.lemma_)
        texts.append(text)
    print(texts)
```

We performed very similar preprocessing when we introduced spaCy. What do our documents look like now?

```
[[u'football', u'club', u'arsenal', u'defeat', u'local', u'rival',
u'weekend'],
[u'weekend', u'football', u'frenzy', u'take', u'london'],
[u'bank', u'open', u'bid', u'lose', u'million'],
[u'london', u'football', u'club', u'bid', u'wembley', u'stadium'],
[u'arsenal', u'bid', u'pound', u'striker', u'kane'],
[u'financial', u'trouble', u'result', u'loss', u'million', u'bank'],
[u'western', u'bank', u'file', u'bankruptcy', u'financial', u'loss'],
[u'london', u'football', u'club', u'take', u'oil', u'millionaire',
u'russia'],
[u'bank', u'finance', u'work', u'russia']]
```

Let's start by whipping up a bag-of-words representation for our mini-corpus. Gensim allows us to do this very conveniently through its `dictionary` class.

```
dictionary = corpora.Dictionary(texts)
print(dictionary.token2id)
```

```
{u'pound': 17, u'financial': 22, u'kane': 18, u'arsenal': 3, u'oil': 27,
u'london': 7, u'result': 23, u'file': 25, u'open': 12, u'bankruptcy': 26,
u'take': 9, u'stadium': 16, u'wembley': 15, u'local': 4, u'defeat': 5,
u'football': 2, u'finance': 31, u'club': 0, u'bid': 10, u'million': 11,
u'striker': 19, u'frenzy': 8, u'western': 24, u'trouble': 21, u'weekend':
6, u'bank': 13, u'loss': 20, u'rival': 1, u'work': 30, u'millionaire': 29,
u'lose': 14, u'russia': 28}
```

There are 32 unique words in our corpus, all of which are represented in our dictionary with each word being assigned an index value. When we refer to a word's word_id henceforth, it means we are talking about the words integer-id mapping made by the dictionary.

We will be using the `doc2bow` method, which, as the name suggests, helps convert our document to bag-of-words.

```
corpus = [dictionary.doc2bow(text) for text in texts]
```

If we print our corpus, we'll have our bag of words representation of the documents we used.

```
[[(0, 1), (1, 1), (2, 1), (3, 1), (4, 1), (5, 1), (6, 1)],
[(2, 1), (6, 1), (7, 1), (8, 1), (9, 1)], [(10, 1), (11, 1), (12, 1), (13,
1), (14, 1)],
[(0, 1), (2, 1), (7, 1), (10, 1), (15, 1), (16, 1)], [(3, 1), (10, 1), (17,
1), (18, 1), (19, 1)],
[(11, 1), (13, 1), (20, 1), (21, 1), (22, 1), (23, 1)],
[(13, 1), (20, 1), (22, 1), (24, 1), (25, 1), (26, 1)],
[(0, 1), (2, 1), (7, 1), (9, 1), (27, 1), (28, 1), (29, 1)], [(13, 1), (28,
1), (30, 1), (31, 1)]]
```

This is a list of lists, where each individual list represents a documents bag-of-words representation. A reminder: you might see different numbers in your list, this is because each time you create a dictionary, different mappings will occur. Unlike the example we demonstrated, where an absence of a word was a 0, we use tuples that represent (word_id, word_count). We can easily verify this by checking the original sentence, mapping each word to its integer ID and reconstructing our list. We can also notice in this case each document has not greater than one count of each word - in smaller corpuses, this tends to happen.

And voila! Our corpus is assembled, and we are ready to work machine learning/information retrieval magic on them whenever we would like. But before we sink our teeth into it... let's spend some more time with some details regarding corpuses.

We previously mentioned how Gensim is powerful because it uses streaming corpuses. But in this case, the entire list is loaded into the RAM. This is not a bother for us because it is a toy example, but in any real-world cases, this might cause problems. How do we get past this?

We can start by storing the corpus, once it is created, to disk. One way to do this is as follows:

```
corpora.MmCorpus.serialize('/tmp/example.mm', corpus)
```

By storing the corpus to disk and then later loading from disk, we are being far more memory efficient, because at most one vector resides in the RAM at a time. The Gensim tutorial [13] on corpora and vector spaces covers a little more than what we discussed so far and may be useful for some readers.

Converting a bag of words representation into TF-IDF, for example, is also made very easy with Gensim. We first choose the model/representation we want from the Gensim models' directory.

```
from gensim import models
tfidf = models.TfidfModel(corpus)
```

This means that `tfidf` now represents a TF-IDF table *trained* on our corpus. Note that in case of TFIDF, the *training* consists simply of going through the supplied corpus once and computing document frequencies of all its features. Training other models, such as latent semantic analysis or latent dirichlet allocation, is much more involved and, consequently, takes much more time. We will explore those transformations on the chapters on topic modelling. It is also important to note that all such vector transformations require the same input feature space - which means the same dictionary (and of course, vocabulary).

So, what does a TF-IDF representation of our corpus look like? All we have to do is this:

```
for document in tfidf[corpus]:
    print(document)
```

This gives us the following:

```
[(0, 0.24046829370585293), (1, 0.48093658741170586), (2,
0.17749938483254057), (3, 0.3292179861221232), (4, 0.48093658741170586),
(5, 0.48093658741170586), (6, 0.3292179861221232)]

[(2, 0.24212967666975266), (6, 0.4490913847888623), (7,
0.32802654645398593), (8, 0.6560530929079719), (9, 0.4490913847888623)]

[(10, 0.29592528218102643), (11, 0.4051424990000138), (12,
0.5918505643620529), (13, 0.2184344336379748), (14, 0.5918505643620529)]

[(0, 0.29431054749542984), (2, 0.21724253258131512), (7,
0.29431054749542984), (10, 0.29431054749542984), (15, 0.5886210949908597),
(16, 0.5886210949908597)]

[(3, 0.354982288765831), (10, 0.25928712547209604), (17,
0.5185742509441921), (18, 0.5185742509441921), (19, 0.5185742509441921)]

[(11, 0.3637247180792822), (13, 0.19610384738673725), (20,
0.3637247180792822), (21, 0.5313455887718271), (22, 0.3637247180792822),
(23, 0.5313455887718271)]

[(13, 0.18286519950508276), (20, 0.3391702611796705), (22,
0.3391702611796705), (24, 0.4954753228542582), (25, 0.4954753228542582),
(26, 0.4954753228542582)]
```

```
[(0, 0.2645025265769199), (2, 0.1952400253294319), (7, 0.2645025265769199),
(9, 0.3621225392416359), (27, 0.5290050531538398), (28,
0.3621225392416359), (29, 0.5290050531538398)]

[(13, 0.22867660961662029), (28, 0.4241392327204109), (30,
0.6196018558242014), (31, 0.6196018558242014)]
```

If you remember what we said about TF-IDF, you will be able to identify the float next to each word_id - it is the product of the TF and IDF scores for that particular word, instead of just the word count which was present before. The higher the score, the more important the word in the document.

We can use this representation as input for our ML algorithms as well, and we can also further chain or link these vector representations by performing another transformation on them.

Let's move on to a small, but interesting (and useful!) part of text analysis - bi-grams and n-grams.

n-grams and some more preprocessing

When working with textual data, context can be very important. As we discussed before, we sometimes lose this context in vector representations, knowing only the count of each word. **N-grams**, and in particular, **bi-grams** are going to help us solve this problem, at least to some extent.

An n-gram is a contiguous sequence of *n* items in the text. In our case, we will be dealing with words being the *item*, but depending on the use case, it could be even letters, syllables, or sometimes in the case of speech, phonemes. A bi-gram is when *n = 2*.

One way bi-grams are calculated in the text is by calculating the conditional probability of a token given by the preceding token. It can also just be calculated by choosing words that appear next to each other, but it is more useful for us to use bi-grams that are more *likely* to appear as a pair. Such a bi-gram is called a collocation. What this means is that we're trying to find pairs of words that are more likely to appear around each other. For example, *New York* or *Machine Learning* could be two possible pairs of words created by bi-grams. In other words, based on the training data (usually the corpus), we identify that it is with high probability that the word *York* follows the word *New*, and that it is worth considering *New York* as one identity. We must be careful to get rid of stop words before running a bi-gram model on our corpus, as there could be meaningless bi-grams formed. The Gensim bi-gram model is basically an implementation of collocation identification.

We can clearly see how this is useful - we can now pick up phrases from our corpus, and *New York* certainly provides us with more information than the words *New* and *York* separately. This means it can be added to our preprocessing pipeline.

Gensim approaches bigrams by simply combining the two high probability tokens with an underscore. The tokens *new* and *york* will now become *new_york* instead. Similar to the TF-IDF model, bigrams can be created using another Gensim model - `Phrases`.

```
import gensim
bigram = gensim.models.Phrases(texts)
```

We now have a trained bi-gram model for our corpus. We can perform our *transformation* on the text the same way we used TF-IDF. We recreate our corpus like this:

```
texts = [bigram[line] for line in texts]
```

Each line will now have all possible bi-grams created. It should be noted that in our toy example, we will have no bi-grams or meaningless bi-grams being created. To see an example where bi-grams provide useful information, the Jupyter notebook [14] written by me on topic modeling serves well.

Since by creating new phrases we add words to our dictionary, this step must be done before we create our dictionary. We would have to run this:

```
dictionary = corpora.Dictionary(texts)

corpus = [dictionary.doc2bow(text) for text in texts]
```

After we are done creating our bi-grams, we can create tri-grams, and other n-grams by simply running the phrases model multiple times on our corpus. Bi-grams still remains the most used n-gram model, though it is worth one's time to glance over the other uses and kinds of n-gram implementations. Again, the Wikipedia page [15] serves as a good introductory resource.

This brings us to the end of the preprocessing techniques covered in this book. It must be noted however that there is no one perfect preprocessing pipeline or set of rules - it depends largely on our use-cases, the kind of data we are working with, and what sort of information we wish to preserve (or lose!).

For example, one popular preprocessing technique involves removing both high frequency and low-frequency words. We can do this in Gensim with the `dictionary` module. Let's say we would like to get rid of words that occur in less than 20 documents, or in more than 50% of the documents, we would add the following:

```
dictionary.filter_extremes(no_below=20, no_above=0.5)
```

We can also remove most frequent tokens or prune out certain token ids. You can refer to the docs [16] to see the full extent of the preprocessing tools the `dictionary` class can provide us.

More often than not, it's after multiple iterations of preprocessing and running our algorithms when we figure out the *correct* preprocessing techniques we wish to use. What is important for us is to know what kind of tools are available to do this, and what is the reason behind doing all of this.

We are now equipped with everything we need for Gensim and scikit-learns' algorithms to get working.

Summary

We've seen in this chapter why it makes sense to change our representation of text from words to numbers, and why this is the only language a computer understands. There are different ways computers can interpret words, and TF-IDF and bag of words are two such vector representations. Gensim is a Python package that offers us ways to generate such vector representations, which are later used as inputs into various machine learning and information retrieval algorithms.

There are further preprocessing techniques such as creating n-grams, collocations and removing low-frequency words, which can help us arrive at better results. The concepts of vectors form a basis in natural language processing and we can now get back to using spaCy's pipelines; indeed, Chapter 5, *POS-Tagging and Its Applications*, Chapter 6, *NER-Tagging and Its Applications*, and Chapter 7, *Dependency Parsing*, all showcase the power of spaCy, and we will start with POS-tagging algorithms using spaCy.

References

[1] Vectors:
https://en.wikipedia.org/wiki/Euclidean_vector

[2] Scalability of Semantic Analysis in Natural Language Processing:
https://radimrehurek.com/phd_rehurek.pdf

[3] Latent Dirichlet allocation:
https://en.wikipedia.org/wiki/Latent_Dirichlet_allocation

[4] Latent semantic indexing:
https://en.wikipedia.org/wiki/Latent_semantic_analysis#Latent_semantic_indexing

[5] Random Projection:
https://en.wikipedia.org/wiki/Random_projection

[6] Stanford TMT:
https://nlp.stanford.edu/software/tmt/tmt-0.4/

[7] Gensim notebooks:
https://github.com/RaRe-Technologies/gensim/tree/develop/docs/notebooks

[8] Jupyter Notebooks:
http://jupyter-notebook.readthedocs.io/en/stable/notebook.html

[9] Vector Space Models:
https://en.wikipedia.org/wiki/Vector_space_model

[10] Bayesian Probability:
https://en.wikipedia.org/wiki/Bayesian_probability

[11] TF-IDF:
https://en.wikipedia.org/wiki/Tf-idf

[12] The Amazing power of word vectors:
https://blog.acolyer.org/2016/04/21/the-amazing-power-of-word-vectors/

[13] Corpora and Vector Spaces:
https://radimrehurek.com/gensim/tut1.html

[14] Bi-Gram example notebook:
https://github.com/bhargavvader/personal/tree/master/notebooks/text_analysis_tutorial

[15] N-grams:
https://en.wikipedia.org/wiki/N-gram

[16] Gensim dictionary:
https://radimrehurek.com/gensim/corpora/dictionary.html

[17] Scalability of Semantic Analysis in Natural Language Processing:
https://radimrehurek.com/phd_rehurek.pdf

5
POS-Tagging and Its Applications

Chapter 1, *What is Text Analysis*, and Chapter 2, *Python Tips for Text Analysis*, introduced text analysis and Python, and Chapter 3, *SpaCy's Language Models*, and Chapter 4, *Gensim - Vectorizing Text and Transformations and n-grams*, helped us set-up our code for more advanced text analysis. This chapter will discuss the first of such advanced techniques – part of speech tagging, popularly called POS-tagging. We will study what parts of speech exist, how to identify them in our documents, and what possible uses these POS-tags have.

- What is POS-tagging?
- spaCy for POS-tagging
- Training your POS-tagger
- POS-tagging examples

What is POS-tagging?

The obvious first step in understanding POS-tagging is to expand the acronym – **Part-Of-Speech** tagging. Now, that makes things a lot easier now, doesn't it? As the name suggests, it is the process of tagging words in a textual input with their appropriate part of speech. We've already discussed this before briefly, particularly when dealing with spaCy and its language models. So, while we know that POS-tagging refers to the action of tagging words with their POS, we haven't talked very much about what exactly a part of speech in natural language (and in particular, English) is, and why it might be relevant to us in the realm of text analysis.

Traditionally, a part of speech is a category of words which have similar grammatical properties or usage. We will be focusing our efforts on the English language (as we have been and will continue to do throughout this book), but generally, these categories can be extended to most, if not all, languages. The commonly listed categories in English are these:

- **Noun** - The name of a person, place, thing, or idea
- **Verb** - The action or being
- **Adjective** - This modifies or describes a noun or a pronoun
- **Adverb** - This modifies or describes a verb, adjective, or another adverb
- **Pronoun** - The word to be used in place of a noun
- **Preposition** - The word placed before a noun or pronoun to form a phrase modifying another word in the sentence
- **Conjunction** - This joins words, phrases, or clauses
- **Interjection** - A word used to express emotion

There are also various subcategories into which a word can be put, and there is no *official* list of all the parts of speech that exist. In fact, for the purpose of text analysis or computational linguistics, we will be concerned with all the possible divisions that a particular tagger can tag a word as! This can range anywhere between the *common* categories or even more detailed categories, as we will see in spaCy.

Since the purpose of this book is not to explain the concepts of linguistics, we will not be describing the various parts of speech in detail, and the reader is encouraged to have a look through what each POS category means. We expect the reader to be comfortable with basic POS categories – this will come in handy later!

The following links will be handy to get more used to parts of speech:

1. The Eight Parts of Speech [1]
2. partofspeech.org [2]

We mentioned earlier that we will be focusing on English and English POS, but most available POS-taggers offer tagging functions for non-English languages as well. It should also be noted that the principles we use to train POS-taggers, as well as the different ways we can use this information tend to remain the same, and one can carry on the lessons we learn here.

What usually remains common between all-natural languages are nouns and verbs, but as we move beyond this it becomes more and more difficult to fix in on different word categories. For some example, some languages don't differentiate between adjectives and adverbs, while Japanese has three different classes just for adjectives.

Even within the English language, POS-tagging isn't always a straightforward task and words have different POS-tags depending on the context. A simple example is the word *refuse*, where if it used as a verb it means to decline an offer, and when used as a noun it is used to refer to something you throw away or rubbish. It is important for us to be able to identify which meaning of the word is being referred to, and the POS-tag can help us here. As for identifying the POS-tag in the first place, the context is crucial – it is not possible for us to tag a word with its part of speech unless it is in a sentence or phrase.

And how does one go about identifying the POS-tag for a word? Traditionally, of course, this was done by hand, but from a computational perspective, we have more than one way to do this. We mentioned before that we have to concern ourselves with many POS-tags as the tagger identifies – in some cases, there are up to 100 different tags, but this isn't always very useful - the spaCy POS-tagger that we will be largely using uses 19 different categories for classifying tokens. In all realistic text analysis scenarios, we will not be dealing with pure textual data – there is likely going to be numbers, symbols, and words that are not recognized, in which case we are likely to have multiple categories.

In spaCy, for a more detailed analysis, we also have the `.tag_` attribute, which adds more information to the previously given `.pos_` attribute. The following table gives the breakup of the categories spaCy has to annotate its words.

POS	DESCRIPTION	EXAMPLES
ADJ	adjective	*big, old, green, incomprehensible, first*
ADP	adposition	*in, to, during*
ADV	adverb	*very, tomorrow, down, where, there*
AUX	auxiliary	*is, has (done), will (do), should (do)*
CONJ	conjunction	*and, or, but*
CCONJ	coordinating conjunction	*and, or, but*
DET	determiner	*a, an, the*
INTJ	interjection	*psst, ouch, bravo, hello*
NOUN	noun	*girl, cat, tree, air, beauty*
NUM	numeral	*1, 2017, one, seventy-seven, IV, MMXIV*
PART	particle	*'s, not,*
PRON	pronoun	*I, you, he, she, myself, themselves, somebody*
PROPN	proper noun	*Mary, John, London, NATO, HBO*
PUNCT	punctuation	*., (,), ?*
SCONJ	subordinating conjunction	*if, while, that*
SYM	symbol	*$, %, §, ©, +, −, ×, ÷, =, :), 🙂*
VERB	verb	*run, runs, running, eat, ate, eating*
X	other	*sfpksdpsxmsa*
SPACE	space	

Fig 5.1 spaCy's list of POS as described in their annotation specifications [3]

Now that we have established *what* POS-tagging is, let's talk about the *how*. Since all the original POS-tagging was done by hand after observation, this leaves us with a lot of classified data to work with when building statistical models. The Brown corpus is one example of a corpus that is very well annotated with POS-tag data. The first few probabilistic models used to train a POS-tagger would use **Hidden Markov Models** [4] to predict the tag.

Hidden Markov Models tend to be used whenever there are sequences present – this turns out to be useful because we can use information about the context of a word to predict what the POS-tag might be. For example, once you've seen an article such as *the*, perhaps the next word is a noun 40% of the time, an adjective 35%, and a number 25%. Knowing this, a program can decide that *refuse* in *the refuse* is far more likely to be a noun than a verb, solving the problem we discussed before.

Apart from statistical models, there are also rule-based POS-taggers, which uses predefined rules to perform the tagging or learns these rules from the corpus. Of course, these methods do not throw away statistical methods, but just relies on them less. One of the most popular of such methods is described by Eric Brill in his 1998 paper titled, *A Simple Rule-Based Part of Speech Tagger* [5].

There are other more naive methods that you can try out, just to attempt to get a feel of the task we are attempting, such as using a regular expressions to evaluate part of speech or simply storing the most likely tag for a word and tag all future occurrences with the same tag. Part of speech tagging has since moved on quite a bit though, and like most computational tasks which are being completed with high levels of accuracy, it is statistical learning or deep learning that is the way to go.

State-of-the-art results have been reached with neural networks on multiple datasets – ACL web maintains a list of this on their website -
https://aclweb.org/aclwiki/POS_Tagging_(State_of_the_art).

It is possible to get close to this kind of results even with a simpler machine learning model such as a perceptron classifier. Indeed, one of spaCy's very first POS-taggers was an averaged perceptron, and their blog features an article detailing the inner workings of their tagger and also serves as a tutorial on how to build it. A perceptron used for POS-tagging works by learning the probability of the tag of the word based on various features, or information – these can include the tag of the previous word or the last few letters of the word. By positively rewarding correct classification and punishing incorrect classification, this model learns weights which it uses to predict the tag of the new word. Indeed, most supervised machine learning algorithms function on similar principles, and these are the algorithms that perform well in POS-tagging tasks.

Now that we have a better idea of the *how,* let's talk about the *why.* While intuitively it may seem that knowing the part of speech of a word may be useful, exactly what can we do with this information? POS tags have been used historically in natural language processing for a variety of reasons and purposes. One interesting such purpose is speech-to-text conversion and language translation, which is when a powerful POS-tagger can be used to disambiguate homonyms. Consider this example when a human says: *I am going to fish a fish,* and wishes this sentence to be translated to another language such as French or Spanish; it is vital to know whether fish here is a noun or a verb – unlike English, it is highly likely that in the target language, the word to describe the act of fishing is quite different from that of the animal.

Similarly, POS-tagging is used for **Dependency Parsing**. As the name suggests, dependency parsing is the process of identifying dependencies, or relationships between words in a sentence or phrase. We will be spending an entire chapter discussing these dependencies and how they work, but it is enough to understand for now that identifying the part of speech of each word is an important part of generating such a dependency tree. If we use the nifty spaCy **displacy** module [6] in our example sentence – *I am going to fish a fish.,* this is what we get.

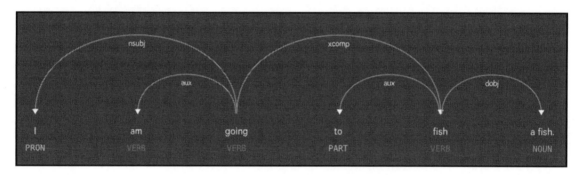

Fig 5.2 The sentence "I am going to fish a fish" after being dependency parsed by spaCY

We can see that POS-tagging has a wealth of applications outside of finding out a part of speech just for the sake of doing this. But even just this information can give us some very fun results, some of which we will see in the very next section.

POS-tagging in Python

It isn't a coincidence that every time we mentioned actually performing POS-tagging, we linked to or mentioned spaCy – it is arguably one of the fastest tokenizer, tagger, and parser out there, and we will be using it for all our examples.

But before we dive into spaCy, we will be briefly discussing its main *rival* when it comes to POS-tagging in Python, which is NLTK. We have already gone through the spaCy versus NLTK debate before, and we will stick to our previous stance of using spaCy for all our real-world application purposes, but it is still worth looking at what NLTK has to offer.

NLTK's fairly straightforward API for playing around or sandboxing is what usually tends to make it an attractive choice for beginners. To get the appropriate tags for a sentence, all we have to run is this:

```
import nltk
text = nltk.word_tokenize("And now for something completely different")
nltk.pos_tag(text)

[('And', 'CC'), ('now', 'RB'), ('for', 'IN'), ('something', 'NN'),
('completely', 'RB'), ('different', 'JJ')]
```

If we wish to use a particular tagger (NLTK offers many options), we simply import that particular tagger. The `train_sents` objects are the training sentences you wish to use to train the `bigram` tagger.

```
bigram_tagger = nltk.BigramTagger(train_sents)
bigram_tagger.tag(text)
```

The following links provide more information about POS-tagging with NLTK if the reader is interested in viewing the same:

1. Official Documentation of tag module [7]
2. Chapter 5 of NLTK book [8]
3. Training NLTK POS-tagger [9]

NLTK isn't the only Python alternative to POS-tagging – *AI in Practice: Identifying Parts of Speech in Python* [10]: takes us through all the different options we can explore in Python. Out of the pick, `TextBlob` is probably the only other tagger worth having a look at. This tagger performs very similar to the one in spaCy, which makes sense as the algorithm is written by the spaCy maintainer. This blog post goes into some more detail about using `TextBlob` [11] to perform your POS-tagging.

This is all we'll discuss when it comes to NLTK and other Python options though – because of its more academic, bloated approach when it comes to POS-tagging, we will stick to spaCy.

POS-tagging with spaCy

POS-tagging with spaCy is like any other basic linguistic function with spaCy – it is one of its core features loaded into its pipeline. If you load up your spaCy module of choice and run the text through the pipeline, you will have that text POS-tagged – as well as tokenized, NER-tagged, and ready to be dependency parsed. We've already seen spaCy's power in this regard in our chapter on our introduction to spaCy's language models.

Setting up our model involves the same steps we saw before.

```
import spacy
nlp = spacy.load('en')
```

Let's now decide some sentence we would like to POS-tag.

```
sent_0 = nlp(u'Mathieu and I went to the park.')
sent_1 = nlp(u'If Clement was asked to take out the garbage, he would
refuse.')
sent_2 = nlp(u'Baptiste was in charge of the refuse treatment center.')
sent_3 = nlp(u'Marie took out her rather suspicious and fishy cat to go
fish for fish.')
```

Sentence 0 is straightforward and will illustrate how a basic sentence will be POS-tagged.

```
for token in sent_0:
    print(token.text, token.pos_, token.tag_)

(u'Mathieu', u'PROPN', u'NNP')
(u'and', u'CCONJ', u'CC')
(u'I', u'PRON', u'PRP')
(u'went', u'VERB', u'VBD')
(u'to', u'ADP', u'IN')
(u'the', u'DET', u'DT')
(u'park', u'NOUN', u'NN')
(u'.', u'PUNCT', u'.')
```

Let's look at a few of the tags here – Mathieu is a name, and it is correctly marked as a proper noun, went is a verb, and the park is a noun – all that we would expect it to be. We previously talked about the word *refuse*, and how it can be both a noun and a verb.

```
for token in sent_1:
    print(token.text, token.pos_, token.tag_)
```

```
(u'If', u'ADP', u'IN')
(u'Clement', u'PROPN', u'NNP')
(u'was', u'VERB', u'VBD')
(u'asked', u'VERB', u'VBN')
(u'to', u'PART', u'TO')
(u'take', u'VERB', u'VB')
(u'out', u'PART', u'RP')
(u'the', u'DET', u'DT')
(u'garbage', u'NOUN', u'NN')
(u',', u'PUNCT', u',')
(u'he', u'PRON', u'PRP')
(u'would', u'VERB', u'MD')
(u'refuse', u'VERB', u'VB')
(u'.', u'PUNCT', u'.')
```

Here, the word `refuse` is a verb, as we expect it to be. The word `garbage` is a noun and is the object which our friend `Clement` is refusing to take out. Our next sentence is also an example involving `garbage`, but here the word `refuse` is the substance being treated in the plant.

```
for token in sent_2:
    print(token.text, token.pos_, token.tag_)
```

```
(u'Baptiste', u'PROPN', u'NNP')
(u'was', u'VERB', u'VBD')
(u'in', u'ADP', u'IN')
(u'charge', u'NOUN', u'NN')
(u'of', u'ADP', u'IN')
(u'the', u'DET', u'DT')
(u'refuse', u'NOUN', u'NN')
(u'treatment', u'NOUN', u'NN')
(u'center', u'NOUN', u'NN')
(u'.', u'PUNCT', u'.')
```

And voila! As we wanted to see, the `refuse` word is now correctly tagged as a noun. With the context of it appearing as something `Baptiste` is in charge of, it is appropriately changed to a noun. In fact, the last three words are all nouns, or is something which we call a **noun phrase**. We will deal with this term in more detail in the chapter on dependency parsing.

Let's now have a look at our last sentence:

```
for token in sent_3:
```

```
print(token.text, token.pos_, token.tag_)
```

```
(u'Marie', u'PROPN', u'NNP')
(u'took', u'VERB', u'VBD')
(u'out', u'PART', u'RP')
(u'her', u'ADJ', u'PRP$')
(u'rather', u'ADV', u'RB')
(u'suspicious', u'ADJ', u'JJ')
(u'and', u'CCONJ', u'CC')
(u'fishy', u'ADJ', u'JJ')
(u'cat', u'NOUN', u'NN')
(u'to', u'PART', u'TO')
(u'fish', u'VERB', u'VB')
(u'for', u'ADP', u'IN')
(u'fish', u'NOUN', u'NN')
(u'.', u'PUNCT', u'.')
```

The purpose of this sentence was to attempt to fool our tagger with different variations of the word `fish`, but our tagger could easily tell the difference in the appropriate context. Our model is a machine learning model which, among other training features, uses the tags of the previous words and upcoming words to decide the new tag – the word `fishy` was tagged as a verb partly because of the fact that a noun comes right after, partly because a conjunction came before, and also possibly because it ends with the letter `y`. Most machine learning models take multiple features into account when deciding a new label.

The other occurrences of the word *fish* were easily predicted, and we saw this earlier on in the chapter as well. spaCy does a very smooth job with this – and we should also remember we have a trove of other data about the tokens in the sentences as well, and not just POS tags. We are killing many metaphorical birds with the same stone!

As impressive as spaCy's pretrained models are, we need not limit ourselves to them. spaCy offers us the functionality to train our models using their machine learning model, and we will have a look at how this is done.

Training our own POS-taggers

The prediction done by spaCy's models with regard to its POS-tag are statistical predictions; unlike, say, whether or not it is a stop word, which is just a check against a list of words. If it is a statistical prediction, this means that we can train a model for it to perform better predictions or predictions that are more relevant to the dataset we are intending to use it on. Here, better isn't meant to be taken too literally – the current spaCy model already comes to 97% in terms of tagging accuracy.

Before we dive in deep into our training process, let's clarify a few commonly used terms when it comes to machine learning, and machine learning for text.

Training - the process of teaching your machine learning model how to make the right prediction. In text analysis, we do this by providing classified data to the model. What does this mean? In the setting of POS-tagging, it would be a list of words and their tagged POS. This labeled information is then used to learn certain *weights*, which are further used to make the prediction. We have used some of this terminology before when describing the perceptron tagger.

So how are these weights learned? We mentioned that we provide classified data to the model – this data is referred to as our training data. Once we start making predictions and making mistakes, the weights are adjusted accordingly to minimize the mistakes. We calculate this feedback through what is called the error gradient of the loss function. The error gradient is larger if the performance is worse and gets smaller as the performance improves - we can also understand it as the direction the weights need to change in so that our predictions are better.

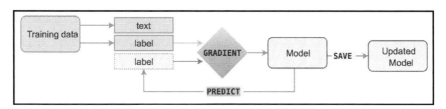

Fig 5.3 An explanation of the training process of spaCy's models as described on their training page [12]

The final jargon that we will come across is *testing data*. This is simply the data that we will finally use after training to see how well our model is performing. This is also a set of labeled or classified data, and by checking the predicted tag by the model versus the actual tag of the word, we can verify how well our model performs. While all of this is in the context of POS-tags, it can be extended to other forms of prediction both inside and outside of text analysis. The spaCy training page [12] is worth having a look and further talks about how training models in spaCy works.

Now that we have theory out of the way – how do we actually train our model?

Getting data can be a pain at times, and for very large-scale projects, this can be a bottleneck. In the training documentation page, there are examples pertaining to large-scale training problems, and the `prodigy` tool [13] is suggested for collecting the said data. Before v2.0, the `GoldParse` [14] object was used for training purposes, but we will rather be exploring the more simple method of using raw text and dictionaries of annotations. Again, we will not be going into details of either prodigy or into how to use `GoldParse`, as they are not the recommended methods – but are still worth knowing.

A simple training loop would look like this:

```
TRAIN_DATA = [
    ("Facebook has been accused for leaking personal data of users.",
{'entities': [(0, 8, 'ORG')]}),
    ("Tinder uses sophisticated algorithms to find the perfect match.",
{'entities': [(0, 6, "ORG")]})]

nlp = spacy.blank('en')
optimizer = nlp.begin_training()
for i in range(20):
    random.shuffle(TRAIN_DATA)
    for text, annotations in TRAIN_DATA:
        nlp.update([text], [annotations], sgd=optimizer)
nlp.to_disk('/model')
```

We can see how simple it is in theory – just provide the sentence, the part we intend to train (this can be: *entities, heads, deps, tags,* and *cats*), and the part of the sentence that corresponds to the entity, or the tag, and the third value in the tuple corresponds to the label we wish to give to the word between the indices marked out in the first and second values of the tuple. In the example given, we can see that `Facebook` and `Tinder` are the two entities that are to be marked as `ORG`, or organization.

Training a POS-tagger isn't any different in theory, and we will be using the example code (`train_tagger.py` [18]) in the spaCy GitHub page which guides us in how to do this.

```
import plac
import random
from pathlib import Path
import spacy

TAG_MAP = {
    'N': {'pos': 'NOUN'},
    'V': {'pos': 'VERB'},
    'J': {'pos': 'ADJ'}
}
```

We've set up our basic imports and have initialized the TAG_MAP dictionary. We need to define a mapping from the data's part-of-speech tag names to the **Universal Part-of-Speech tag** set [15], as spaCy includes an enum of these tags. In this example, we only intend to train nouns, verbs, and adjectives, so we include these in our tag map.

```
TRAIN_DATA = [
    ("I like green eggs", {'tags': ['N', 'V', 'J', 'N']}),
    ("Eat blue ham", {'tags': ['V', 'J', 'N']})
]
```

Of course, this amount of training data isn't going to train ourselves a very good model; as in most machine learning problems, more data results in a better model, and the data present here is to only give an idea of how the training data should look like.

```
@plac.annotations(
    lang=("ISO Code of language to use", "option", "l", str),
    output_dir=("Optional output directory", "option", "o", Path),
    n_iter=("Number of training iterations", "option", "n", int))
```

We set up some annotations for the language, output directory, and a number of training iterations.

```
def main(lang='en', output_dir=None, n_iter=25):
    """Main function to create a new model, set up the pipeline and train
    the tagger. In order to train the tagger with a custom tag map,
    we're creating a new Language instance with a custom vocab.
    """
    nlp = spacy.blank(lang)
    tagger = nlp.create_pipe('tagger')
```

We have now created a new blank language model and added the tagger to the pipeline using the create_pipe method. Note that this works for built-ins that are registered with spaCy.

```
for tag, values in TAG_MAP.items():
    tagger.add_label(tag, values)
nlp.add_pipe(tagger)
```

We have now added the tags. This needs to be done before you start training.

```
optimizer = nlp.begin_training()
for i in range(n_iter):
    random.shuffle(TRAIN_DATA)
    losses = {}
    for text, annotations in TRAIN_DATA:
        nlp.update([text], [annotations], sgd=optimizer, losses=losses)
    print(losses)
```

We've seen this part of the training process before in the example.

```
test_text = "I like blue eggs"
doc = nlp(test_text)
print('Tags', [(t.text, t.tag_, t.pos_) for t in doc])
```

Let's do a quick sanity check where we test our model, before saving it to the output directory.

```
if output_dir is not None:
    output_dir = Path(output_dir)
    if not output_dir.exists():
        output_dir.mkdir()
    nlp.to_disk(output_dir)
    print("Saved model to", output_dir)

    # test the save model
    print("Loading from", output_dir)
    nlp2 = spacy.load(output_dir)
    doc = nlp2(test_text)
    print('Tags', [(t.text, t.tag_, t.pos_) for t in doc])

if __name__ == '__main__':
    plac.call(main)

# Expected output:
# [
#   ('I', 'N', 'NOUN'),
#   ('like', 'V', 'VERB'),
#   ('blue', 'J', 'ADJ'),
#   ('eggs', 'N', 'NOUN')
# ]
```

And there we have it; our own custom-trained POS-tagger! Of course, this will not be the best POS-tagger, unless our corpus is a tiny corpus of our opinions on different breakfast foods – but this is not usually the case. For all real-world scenarios, the training data will be a lot more massive and assembling this data will be a huge part of our training task.

In our case of training a spaCy model, the machine learning model which we used to train the POS-tagger was abstracted to us. We only used the update() method to train our model, and don't know about the *nature* of the model, apart from the fact that it works well, and is a neural network. While for all practical cases this works more than well, if we do wish to train our *own* classifier, it isn't terribly hard to do so.

For more advanced users who are aware of how scikit-learn works, the blog post [16] illustrates an example using NLTK to generate data to train a classifier yourself using scikit-learn. We will be coming across scikit-learn and how to train such models later on in the book, but curious readers can check the link to have an idea of how to build it.

But for the definitive *how to build your own POS-tagger* tutorial, the spaCy blog has an article describing the very same – *A Good Part-of-Speech Tagger in about 200 Lines of Python* [17]. We've previously linked to the article when describing the perceptron-based tagger, and this is also the tagger that TextBlob uses.

And there we go! We are now sufficiently armed with the knowledge to train our own spaCy POS-tagger, use it in our pipelines, and more importantly, are aware of why it is a crucial part of text analysis. Our final, short section illustrates some code snippets describing what we can do with knowledge of POS-tags.

POS-tagging code examples

The following code snippets illustrate some of the simple tasks we can do with knowledge of POS-tags. These examples don't achieve too much in terms of in-depth text analysis, but offer a quick glance at text manipulation once we have our text processed.

```
def make_verb_upper(text, pos):
    return text.upper() if pos == "VERB" else text
doc = nlp(u'Tom ran swiftly and walked slowly')
text = ''.join(make_verb_upper(w.text_with_ws, w.pos_) for w in doc)
print(text)
```

As the function name suggests, the preceding code is to change all the verbs of the sentence into uppercase. By doing a quick check of the POS-tag and the basic string function upper, we can achieve this in 5 lines!

Another popular task often done during analysis of text is to count the occurrences of each kind of POS. This can be done quite quickly with the following code snippet, where we find out the number of occurrences of these words in the 1st Harry Potter book (which you would buy/download and save as a text file):

```
import pandas as pd

harry_potter = open("HP1.txt").read()
hp = nlp(harry_potter)
hpSents = list(hp.sents)
hpSentenceLengths = [len(sent) for sent in hpSents]
[sent for sent in hpSents if len(sent) == max(hpSentenceLengths)]
```

```
hpPOS = pd.Series(hp.count_by(spacy.attrs.POS))/len(hp)

tagDict = {w.pos: w.pos_ for w in hp}
hpPOS = pd.Series(hp.count_by(spacy.attrs.POS))/len(hp)
df = pd.DataFrame([hpPOS], index=['Harry Potter'])
df.columns = [tagDict[column] for column in df.columns]
df.T.plot(kind='bar')
```

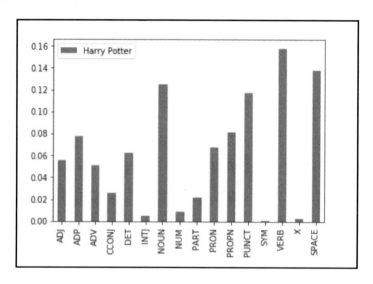

The *y*-axis is the percentage of that POS-tag appearing in the text.

What if we want to find the most commonly used pronouns? We only need two lines for this task:

```
hpAdjs = [w for w in hp if w.pos_ == 'PRON']
Counter([w.string.strip() for w in hpAdjs]).most_common(10)
```

```
[(u'he', 1208),
 (u'I', 923),
 (u'it', 898),
 (u'you', 846),
 (u'He', 549),
 (u'they', 507),
 (u'him', 493),
 (u'them', 325),
 (u'It', 287),
 (u'me', 215)]
```

Knowledge of POS-tags can help us with a more in-depth text analysis. It is a pillar of natural language processing, and after the tokenizing text is usually the first piece of analysis which we carry out. spaCy offers us the best way to perform POS-tagging, but we have had a look at all the other options that Python gives us as well. We will be sticking with spaCy for the rest of the computational linguistics tasks we will be exploring, such as NER-tagging and dependency parsing in the next chapters.

Summary

We've explored in this chapter how to use spaCy as part of our pipelines, and in particular how to extract POS-tags. We discussed what POS-tags are, and how they can be useful in different kinds of analysis. We soon moved on to training your own POS-tagger in spaCy and looked at different examples where we use POS-tags. We will now explore other spaCy functionalities such as NER-tagging and dependency parsing.

References

[1] 8 Parts of Speech:
http://www.butte.edu/departments/cas/tipsheets/grammar/parts_of_speech.html

[2] Parts of Speech overview:
http://partofspeech.org/

[3] spaCy Annotation Specifications:
https://spacy.io/api/annotation#pos-tagging

[4] Hidden Markov Model:
https://en.wikipedia.org/wiki/Hidden_Markov_model

[5] A simple rule-based part of speech tagger:
http://www.aclweb.org/anthology/A92-1021

[6] displaCy:
https://explosion.ai/demos/displacy

[7] ntlk tag module:
https://www.nltk.org/api/nltk.tag.html

[8] nltk chapter 5:
https://www.nltk.org/book/ch05.html

[9] Training NLTK tagger:
http://textminingonline.com/dive-into-nltk-part-iii-part-of-speech-tagging-and-pos-tagger

[10] AI in Practice: Identifying Parts of Speech in Python:
https://medium.com/@brianray_7981/ai-in-practice-identifying-parts-of-speech-in-python-8a690c7a1a08

[11] Speech Tagging in TextBlob:
https://stevenloria.com/pos-tagging/

[12] spaCy training:
https://spacy.io/usage/training

[13] prodigy:
https://prodi.gy/

[14] Gold Standard:
https://spacy.io/api/goldparse

[15] Universal POS tags:
http://universaldependencies.org/docs/u/pos/index.html

[16] Training your POS-tagger:
https://nlpforhackers.io/training-pos-tagger/

[17] A Good Part-of-Speech Tagger in about 200 Lines of Python:
https://explosion.ai/blog/part-of-speech-pos-tagger-in-python

[18] train_tagger.py:
https://github.com/explosion/spacy/blob/master/examples/training/train_tagger.py

6
NER-Tagging and Its Applications

We saw in the previous chapter how we can use spaCy's language pipeline – POS-tagging, which is a very powerful tool, and we will now explore another interesting usage, NER-tagging. We will discuss what exactly this is from both a linguistic and text analysis point of view, as well as detailed examples of its usage, and how to train our own NER-tagger with spaCy. Following are the topics we will cover in this chapter:

- What is NER-tagging?
- NER-tagging in Python
- Training your NER-tagger
- NER-tagging examples and visualization

What is NER-tagging?

We started our chapter on POS-tagging by expanding an acronym, and we'll be doing the same here as well. **NER** stands for **Named Entity Recognition**, and along with part of speech tagging, it is one of the pillars of natural language processing.

Let's us start by understanding what a *named entity* is. A named entity is a real-world object with a proper name – examples are France, Donald Trump, and Twitter. In these examples, France is a country and would be identified as a **GPE (Geopolitical Entity)**, Donald Trump as **PER** (a person), and Twitter is a company, so identified as an **ORG (Organization)**. In a study titled *A survey of named entity recognition and classification* by David Nadeau and Satoshi Sekine (New York University) [1], we get a more rigorous definition:

In the expression "Named Entity", the word "Named" aims to restrict the possible set of entities to only those for which one or many rigid designators stands for the referent. A designator is rigid when it designates the same thing in every possible world.

What we have to understand from this is that it refers to a *particular* object or person. For example, if we NER-tagged the sentence, *Emmanuel Macron is the current president of France.*, we would recognize Emmanuel Macron as a person, and France as a country – but not *president* because it can refer to many objects, such as presidents in different countries or even of an organization.

How many different categories of named entities exist? Again, much like parts of speech, this really depends on us. We can choose to be vague with our entities, only recognizing a few, or have a really fine-grained set of categories. We have to remember that most modern NER-taggers, similar to POS-taggers, are statistically trained models where the number of classes is equal to the number we *want* them to be, and depending on the problem, this is likely to keep changing.

But with this being said, there are a few categories we will expect to see more often than not, like the ones we have discussed before. These would be a person (PER), location (LOC), organization (ORG), and other miscellaneous entities (MISC).

TYPE	DESCRIPTION
PER	Named person or family.
LOC	Name of politically or geographically defined location (cities, provinces, countries, international regions, bodies of water, mountains).
ORG	Named corporate, governmental, or other organizational entity.
MISC	Miscellaneous entities, e.g. events, nationalities, products or works of art.

Fig 6.1 spaCy's lightweight Wikipedia trained tagger, only featuring basic entity types

You may be wondering why in the previous section we have used the particular acronyms (PER, LOC, ORG, and MISC). This is because, like we explored in the previous chapter on POS-tagging, we will largely be discussing spaCy when we perform our NER-tagging. These acronyms also tend to pop up in other taggers and schemes.

Apart from these rather obvious entity types, what other categories are we expected to identify when carrying out this task? Temporal expressions and numerical expressions often come up in this context. But if we adhere to our definition of named entities or rigid designators very closely, this might confuse things for us. For example, think of the year 2016. It designates a particular year, and we can consider it a named entity. But what if we have this sentence –

I enjoy going to the beach in the month of July.

Here, any month can be in the place of July, and without context, it would be difficult to call it a **rigid designator**, or something that refers to a *particular* month. But, on that note, consider this sentence:

I enjoyed going to the beach last July.

Suddenly, the word July now refers to a particular month, is a rigid designator, and should be considered a named entity type. However, it might be difficult to always recognize the context in such a case, and we might have an *incorrect* label. It is during such situations when we have to decide that it isn't always wise to stick to strict definitions when we are performing textual analysis tasks, and that being a little flexible in such situations, can lead to a better performing, more practical machine.

TYPE	DESCRIPTION
PERSON	People, including fictional.
NORP	Nationalities or religious or political groups.
FACILITY	Buildings, airports, highways, bridges, etc.
ORG	Companies, agencies, institutions, etc.
GPE	Countries, cities, states.
LOC	Non-GPE locations, mountain ranges, bodies of water.
PRODUCT	Objects, vehicles, foods, etc. (Not services.)
EVENT	Named hurricanes, battles, wars, sports events, etc.
WORK_OF_ART	Titles of books, songs, etc.
LAW	Named documents made into laws.
LANGUAGE	Any named language.
DATE	Absolute or relative dates or periods.
TIME	Times smaller than a day.
PERCENT	Percentage, including "%".
MONEY	Monetary values, including unit.
QUANTITY	Measurements, as of weight or distance.
ORDINAL	"first", "second", etc.
CARDINAL	Numerals that do not fall under another type.

Fig 6.2 A full list of entity types that spaCy offers

BBN technologies have released a list of entities and subentities used for question answering, and this can be found at – Annotation sub-types [2]. spaCy features 18 different categories for its named entity classification, and we will be using these for the rest of the chapter.

So once again, we've got the *what* out of the way. *Why* should we now be interested in NER-tagging? As usual, simply identifying named entities in text is not often the end result of our task, but it ends up being an important building block for further tasks. Entity linking is a task where we use entity recognition and then attempt to derive relationships between them. Consider this sentence:

Rome is the capital of Italy.

Any NER-tagger would recognize Rome as a place (GPE), as well as Italy. To be able to draw the conclusion that Rome is a city, which is linked to the country Italy, and not Rome, an American R&B artist, are the kind of tasks that we call as **Named Entity Disambiguation (NED)**.

This is also of great value in biomedical research, where scientists attempt to identify genes and gene products. It can be used by the businesses to help identify which organizations are most important by analyzing and identifying links between other organizations and revenue. Both of these examples are domain-specific though; do not expect a tagger trained on medical journal data to perform well on financial documents! This is one difference between NER-tagging and POS-tagging; while POS tend to be more or less across different kinds of literature, named entities can differ entirely based on the context. This results in even really well-trained models to be brittle; this means that it *breaks* easily when used in a different domain.

In analyzing literature and styles of writing, NER-tagging can again come in handy, which we see in the study, *Named Entity Recognition and Resolution for Literary Studies*, by Van Dale and co. [3]. The most popular usage of NER-tagging in science still remains in the field of medicine and biology, which is also evident by the existence of competitions [18] just devoted to extracting entities from medical documents.

There's enough motivation for us to build an NER-tagger; so, to the next question, exactly how are we going to be doing this?

Much like most of the problems we have been attempting to solve so far (and like the ones we will continue to solve throughout this book!), the answer is statistical modeling. Similar to our POS-taggers where we used annotated data-sets and extracted relevant features, we will be doing the same, but with the dataset annotated with entities. It is worth noting that in this context when we talk about relevant features, we are discussing possible information which we can use to predict the class of an unknown object that we wish to identify. And *in our context of NER-tagging, the POS-tag of the word, as well as the POS-tags of the surrounding words can be used as a predictor!*

This is also why in our pipelines we perform POS-tagging before NER-tagging; though, in the case of spaCy, where it is a pretrained statistical model, this doesn't really matter. Other possible features that can be used to predict whether a word is a named entity or not is the prefix or suffix of the word (for example, -ion), whether it contains a special symbol, or whether it is in uppercase or not.

Once we have our features ready, there is a multitude of machine learning algorithms which we can use to train our model – **CRFs** (**Conditional Random Fields**, described in *Conditional Random Fields: Probabilistic Models for Segmenting and Labeling Sequence Data* by John Lafferty and co. [4]) are often a popular choice for NER-tagging, and as are deep learning methods, similar to the one we discussed for POS-tagging.

Of course, much like most tasks that are carried out in natural language processing, we can also attempt more rule-based approaches. Section 13.2.1 of the book *Natural Language Processing: Semantic Aspects* by Epaminondas Kapetanios and co. [5] lists and references multiple such approaches. One such example rule is this one:

Identify a match of a dictionary of salutations followed by a match of a dictionary of last names and mark the entire region as a candidate person.

This technique requires us to have dictionaries where we store salutations, as well as a dictionary of last names. This makes this method quite undesirable; dictionaries can grow to be quite large and take space, can become redundant if not updated regularly, and can make our approach rather domain-specific, or more importantly, data-specific.

It can be seen why we prefer to stick to statistical models throughout this book, and it definitely helps that statistical methods tend to far outperform rule-based methods.

We have a feel of the what, why, and how of NER-tagging, and it is time to get cracking and learn to build models ourselves in Python, as well as how to train these NER-taggers ourselves.

NER-tagging in Python

Our approach with NER-tagging is going to mirror our approach to POS-tagging; after all, they are very similar tasks, and both of them can be compared to the machine learning task of classification, where we assign an unknown object to the class it has the highest probability of belonging to.

Another similarity in our approaches to this task is the fact that we will be using spaCy to conduct our NER-tagging. Again, this does not mean that spaCy is the only way to perform NER-tagging; there are two popular alternatives, one is NLTK, and the other is the Stanford NER-tagger.

Before we start with our explanations, it is worth our while to briefly understand the term, *chunking*. It is the process of breaking up your sentence into constituent parts after the POS-tagging of the sentence is completed. Examples of these constituent parts are noun phrases or verb phrases. For example, consider the following sentence:

The little brown dog barked at the black cat.

In this case, we can identify the two noun phrases quite easily: the *little brown dog* and *the black cat*. These chunks can come in handy when we're doing NER-tagging, and we will explore these topics in a lot more detail in `Chapter 7`, *Dependency Parsing*. In fact, chunking is also referred to as shallow parsing.

So why exactly is it relevant to us during NER-tagging? If you remember, when we were citing examples of NER tags, we said that *Donald Trump* would be tagged as a person; not just *Donald*, or *Trump*, but the entire phrase. This knowledge of a group of words as a noun phrase can help make decisions when we are tagging.

In most taggers we find online, we can find tagging systems such as the IOB tagging system. This is just a way to further identify or represent tokens when we are NER-tagging. This is what **IOB** simply stands for:

B-{CHUNK_TYPE} - for the word in the Beginning chunk

I-{CHUNK_TYPE} - for words Inside the chunk

O - Outside any chunk

spaCy also uses such a system; it adds L and U, and since we deal with tokens in spaCy, it is considered a **BILOU** system.

TAG	DESCRIPTION
B EGIN	The first token of a multi-token entity.
I N	An inner token of a multi-token entity.
L AST	The final token of a multi-token entity.
U NIT	A single-token entity.
O UT	A non-entity token.

Fig 6.3 spaCy's own BILOU system for its NER tags

Even though we will largely use spaCy, let's briefly discuss NLTK: NLTK uses these chunks as part of a tree-like system to do its tagging, though it also has a tagger which follows an IOB system. Here are some code snippets explaining how to use both, and how to convert between them:

```
from nltk.chunk import conlltags2tree, tree2conlltags
from nltk import pos_tag
from nltk import word_tokenize
from nltk.chunk import ne_chunk
```

Our imports, where these models are trained on the CoNLL (from the CoNLL conference) corpus in NLTK. Since we already did our tokenizing, POS-tagging and chunking, all we need to do for the tree-based tagging is to use the `conlltags2tree` method to see our tags.

```
sentence = "Clement and Mathieu are working at Apple."
ne_tree = ne_chunk(pos_tag(word_tokenize(sentence)))

iob_tagged = tree2conlltags(ne_tree)
print(iob_tagged)

[('Clement', 'NNP', u'B-PERSON'), ('and', 'CC', u'O'), ('Mathieu', 'NNP',
u'B-PERSON'), ('are', 'VBP', u'O'), ('working', 'VBG', u'O'), ('at', 'IN',
u'O'), ('Apple', 'NNP', u'B-ORGANIZATION'), ('.', '.', u'O')]
```

Notice here how we first tokenized our sentence, then POS-tagged it, and chunked it before passing it to the tree-based tagger. Our output is each word tagged appropriately with both the part of speech and named entity class.

```
ne_tree = conlltags2tree(iob_tagged)
print(ne_tree)

(S
  (PERSON Clement/NNP)
  and/CC
  (PERSON Mathieu/NNP)
  are/VBP
  working/VBG
  at/IN
  (ORGANIZATION Apple/NNP)
  ./.)
```

The other popular tagger is the **Stanford Named Entity Recognizer** (**NER**) tagger [6]. We previously mentioned **CRFs** (**Conditional Random Fields**) and how they are a machine learning constructs that are often used to train classifiers related to text-based problems; Stanford's tagger uses the same algorithm. While it is written in Java and to use it you must download the JAR files to use it (you can find these files on the website), NLTK offers us a Python interface to access the tagger.

After downloading the JAR files, we must link to them from NLTK. JAR files are Java files that are created by the Java code - we can understand them as libraries which we load through Python, in our case.

```
from nltk.tag import StanfordNERTagger
st = StanfordNERTagger('/usr/share/stanford-
ner/classifiers/english.all.3class.distsim.crf.ser.gz',
'/usr/share/stanford-ner/stanford-ner.jar', encoding='utf-8')
```

Be careful to note the URLs you must refer to. Since our examples will only deal with English, we only load the English class.

Let's use it is as straightforward as when using the other NLTK taggers:

```
st.tag('Baptiste Capdeville is studying at Columbia University in
NY'.split())

[('Baptiste', 'PERSON'), ('Capdeville', 'PERSON'), ('is', 'O'),
('studying', 'O'),
('at', 'O'), ('Columbia', 'ORGANIZATION'), ('University', 'ORGANIZATION'),
('in', 'O'), ('NY', 'LOCATION')]
```

We see that once again, similar to our POS-tagging example, NLTK can be tempting because of the simple API it offers, but this is still not what we would want to use in any production level software. Before we jump into using spaCy to do our NER-tagging, we encourage the reader to browse the following links regarding NLTK and what it offers:

1. Testing NLTK and Stanford NER Taggers for Accuracy [7]
2. How to Use Stanford Named Entity Recognizer (NER) in Python NLTK and Other Programming Languages [8]
3. Chapter 7 (NLTK book) – Extracting Information from Text [9]
4. Named Entity Recognition On Large Collections From Python (PyNER) [10]

NER-tagging with spaCy

We've discussed the incredible power and simplicity of spaCy before when we talked about POS-tagging – and we will cite the same reasons when using spaCy for NER-tagging. In practice, if you've followed the previous chapter on POS-tagging, we have already finished our POS-tagging; since NER-tagging is part of spaCy's natural pipeline, simply processing a document with the pipeline means that along with being tokenized and POS-tagged, it has already been NER-tagged (not to mention dependency parsed too!).

Setting up our model involves the same steps we saw before.

```
import spacy
nlp = spacy.load('en')
```

Let's now decide some sentences we would like to NER-tag.

```
sent_0 = nlp(u'Donald Trump visited at the government headquarters in
France today.')

sent_1 = nlp(u'Emmanuel Jean-Michel Frédéric Macron is a French politician
serving as President of France and ex officio Co-Prince of Andorra since 14
May 2017.')

sent_2 = nlp(u"He studied philosophy at Paris Nanterre University,
completed a Master's of Public Affairs at Sciences Po, and graduated from
the École nationale d'administration (ÉNA) in 2004.")

sent_3 = nlp(u'He worked at the Inspectorate General of Finances, and later
became an investment banker at Rothschild & Cie Banque.')
```

The sent_0 sentence is straightforward and will illustrate how we expect a basic sentence to be NER-tagged by spaCy.

When spaCy processes a document, the named entities are stored in the `ents` property of a `Doc` class. We can still access the entities through the token, which is stored in the `ent_type`. Here is an example illustrating the use of both:

```
for token in sent_0:
    print(token.text, token.ent_type_)

(u'Donald', u'PERSON')
(u'Trump', u'PERSON')
(u'visited', u'')
(u'at', u'')
(u'the', u'')
(u'government', u'')
(u'headquarters', u'')
(u'in', u'')
(u'France', u'GPE')
(u'today', u'DATE')
(u'.', u'')
```

For those words that were not identified as named entities, an empty string is returned. For those identified as named entities, the appropriate tag is returned. In our example, we have just three entities, `Donald Trump`, `France`, and `today`, which are correctly identified as `PERSON`, `GPE`, and `DATE`, respectively. Because government headquarters doesn't refer to a particular one, it isn't identified as a named entity. We could argue that because `France` is mentioned, one could assume that the government headquarters should also be tagged, but this is a grey area and we could give our tagger a pass here.

Remember that spaCy intends us to access the entities in the `doc.ents` streamable object. This slice of the `Doc` class is called a `Span` class [11].

```
for ent in sent_0.ents:
    print(ent.text, ent.label_)

(u'Donald Trump', u'PERSON')
(u'France', u'GPE')
(u'today', u'DATE')
```

You can see that only the entities are picked up by the span, and the three entities are printed. Note that `Donald Trump` is one entity and how this was not inherently captured when just printing out tokens.

Let's try the next sentence, which is longer and contains a French name, which might potentially throw off our English tagger.

```
for token in sent_1:
    print(token.text, token.ent_type_)
```

```
(u'Emmanuel', u'PERSON')
(u'Jean', u'PERSON')
(u'-', u'PERSON')
(u'Michel', u'PERSON')
(u'Frxe9dxe9ric', u'')
(u'Macron', u'')
(u'is', u'')
(u'a', u'')
(u'French', u'NORP')
(u'politician', u'')
(u'serving', u'')
(u'as', u'')
(u'President', u'')
(u'of', u'')
(u'France', u'GPE')
(u'and', u'')
(u'ex', u'')
(u'officio', u'')
(u'Co', u'PERSON')
(u'-', u'PERSON')
(u'Prince', u'PERSON')
(u'of', u'')
(u'Andorra', u'')
(u'since', u'')
(u'14', u'DATE')
(u'May', u'DATE')
(u'2017', u'DATE')
(u'.', u'')
```

Here, we notice a few peculiarities. The accent on the é character throws off the Unicode here, so `Macron` isn't captured as part of the entity. We will see later on in this chapter that if not for the accent, or for the way Unicode is read in this example, `Macron` would have been included as part of the entity. We can see that `Co-Prince of Andorra` isn't identified as the best possible way, too.

Let's look at the same example, but only printing the entities:

```
for ent in sent_1.ents:
    print(ent.text, ent.label_)

(u'Emmanuel Jean-Michel', u'PERSON')
(u'French', u'NORP')
(u'France', u'GPE')
(u'Co-Prince', u'PERSON')
(u'14 May 2017', u'DATE')
```

We see the mistakes here quite clearly. That being said, let's remove occurrences of accents before we run the next example:

```
for token in sent_2:
    print(token.text, token.ent_type_)

(u'He', u'')
(u'studied', u'')
(u'philosophy', u'')
(u'at', u'')
(u'Paris', u'ORG')
(u'Nanterre', u'ORG')
(u'University', u'ORG')
(u',', u'')
(u'completed', u'')
(u'a', u'')
(u'Masters', u'ORG')
(u'of', u'ORG')
(u'Public', u'ORG')
(u'Affairs', u'ORG')
(u'at', u'')
(u'Sciences', u'')
(u'Po', u'')
(u',', u'')
(u'and', u'')
(u'graduated', u'')
(u'from', u'')
(u'the', u'ORG')
(u'Ecole', u'ORG')
(u'Nationale', u'ORG')
(u'Administration', u'ORG')
(u'(', u'')
(u'ENA', u'ORG')
(u')', u'')
(u'in', u'')
(u'2004', u'DATE')
(u'.', u'')
```

We see no errors in this example - let's examine only the spans to see if it's picked up all the phrases.

```
(u'Paris Nanterre University', u'ORG')
(u'Masters of Public Affairs', u'ORG')
(u'the Ecole Nationale Administration', u'ORG')
(u'ENA', u'ORG')
(u'2004', u'DATE')
```

And voila! We see once we've removed the pesky accents it's smooth.

```
for token in sent_3:
    print(token.text, token.ent_type_)

(u'He', u'')
(u'worked', u'')
(u'at', u'')
(u'the', u'ORG')
(u'Inspectorate', u'ORG')
(u'General', u'ORG')
(u'of', u'ORG')
(u'Finances', u'ORG')
(u',', u'')
(u'and', u'')
(u'later', u'')
(u'became', u'')
(u'an', u'')
(u'investment', u'')
(u'banker', u'')
(u'at', u'')
(u'Rothschild', u'ORG')
(u'&', u'ORG')
(u'Cie', u'ORG')
(u'Banque', u'ORG')
(u'.', u'')

for ent in sent_3.ents:
    print(ent.text, ent.label_)

(u'the Inspectorate General of Finances', u'ORG')
(u'Rothschild & Cie Banque', u'ORG')
```

And there we go – we've seen how spaCy works in a variety of settings, and the possible things that can confuse it. Overall, it works quite well, and we encourage the reader to try out a few of their examples.

Much like the POS-taggers of spaCy's model, we are also encouraged to train spaCy's own NER model.

Training our own NER-taggers

In the previous chapter on POS-tagging, we discussed in detail the training process of a statistical model used for tagging. The idea for NER-tagging remains the same – we select features we believe are indicative of a named entity tag, plug these features into a machine learning model, feed it annotated data, and let the machine learn from the examples provided.

 If you are in the need of a refresher of how the training process happens in a spaCy model, we recommend that you re-read *Training our own POS-taggers* section from the Chapter 5, *POS-Tagging and Its Applications* of the book.

We will now examine two code files present in the spaCy examples folder: one which trains a blank model to perform NER-tagging, and another which adds a new entity to an existing model.

The following code appears in the train_ner.py file [12]:

```
import plac
import random
from pathlib import Path
import spacy

# training data
TRAIN_DATA = [
    ('Who is Shaka Khan?', {
        'entities': [(7, 17, 'PERSON')]
    }),
    ('I like London and Berlin.', {
        'entities': [(7, 13, 'LOC'), (18, 24, 'LOC')]
    })
]
```

We've set up our basic imports and our training examples. A friendly reminder that these are far too few examples for any serious training to happen, and that is merely a representative example.

```
@plac.annotations(
    model=("Model name. Defaults to blank 'en' model.", "option", "m",
str),
    output_dir=("Optional output directory", "option", "o", Path),
    n_iter=("Number of training iterations", "option", "n", int))
def main(model=None, output_dir=None, n_iter=100):
    """Load the model, set up the pipeline and train the
        entity recognizer."""
    if model is not None:
        nlp = spacy.load(model)  # load existing spaCy model
        print("Loaded model '%s'" % model)
    else:
        nlp = spacy.blank('en')  # create blank Language class
        print("Created blank 'en' model")
```

We've set up annotations for where our model will be saved, as well as the number of iterations. Our model is loaded, and we have now created a blank model.

```
# create the built-in pipeline components and add them to the pipeline
# nlp.create_pipe works for built-ins that are registered with spaCy
    if 'ner' not in nlp.pipe_names:
        ner = nlp.create_pipe('ner')
        nlp.add_pipe(ner, last=True)
# otherwise, get it so we can add labels
    else:
        ner = nlp.get_pipe('ner')
# add labels
    for _, annotations in TRAIN_DATA:
        for ent in annotations.get('entities'):
            ner.add_label(ent[2])
# get names of other pipes to disable them during training
other_pipes = [pipe for pipe in nlp.pipe_names if pipe != 'ner']
    with nlp.disable_pipes(*other_pipes):  # only train NER
        optimizer = nlp.begin_training()
        for itn in range(n_iter):
            random.shuffle(TRAIN_DATA)
            losses = {}
            for text, annotations in TRAIN_DATA:
                nlp.update(
                    [text], # batch of texts
                    [annotations], # batch of annotations
                    drop=0.5, # dropout-make it harder to memorise data
                    sgd=optimizer, # callable to update weights
                    losses=losses)
            print(losses)
```

We notice here that it follows the exact same training principles as the POS-tagger. We start by adding the `ner` label to the pipeline, and then disabling all the other components of the pipe so that we only train/update the NER-tagger. The training itself is straightforward, and the `nlp.update()` method abstracts everything for us, letting spaCy deal with the actual machine learning and heavy lifting.

```
# test the trained model
for text, _ in TRAIN_DATA:
    doc = nlp(text)
    print('Entities', [(ent.text, ent.label_) for ent in doc.ents])
    print('Tokens', [(t.text, t.ent_type_, t.ent_iob) for t in doc])
# save model to output directory
    if output_dir is not None:
        output_dir = Path(output_dir)
        if not output_dir.exists():
            output_dir.mkdir()
    nlp.to_disk(output_dir)
    print("Saved model to", output_dir)
# test the saved model
    print("Loading from", output_dir)
    nlp2 = spacy.load(output_dir)
    for text, _ in TRAIN_DATA:
        doc = nlp2(text)
        print('Entities', [(ent.text, ent.label_) for ent in doc.ents])
        print('Tokens', [(t.text, t.ent_type_, t.ent_iob) for t in
doc])

if __name__ == '__main__':
    plac.call(main)
```

Soon after our training is done, we test our model and then save it to the directory specified. If we run the file without any errors, we should expect the following output:

```
Entities [('Shaka Khan', 'PERSON')]
Tokens [('Who', '', 2), ('is', '', 2), ('Shaka', 'PERSON', 3),
('Khan', 'PERSON', 1), ('?', '', 2)]
Entities [('London', 'LOC'), ('Berlin', 'LOC')]
Tokens [('I', '', 2), ('like', '', 2), ('London', 'LOC', 3),
('and', '', 2), ('Berlin', 'LOC', 3), ('.', '', 2)]
```

Let's now look at adding a new class to a model. The principle remains the same here; we load the model, disable the pipes we won't be updating, add the new label, and then loop over the examples and update them. Again, exactly like the old example, don't expect the trained model to do any wonders – we don't have enough training examples.

The actual training is performed by looping over the examples and calling `nlp.entity.update()`. The `update()` method steps through the words of the input. At each word, it makes a prediction. It then consults the annotations provided on the `GoldParse` instance, to see whether it was right. If it was wrong, it adjusts its weights so that the correct action will score higher next time.

```
import plac
import random
from pathlib import Path
import spacy

# new entity label
LABEL = 'ANIMAL'

TRAIN_DATA = [
    ("Horses are too tall and they pretend to care about your feelings", {
        'entities': [(0, 6, 'ANIMAL')]
    }),

    ("Do they bite?", {
        'entities': []
    }),

    ("horses are too tall and they pretend to care about your feelings", {
        'entities': [(0, 6, 'ANIMAL')]
    }),

    ("horses pretend to care about your feelings", {
        'entities': [(0, 6, 'ANIMAL')]
    }),

    ("they pretend to care about your feelings, those horses", {
        'entities': [(48, 54, 'ANIMAL')]
    }),

    ("horses?", {
        'entities': [(0, 6, 'ANIMAL')]
    })
]
```

We've set up our imports and our training examples.

> If you're using an existing model, make sure to mix in examples of other entity types that spaCy correctly recognized before. Otherwise, your model might learn the new type, but *forget* what it previously knew.

This blog post link explains this mistake of forgetting old functions, https://explosion.ai/blog/pseudo-rehearsal-catastrophic-forgetting.

```
@plac.annotations(
    model=("Model name. Defaults to blank 'en' model.", "option", "m",
str),
    new_model_name=("New model name for model meta.", "option", "nm", str),
    output_dir=("Optional output directory", "option", "o", Path),
    n_iter=("Number of training iterations", "option", "n", int))
def main(model=None, new_model_name='animal', output_dir=None, n_iter=20):
    """Set up the pipeline and entity recognizer, and train
        the new entity."""
    if model is not None:
        nlp = spacy.load(model)  # load existing spaCy model
        print("Loaded model '%s'" % model)
    else:
        nlp = spacy.blank('en')  # create blank Language class
        print("Created blank 'en' model")
    # Add entity recognizer to model if it's not in the pipeline
    # nlp.create_pipe works for built-ins that are registered with spaCy
    if 'ner' not in nlp.pipe_names:
        ner = nlp.create_pipe('ner')
        nlp.add_pipe(ner)
    # otherwise, get it, so we can add labels to it
    else:
        ner = nlp.get_pipe('ner')
```

The preceding steps are similar to the previous example. Pay attention to the next line carefully – it's where we add our label.

```
        ner.add_label(LABEL)   # add new entity label to entity recognizer
        if model is None:
            optimizer = nlp.begin_training()
        else:
            # Note that 'begin_training' initializes the models, so it'll
            # zero out existing entity types.
            optimizer = nlp.entity.create_optimizer()
    # get names of other pipes to disable them during training
        other_pipes = [pipe for pipe in nlp.pipe_names if pipe != 'ner']
        with nlp.disable_pipes(*other_pipes):  # only train NER
        for itn in range(n_iter):
```

```
random.shuffle(TRAIN_DATA)
losses = {}
for text, annotations in TRAIN_DATA:
    nlp.update([text], [annotations], sgd=optimizer,
            drop=0.35, losses=losses)
print(losses)
```

We trained our model the same way we trained the previous model; after all, the training process remains the same.

```
# test the trained model
test_text = 'Do you like horses?'
doc = nlp(test_text)
print("Entities in '%s'" % test_text)
for ent in doc.ents:
    print(ent.label_, ent.text)

# save model to output directory
if output_dir is not None:
    output_dir = Path(output_dir)
    if not output_dir.exists():
        output_dir.mkdir()
    nlp.meta['name'] = new_model_name  # rename model
    nlp.to_disk(output_dir)
    print("Saved model to", output_dir)
# test the saved model
    print("Loading from", output_dir)
    nlp2 = spacy.load(output_dir)
    doc2 = nlp2(test_text)
    for ent in doc2.ents:
        print(ent.label_, ent.text)

if __name__ == '__main__':
    plac.call(main)
```

The rest of the code again remains the same; the crucial difference is in the training data, adding the new class, and considering we need to add older examples too.

It is worth looking at spaCy's *NER linguistic features* page [16] – they also offer useful advice on how to set entity annotations.

spaCy offers us an easy way to train our models, though it's existing models do a good job too. We should not forget what lies underneath the hood – a statistical model that accepts features and makes predictions. Even NLTK offers us the ability to train their models. There are a number of tutorials that explain how to build your own classifier, or how to update your NLTK classifier. While these are interesting to understand the concepts behind training an NER classifier, it is not relevant to our immediate cause. We offer a list of these tutorials in case the reader is interested:

1. A complete guide to building your own Named Entity Recognizer with Python [13]
2. Introduction To Named Entity Recognition In Python [14]
3. Performing Sequence Labelling using CRF in Python [15]

NER-tagging examples and visualization

One of spaCy's most impressive offerings is its visualization suites and API, and in particular `displaCy` [17]. We discussed this in the previous chapter when visualizing part of speech tags. While it is most impressive in visualizing dependency parsing (which we will see next chapter), it doesn't do a half bad job with entities either.

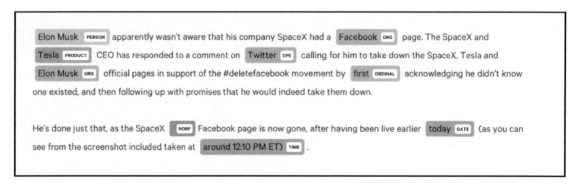

Fig 6.4 An example from a news excerpt from an Elon Musk article on https://www.wired.com

We can see in the above example that spaCy has caught the entities quite well. Indeed, even the Elon Musk page is marked as an organization, which could be considered an organization. It could be the context of Tesla before it or *official pages* after it – we cannot be sure. We do have an interesting mistake caught again here, where Twitter is a geopolitical entity. Again, we could let this slide if we are considering that Facebook and Twitter are becoming big enough to be a country! But jokes aside, it is not always easy to deal with such words unless the corpus was trained on a similar domain. Let's look at the sentences we NER-tagged before:

Emmanuel Jean-Michel Frédéric Macron (French pronunciation: [ɛmanɥɛl makʁɔ̃]; born 21 December 1977) is a French politician serving as President of France and ex officio Co-Prince of Andorra since 14 May 2017.

Before entering politics, he was a senior civil servant and investment banker. Macron studied philosophy at Paris Nanterre University, completed a Master's of Public Affairs at Sciences Po, and graduated from the École nationale d'administration (ÉNA) in 2004. He worked at the Inspectorate General of Finances, and later became an investment banker at Rothschild & Cie Banque.

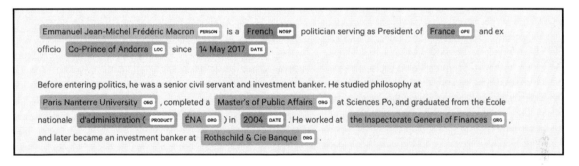

Fig 6.5 An example visualizing entities from the wiki page of French President, Emmanuel Macron

We can see here that Macron's whole name is caught – the accent didn't throw off the web-app!

Apart from neat visualizations, we can also use NERs for simple, more possibly pointless tasks, such as swapping two NERs in a sentence around.

```
words, indices = [], []
for i, w in enumerate(nlp(u'Tom went to London before going to Paris.')):
    words.append(w.text_with_ws), indices.append(i) if w.ent_type_ == "GPE"
else words.append(w.text_with_ws)
```

```
words[indices[0]], words[indices[1]] = words[indices[1]], words[indices[0]]
print(''.join(words))
```

Tom went to Paris before going to London.

In five sentences, we've swapped London for Paris – might not be the most useful manipulation of sentence we've seen so far, but it illustrates the ease of spaCy quite well.

Summary

We've seen once again how well spaCy deals with computational linguistic tasks and also how useful NER-tagging can be. While being a task that is used in text analysis, the model itself is a statistical one – understanding this helps in setting the context for building our own models if we would like, or in updating the existing model that spaCy uses.

In the next chapter, we will see how spaCy deals with our final section on computational linguistics – dependency parsing.

References

[1] A survey of named entity recognition and classification:
https://nlp.cs.nyu.edu/sekine/papers/li07.pdf

[2] Annotation Sub-Types:
https://catalog.ldc.upenn.edu/docs/LDC2005T33/BBN-Types-Subtypes.html

[3] Named Entity Recognition and Resolution for Literary Studies:
https://pure.uva.nl/ws/files/2676433/168352_2014_VanDalenOskam_07_Namescape.pdf

[4] Conditional Random Fields: Probabilistic Models for Segmenting and Labeling Sequence Data:
https://repository.upenn.edu/cgi/viewcontent.cgi?referer=&httpsredir=1&article=1162&context=cis_papers

[5] Natural Language Processing: Semantic Aspects:
https://books.google.fr/books?id=YXv6AQAAQBAJ&source=gbs_navlinks_s

[6] Stanford NER:
https://nlp.stanford.edu/software/CRF-NER.shtml

[7] Testing NLTK and Stanford NER Taggers for Accuracy:
`https://pythonprogramming.net/testing-stanford-ner-taggers-for-accuracy/?comple ted=/named-entity-recognition-stanford-ner-tagger/`

[8] How to Use Stanford Named Entity Recognizer (NER) in Python NLTK and Other Programming Languages:
`http://textminingonline.com/how-to-use-stanford-named-entity-recognizer-ner-in- python-nltk-and-other-programming-languages`

[9] Chapter 7 (NLTK book) - Extracting Information from Text:
`http://www.nltk.org/book/ch07.html`

[10] Named Entity Recognition On Large Collections From Python (PyNER):
`http://erickpeirson.github.io/pythia/python/2015/05/01/named-entity-recognition -on-large-collections.html`

[11] span:
`https://spacy.io/api/span`

[12] train_ner.py:
`https://github.com/explosion/spacy/blob/master/examples/training/train_ner.py`

[13] A complete guide to build your own Named Entity Recognizer with Python:
`https://nlpforhackers.io/named-entity-extraction/`

[14] Introduction To Named Entity Recognition In Python:
`https://www.depends-on-the-definition.com/introduction-named-entity-recognition -python/`

[15] Performing Sequence Labelling using CRF in Python:
`http://www.albertauyeung.com/post/python-sequence-labelling-with-crf/`

[16] spaCy NER:
`https://spacy.io/usage/training#section-ner`

[17] dispaCy:
`https://explosion.ai/demos/displacy`

[18] Biocreative:
`http://www.biocreative.org/`

Dependency Parsing

We saw in Chapter 5, *POS-Tagging and Its Applications* and Chapter 6, *NER-Tagging and Its Applications*, how spaCy's language pipeline performs a variety of complex computational linguistics algorithms, such as POS-tagging and NER-tagging. This isn't all spaCy packs though, and in this chapter, we will explore the power of dependency parsing and how it can be used in a variety of contexts and applications. We will have a look at the theory of dependency parsing before moving on to using it with spaCy, as well as training our own dependency parsers. Following are the topics we will cover in this chapter:

- Dependency parsing
- Dependency parsing with Python
- Training our dependency parsers
- Summary
- References

Dependency parsing

Parsing remains one of the most important processes we can carry out in the text. It isn't limited to natural languages though and has a history of computer languages as well, and the ideologies can also be extended to any kind of data structure that conforms to certain formal grammatical rules.

This means that to be able to do any kind of parsing, we would need two things – a parser and a grammar. But wait, what *exactly* is parsing?

We can understand it is a way to analyze a sentence or breaking up a sentence to understand the structure of a sentence. The way we break up the sentence to understand its underlying structures is what makes up the crix of parsing, and there are many different ways we can attempt to interpret a sentence's structure.

We mention sentence here because it is relevant to us because of natural languages, but parsing is an activity that can be performed on any statement with a formal grammar. For example, let's look at this simple arithmetic statement: *((7 + 3) * (5 - 2))*

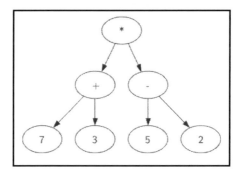

Fig 7.1 An example of parsing a simple mathematical statement

How would we break this up? The four numbers would be our four main constituents, and the other symbols represent the actions between these numbers. Following standard **BODMAS** rules of arithmetic, we would first finish the actions in between brackets. We then describe how the mathematical symbols (**+**, **-**, *****) relate the leaves of the tree - here the leaves are the nodes at the very bottom of the tree, and are the numbers **7**, **3**, **5**, and **2**. The figure explains how we would parse such a statement.

Now that we know what the idea of parsing is, we can focus on how it is relevant to us. Even in the world of natural language processing, the term parsing could mean two different things - while traditional sentence parsing refers to the understanding of the meaning of a sentence of a word, in the context of computational linguistics it can also refer to the formal analysis by an algorithm that results in a parse tree (not dissimilar from the tree we saw earlier).

In our discussions throughout this chapter, whenever we refer to parsing, we will refer to the traditional sentence parsing. In the realm of traditional sentence parsing, there are many schools of thought, out of which two are the most popular - dependency parsing and phrase structure parsing. We will be largely using dependency parsing in our textual analysis, but it is worth our while to understand both kinds of parsing.

A little bit of history - dependency parsing is a rather new approach to parsing, and the French linguist Lucien Tesnière [1] is credited with introducing this school of thought. **Constituency Parsing**, on the other hand, has been around for much longer, with Aristotle's ideas on **term logic** [2] said to resemble the way we understand constituencies. It is formally credited to Noam Chomsky [3], who is considered the father of linguistics.

As the name suggests, dependency parsing refers to understanding the structure of a sentence via the dependencies between words in a sentence. Dependency is the idea that words in a sentence are connected to each other with directed links. Phrase structure parsing, on the other hand, breaks up sentences into phrases, or separate constituents, and can also be referred to as constituency parsing. So, while a sentence that is dependency parsed would give us information about the relationships between words in a sentence, a sentence that is parsed using constituency relationships will help us understand how we can group our sentences.

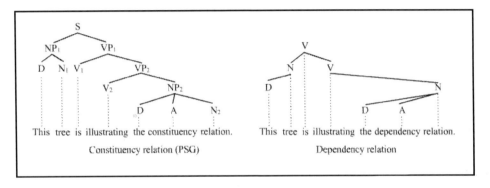

Fig 7.2 Illustrating the differences between constituency and dependency parsing. Credits: Wikipedia editor Tjo3ya [4]

What kind of information can we extract from a sentence parsed using phrases or constituencies? This kind of parsing depends on splitting up a sentence into phrases, particularly into a subject (usually the **noun phrase (NP)**) and a predicate (the **verb phrase (VP)**). Note from the diagram that the relationships between words involve multiple links. Indeed, in the example, we see an almost recursive structure. The words of the sentence are also called the leaves of the tree, and each of the phrases here is the nodes. It is useful in finding out what kind of phrases exist in a sentence, and the sub-phrases as well. Since this results in us identifying the subject and the object as well, we have some semantic information about the context of words which might be previously unknown. For example, consider the sentence: *The lion ate the zebra.*

We have previously discussed how to represent words as vectors (Chapter 3, *spaCy's Language Models*), and one of these representations was the bag of words representation. In such a case, we would only be aware of the presence of the words (assuming that the stopwords are removed) *lion*, *ate*, and *zebra*. While it is likely that the lion did indeed eat the zebra, we cannot *really* be sure unless we know the order and structure of the sentence - a phrasal parsing of the sentence will deliver us with the subject (lion) and object (zebra), which would allow us to confirm our intuition that the lion did indeed eat the zebra.

Again, since this is not a linguistics book, we will not be further focusing on the kinds of grammars that exist, or indeed even the parsing techniques being used (and there are many! The Wikipedia article on phrase structure grammar [5] on the same has a helpful summary), but rather on how to actually perform the parsing, and on how to interpret and use the results.

Dependency parsing focuses on the relationships or dependencies between the words in a sentence. That being said, there are many kinds of dependencies which can be represented during such a parsing; the popular ones being semantic dependencies, morphological dependencies, prosodic dependencies, and syntactic dependencies (the article [6] by Joakim Nivre sums up the theory behind some of these, as does the Wikipedia page on dependency grammar [7]).

Throughout this chapter, we will focus on one particular kind of dependency parsing - syntactic dependency parsing. This is in part because most work in dependency parsing refers to the syntactic dependency parsing, and also in part because spaCy's parsing algorithm is a syntactic dependency parser. This kind of parsing, as the name suggests, assigns a syntactic structure to a sentence, and in our case, this will be a tree.

Let's sum up some of the differences between the two kinds of parsing methods. Constituency parsing breaks up a sentence into sub-phrases, where the non-terminal nodes are the types of phrases, and the terminal nodes (leaves) are the words in the sentence, and the edges are unlabeled. We would use them to understand the phrases a sentence has, as well as the subject and objects.

Dependency parsing connects words according to relationships, and each vertex in the tree represents a word. There are child words and parent nodes, and each edge is labeled to explain the relationship between the words.

Constituency parsers and dependency parsers also differ in the first break-up or split between the sentences; constituency parsers break up a sentence into a subject and an object, which is usually a noun phrase and a verb phrase. Dependency parsers, on the other hand, consider the verb as the head of the sentence, and all dependencies are built around it.

We have spoken a lot about these dependencies - but what exactly are they? spaCy uses the *CLEAR style* [8] for marking its dependencies. We would again like to stress that understanding the linguistic dependencies and what they imply is beyond the scope of the book, and we encourage the reader to use the aforementioned links and research articles to refresh their knowledge on dependencies. That being said, let's look at this simple example:

The dog is faster than the cat.

If we dependency parse this sentence and visualize it (again, using the always useful `displaCy` [9]), this is what we see.

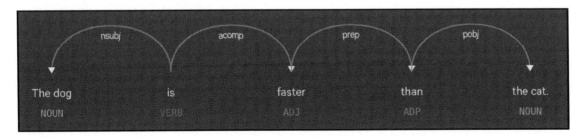

Fig 7.3 Visualizing dependency parsing

In this example, the root word is *is*, which is the main verb of the sentence. The dog is the noun phrase which is marked as **nsubj**, which refers to the nominal subject of the sentence. **Acomp** means adjectival complement, which means that it is a clause or phrase that modifies an adjective or adds to the meaning to an adjective. The word *than* is our preposition; and **pobj** stands for the object of a preposition, which is here *the cat*.

For a faster round-up of what labels spaCy assigns, the annotation page [10] is very useful.

We now have an idea of what exactly dependency parsing and have a peek into why they can be very useful for us in our text analysis tasks. But where exactly is this information of phrases or of dependencies going to come in handy?

Like most NLP tasks, finishing one task can greatly help in other tasks. In this case, having a sentence parsed with phrasal rules can help us in NER-tagging. We remember from the previous chapter that often noun chunks are tagged as an entire entity, and these chunks are often identified post-parsing. The other major use of parsers is in machine translation, where semantic and syntactic information is very important. Since we are constructing trees when we perform parsing, we can convert this tree and represent it as a knowledge graph where we have information regarding the words and how they relate to one another. Using such a knowledge graph as an intermediate step, we can attempt to perform language agnostic translation.

This kind of knowledge graph representation of a sentence can also be helpful when constructing chatbots or a system where we have to understand tasks that need to be performed - in this case, identifying actions are very important. Parsing can also help verify the grammatical correctness of a sentence.

But let's move beyond grammatical correctness and attempt to solve another problem: ambiguity. Like most languages, the English language isn't always straightforward, and a single comma can change the meaning of a sentence. Consider the following two sentences:

I saw a girl with a telescope.

I saw a girl, with a telescope.

While both sentences seemingly appear to mean the same thing, the comma in the second sentence changes this entirely. The first sentence implies that the subject, *I saw a girl who has a telescope.* The second sentence, on the other hand, suggests that the subject saw a girl *using* a telescope. How does spaCy's dependency parser deal with this?

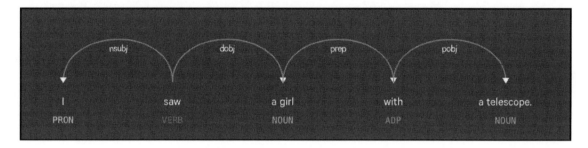

Fig 7.4 Visualizing without a comma

As expected, without a comma, the dependency links *a girl*, *with* and *telescope*, suggesting that the girl is in possession of the telescope.

When we visualize it again, but this time with a comma in the sentence:

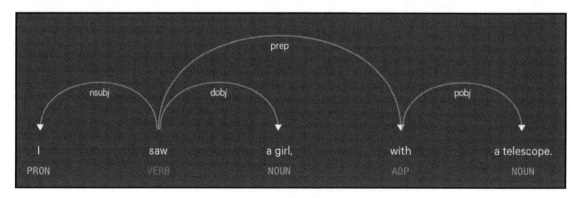

Fig 7.5 Visualizing with a comma

We immediately see how the word *with*, and by extension *a telescope* are linked to the root verb, *saw*. This is because the act of seeing was done using a telescope.

Here, dependencies helped resolve ambiguities between two very similar sentences.

It is clear that dependency parsing has a wealth of applications. Constructing such parsers have long been a problem in natural language processing, and also one that we will not attempt to explain or solve, as they merit their own chapters and theoretical underpinnings. Older methods used heavily rule-based parsing techniques which were dependent on the grammar used. We have now, much like POS-tagging and NER-tagging, shifted to statistical methods to parse, where we tag our phrases and dependencies, using a probabilistic measure which tells us the most likely way a sentence should be parsed based on historical training data and a few basic rules. We have already seen two instances of training such models in Chapter 5, *POS-Tagging and Its Applications* and Chapter 6, *NER-Tagging and Its Applications*, so you should now be comfortable with the process.

As usual, the Python programming language provides us with rich tools and libraries to perform dependency parsing - let's move to the next section where we will discuss this.

Dependency parsing in Python

It's easy to spot the trend in Chapter 4, *Gensim - Vectorizing Text and Transformations and n-grams*, Chapter 5, *POS-Tagging and Its Applications*, and Chapter 6, *NER-Tagging and Its Applications* - all of which choose spaCy as the preferred implementation, not just for the accuracy and speed, but for the way it naturally fits into our text analysis pipelines. We still discussed the other Python libraries available to perform the task, and we will do the same for dependency Parsing.

As usual, we will start with NLTK, which provides the most options regarding parsing methods, but unlike the previous cases, a not so intuitive API and one where we are forced to pass our own grammar for effective results. It is not our purpose to learn grammars before we run computational linguistic algorithms, and this is another reason we will always prefer spaCy for industry strength code.

What we will do however is to demonstrate how to use the **Stanford Dependency Parser** wrapped using NLTK.

The first step would be to download the necessary JAR files from the *Stanford Dependency Parser* page [11] (it would also be worth your while to check out Stanford's other *Statistical Parser* [12], simply for the historical value.).

```
from nltk.parse.stanford import StanfordDependencyParser
path_to_jar = 'path_to/stanford-parser-full-2014-08-27/stanford-parser.jar'
path_to_models_jar = 'path_to/stanford-parser-full-2014-08-27/stanford-
parser-3.4.1-models.jar'
dependency_parser = StanfordDependencyParser(path_to_jar=path_to_jar,
path_to_models_jar=path_to_models_jar)
```

The preceding lines of code demonstrate how to load the Stanford JAR files into our Python NLTK interface, which like the previous POS-tagging and NER-tagging examples, link to the JAR files on your machine. Be sure to post the path to the directory of your files.

```
result = dependency_parser.raw_parse('I shot an elephant in my sleep')
dep = result._next_()
list(dep.triples())
```

If you print the list, this is the output we expect:

```
[((u'shot', u'VBD'), u'nsubj', (u'I', u'PRP')),
((u'shot', u'VBD'), u'dobj', (u'elephant', u'NN')),
((u'elephant', u'NN'), u'det', (u'an', u'DT')),
((u'shot', u'VBD'), u'prep', (u'in', u'IN')),
((u'in', u'IN'), u'pobj', (u'sleep', u'NN')),
((u'sleep', u'NN'), u'poss', (u'my', u'PRP$'))]
```

We can see that `shot`, the verb, takes the root of the tree.

This is the extent of what we will demonstrate with NLTK, but if the reader wishes to define a grammar and use more academic statistical or rule-based parsing techniques, the following links illustrate this:

1. NLTK Dependency Grammars [13]
2. NLTK Book Chapter 8: Analyzing Sentence Structure [14]
3. Configuring Stanford Parser and Stanford NER Tagger with NLTK in Python on Windows and Linux [15]

We will now jump straight to spaCy's dependency parsing API.

Dependency parsing with spaCy

If you've followed every chapter of this book until this one, you would already have finished dependency parsing your data, multiple times; each run of your text through the pipeline had already annotated the words in the sentences in your document with their dependencies to the other words in the sentence. Let's set-up our models again, similar to how we did in the previous chapters.

```
import spacy
nlp = spacy.load('en')
```

Now that our pipeline is ready, we can begin analyzing our sentences.

spaCy's parsing portion of the pipeline does both phrasal parsing and dependency parsing - this means that we can get information about what the noun and verb chunks in a sentence are, as well as information about the dependencies between words.

Phrasal parsing can also be referred to as chunking, as we get *chunks* that are part of sentences, which are phrases. These chunks are stored in each sentence noun_chunks attribute.

Let's illustrate this with three simple sentences:

```
sent_0 = nlp(u'Myriam saw Clement with a telescope.')
sent_1 = nlp(u'Self-driving cars shift insurance liability
             toward manufacturers.')
sent_2 = nlp(u'I shot the elephant in my pyjamas.')

for chunk in sent_0.noun_chunks:
    print(chunk.text, chunk.root.text, chunk.root.dep_,
          chunk.root.head.text)

(u'Myriam', u'Myriam', u'nsubj', u'saw')
(u'Clement', u'Clement', u'dobj', u'saw')
(u'a telescope', u'telescope', u'pobj', u'with')
```

We can see here that we now have the chunks, the root text (we can see this in the a telescope chunk, whose root is telescope), the dependency type, and the head. As expected, as the verb is saw, it is the head for both Myriam and Clement, where Myriam is the subject and Clement is the object.

The next sentence encapsulates the idea of chunking far better.

```
for chunk in sent_1.noun_chunks:
    print(chunk.text, chunk.root.text, chunk.root.dep_,
        chunk.root.head.text)

(u'Self-driving cars', u'cars', u'nsubj', u'shift')
(u'insurance liability', u'liability', u'dobj', u'shift')
(u'manufacturers', u'manufacturers', u'pobj', u'toward')
```

We have three noun phrases, out of which `Self-driving cars` and `insurance liability` give us a clearer idea of what noun phrases are - here `Self-driving` and `insurance` qualify the root nouns `car` and `liability`. The `manufacturers` is the final noun of the sentence, being the object of the verb, `toward`.

Our last example is a lot more straightforward:

```
for chunk in sent_2.noun_chunks:
    print(chunk.text, chunk.root.text, chunk.root.dep_,
        chunk.root.head.text)

(u'I', u'I', u'nsubj', u'shot')
(u'the elephant', u'elephant', u'dobj', u'shot')
(u'my pyjamas', u'pyjamas', u'pobj', u'in')
```

The words `the` and `my` identify both the elephant and the pajamas and are included as part of our noun phrases.

Let's now look at our sentences again, but with individual words instead of phrases. Make a note of how we accessed chunks in the previous examples, and how we will be instead accessing tokens in the coming examples.

```
for token in sent_0:
    print(token.text, token.dep_, token.head.text, token.head.pos_,
        [child for child in token.children])

(u'Myriam', u'nsubj', u'saw', u'VERB', [])
(u'saw', u'ROOT', u'saw', u'VERB', [Myriam, Clement, with, .])
(u'Clement', u'dobj', u'saw', u'VERB', [])
(u'with', u'prep', u'saw', u'VERB', [telescope])
(u'a', u'det', u'telescope', u'NOUN', [])
(u'telescope', u'pobj', u'with', u'ADP', [a])
(u'.', u'punct', u'saw', u'VERB', [])
```

The output is similar to the noun chunk examples, with the addition of a list that contains the children (if any) of the nodes. We can see immediately with the preceding example that the word `saw`, the root verb, is the head node, with four children nodes that are dependent on it, which is visible in the list.

The dependencies are the same as we previously observed in the example with the noun chunks.

```
for token in sent_1:
    print(token.text, token.dep_, token.head.text, token.head.pos_,
        [child for child in token.children])
```

```
(u'Autonomous', u'amod', u'cars', u'NOUN', [])
(u'cars', u'nsubj', u'shift', u'VERB', [Autonomous])
(u'shift', u'ROOT', u'shift', u'VERB', [cars, liability, .])
(u'insurance', u'compound', u'liability', u'NOUN', [])
(u'liability', u'dobj', u'shift', u'VERB', [insurance, toward])
(u'toward', u'prep', u'liability', u'NOUN', [manufacturers])
(u'manufacturers', u'pobj', u'toward', u'ADP', [])
(u'.', u'punct', u'shift', u'VERB', [])
```

With more verbs our parsing looks more interesting - we can see how the verb `shift` is linked to a variety of words in the sentence. We now have an exercise for the user - using the information presented above, draw your own dependency graph for the sentence, and verify this using displaCy.

```
for token in sent_2:
    print(token.text, token.dep_, token.head.text, token.head.pos_,
        [child for child in token.children])
```

```
(u'I', u'nsubj', u'shot', u'VERB', [])
(u'shot', u'ROOT', u'shot', u'VERB', [I, elephant, .])
(u'the', u'det', u'elephant', u'NOUN', [])
(u'elephant', u'dobj', u'shot', u'VERB', [the, in])
(u'in', u'prep', u'elephant', u'NOUN', [pyjamas])
(u'my', u'poss', u'pyjamas', u'NOUN', [])
(u'pyjamas', u'pobj', u'in', u'ADP', [my])
(u'.', u'punct', u'shot', u'VERB', [])
```

Our last example is simple and does present anything out of the ordinary.

Let's now look at other ways we can navigate this tree. We've spoken about how each sentence has exactly one head, and sometimes we would want to identify this. One way to do this is to iterate from below, that is, to iterate over possible subjects instead of possible verbs.

For example, iterating through subjects would look like this:

```
from spacy.symbols import nsubj, VERB

verbs = set()
for possible_subject in sent_1:
    if possible_subject.dep == nsubj and possible_subject.head.pos == VERB:
        verbs.add(possible_subject.head)
```

We've iterated through all the words and checked cases where we have a nominal subject (`nsubj`), and where the head of that word is a verb. Running this for sentence 1 gives us the following result when we print `verbs`:

```
{shift}
```

This is what we expect to see!

It is also possible to search for verbs directly instead, but this takes double the iterations.

 The `doc` variable is a placeholder variable and you will need to pass your own document.

```
verbs = []
for possible_verb in doc:
    if possible_verb.pos == VERB:
        for possible_subject in possible_verb.children:
            if possible_subject.dep == nsubj:
                verbs.append(possible_verb)
                break
```

While this gives us the same result, note that there are two for loops.

spaCy also provides us with some useful attributes such as `lefts`, `rights`, `n_rights`, and `n_lefts`. This gives us information about what is on the left of a particular token in a tree, the right, and the number of either.

Let's take a look at this example to find phrases using the syntactic head.

```
root = [token for token in sent_1 if token.head == token][0]
subject = list(root.lefts)[0]
for descendant in subject.subtree:
    assert subject is descendant or subject.is_ancestor(descendant)
    print(descendant.text, descendant.dep_, descendant.n_lefts,
        descendant.n_rights, [ancestor.text for ancestor in
        descendant.ancestors])
```

We find the root by checking where the head is the token itself. The subject would be to the left of this tree, so we run a check for this. We then iterate through the subject and print the appropriate descendants and the number of other leaves. Let's look at an output from one of our sentences after running the preceding code:

```
(u'Autonomous', u'amod', 0, 0, [u'cars', u'shift'])
(u'cars', u'nsubj', 1, 0, [u'shift'])
```

spaCy's section on dependency parsing [16] has these examples and more (albeit with fewer explanations), and we highly recommend that you visit the page. The annotation page [10] is further recommended for reading.

An example of how we can use this in a more realistic example is, for example, in identifying commonly used adjectives to describe a character in a book.

 The book variable is a placeholder variable and you will need to pass your own document.

```
adjectives = []
for sent in book.sents:
    for word in sent:
        if 'Character' in word.string:
            for child in word.children:
                if child.pos_ == 'ADJ':
                    adjectives.append(child.string.strip())
Counter(adjectives).most_common(10)
```

The code itself remains very simple but does the job effectively. We iterate over our books sentences, look for our character in the sentence, look for the children of that character, and check if the child is an adjective. It being a child means the word is likely to have been marked as a dependency, with the root word (here, the *Character* depending on who it is) being described by the child. By checking the most common adjectives, we can do a mini-analysis of the characters in our books.

Let's now move on to training our own parsers!

Training our dependency parsers

Again, if you have read Chapter 4, *Gensim - Vectorizing Text and Transformations and n-grams*, Chapter 5, *POS-Tagging and Its applications*, and Chapter 6, *NER-Tagging and Its applications*, then you would be comfortable with the theory behind training our own models in spaCy. We would recommend that you go back and read *Vector transformations in Gensim* section from chapter 4 and *Training our own POS-taggers* section from chapter 5 to refresh your ideas on what exactly training means in context with machine learning and in particular, spaCy.

Again, the advantage with spaCy is that we don't need to care about the algorithm being used under the hood, or which features are the best to select for dependency parsing - this is usually the hardest part of machine learning research. We know that an optimal learning algorithm has been selected, and all we have to care about is in passing appropriate training examples and in setting up of the API so that we appropriately update our models. This is what we will be doing in the next two code examples.

The first among the two tells us how to update a dependency parser starting off with a blank model, and the source code can be found in the `train_parser.py` file [17].

```
from __future__ import unicode_literals, print_function

import plac
import random
from pathlib import Path
import spacy
```

As usual, we start with imports, before moving on to our training data.

```
# training data
TRAIN_DATA = [
    ("They trade mortgage-backed securities.", {
        'heads': [1, 1, 4, 4, 5, 1, 1],
        'deps': ['nsubj', 'ROOT', 'compound', 'punct', 'nmod', 'dobj',
                 'punct']
    }),
    ("I like London and Berlin.", {
        'heads': [1, 1, 1, 2, 2, 1],
        'deps': ['nsubj', 'ROOT', 'dobj', 'cc', 'conj', 'punct']
    })
]
```

We need to give examples of heads and dependency label in our training data. A quick glance at our training data can confirm this; in both examples, the verb is the word at index 0, and the dependencies are fairly straightforward.

```
@plac.annotations(
    model=("Model name. Defaults to blank 'en' model.", "option", "m",
           str),
    output_dir=("Optional output directory", "option", "o", Path),
    n_iter=("Number of training iterations", "option", "n", int))
def main(model=None, output_dir=None, n_iter=10):
    """Load the model, set up the pipeline and train the parser."""
    if model is not None:
        nlp = spacy.load(model)  # load existing spaCy model
        print("Loaded model '%s'" % model)
    else:
        nlp = spacy.blank('en')  # create blank Language class
        print("Created blank 'en' model")
```

This step is again similar to our other training examples, where we load a blank model.

```
# add the parser to the pipeline if it doesn't exist
# nlp.create_pipe works for built-ins that are registered with spaCy
if 'parser' not in nlp.pipe_names:
    parser = nlp.create_pipe('parser')
    nlp.add_pipe(parser, first=True)
# otherwise, get it, so we can add labels to it
else:
    parser = nlp.get_pipe('parser')
```

The comments are fairly self-explanatory here; we add a parser to the pipeline if it doesn't exist, and if it does, we add labels.

```
# add labels to the parser
for _, annotations in TRAIN_DATA:
    for dep in annotations.get('deps', []):
        parser.add_label(dep)
# get names of other pipes to disable them during training
other_pipes = [pipe for pipe in nlp.pipe_names if pipe != 'parser']
with nlp.disable_pipes(*other_pipes):  # only train parser
    optimizer = nlp.begin_training()
    for itn in range(n_iter):
        random.shuffle(TRAIN_DATA)
        losses = {}
        for text, annotations in TRAIN_DATA:
            nlp.update([text], [annotations], sgd=optimizer,
                        losses=losses)
        print(losses)
```

We follow the same process of the training examples of the previous chapter, where we add labels, disable the other parts of the pipe so that we're only training the parser.

```
# test the trained model
test_text = "I like securities."
doc = nlp(test_text)
print('Dependencies', [(t.text, t.dep_, t.head.text) for t in doc])
# save model to output directory
if output_dir is not None:
    output_dir = Path(output_dir)
    if not output_dir.exists():
        output_dir.mkdir()
    nlp.to_disk(output_dir)
    print("Saved model to", output_dir)
    # test the saved model
    print("Loading from", output_dir)
    nlp2 = spacy.load(output_dir)
    doc = nlp2(test_text)
    print('Dependencies', [(t.text, t.dep_, t.head.text) for t in doc])
```

The final steps involve training our model and saving it to our appropriate directory.

```
if __name__ == '__main__':
    plac.call(main)
```

On running the main file, we should expect to see the following output:

```
[
    ('I', 'nsubj', 'like'),
    ('like', 'ROOT', 'like'),
    ('securities', 'dobj', 'like'),
    ('.', 'punct', 'like')
]
```

While the preceding training example was rather vanilla, with it following the exact same style as the POS and NER-taggers, we can do a lot more interesting things with parsing; for example, adding our own custom semantics.

What does this mean? We can now train our parsers to understand new semantic relationships or dependencies between words. The spaCy documentation page gives us the following example to illustrate this:

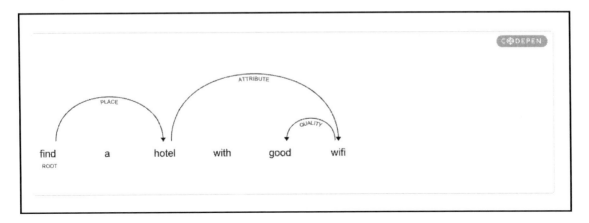

Fig 7.6 Dependency parsing with an additional dependency, "quality"

This is particularly interesting because we can model our own dependencies that are useful for our particular use-cases; though we must keep in mind that it may not always result in *correct* dependency parsing, but it is still useful in encapsulating relationships between words.

The code to do this training can be found in the `train_intent_parser.py` [18] file.

From the comments in the file, in this example, we'll build a message parser for a common *chat intent*: finding local businesses. Our message semantics will have the following types of relations: ROOT, PLACE, QUALITY, ATTRIBUTE, TIME, and LOCATION.

```
"show me the best hotel in berlin"

('show', 'ROOT', 'show')
('best', 'QUALITY', 'hotel') --> hotel with QUALITY best
('hotel', 'PLACE', 'show') --> show PLACE hotel
('berlin', 'LOCATION', 'hotel') --> hotel with LOCATION berlin
```

Let's now start with the code.

```
from __future__ import unicode_literals, print_function

import plac
import random
import spacy
from pathlib import Path

# training data: texts, heads and dependency labels
# for no relation, we simply chose an arbitrary dependency label, e.g. '-'
TRAIN_DATA = [
```

```
    ("find a cafe with great wifi", {
        'heads': [0, 2, 0, 5, 5, 2],   # index of token head
        'deps': ['ROOT', '-', 'PLACE', '-', 'QUALITY', 'ATTRIBUTE']
    }),
    ("find a hotel near the beach", {
        'heads': [0, 2, 0, 5, 5, 2],
        'deps': ['ROOT', '-', 'PLACE', 'QUALITY', '-', 'ATTRIBUTE']
    }),
    ("find me the closest gym that's open late", {
        'heads': [0, 0, 4, 4, 0, 6, 4, 6, 6],
        'deps': ['ROOT', '-', '-', 'QUALITY', 'PLACE', '-', '-',
                 'ATTRIBUTE', 'TIME']
    }),
    ("show me the cheapest store that sells flowers", {
        'heads': [0, 0, 4, 4, 0, 4, 4, 4],   # attach "flowers" to store!
        'deps': ['ROOT', '-', '-', 'QUALITY', 'PLACE', '-', '-', 'PRODUCT']
    }),
    ("find a nice restaurant in london", {
        'heads': [0, 3, 3, 0, 3, 3],
        'deps': ['ROOT', '-', 'QUALITY', 'PLACE', '-', 'LOCATION']
    }),
    ("show me the coolest hostel in berlin", {
        'heads': [0, 0, 4, 4, 0, 4, 4],
        'deps': ['ROOT', '-', '-', 'QUALITY', 'PLACE', '-', 'LOCATION']
    }),
    ("find a good italian restaurant near work", {
        'heads': [0, 4, 4, 4, 0, 4, 5],
        'deps': ['ROOT', '-', 'QUALITY', 'ATTRIBUTE', 'PLACE', 'ATTRIBUTE',
                 'LOCATION']
    })
]
```

It is worth our while to take a close look at the training examples. Like mentioned in the comments, ROOT, PLACE, QUALITY, ATTRIBUTE, TIME, and LOCATION is our new dependencies. Our examples illustrate this, with some of the qualities in our examples being `coolest`, `good`, `great`, and `closest`. Words like `near` and `open` are marked as an attribute to distinguish it from qualities. Place, time, and location are dependencies that are quite clear as well. This kind of information can be very useful when building a semantic information graph.

```
@plac.annotations(
    model=("Model name. Defaults to blank 'en' model.", "option", "m",
            str),
    output_dir=("Optional output directory", "option", "o", Path),
    n_iter=("Number of training iterations", "option", "n", int))
def main(model=None, output_dir=None, n_iter=5):
    """Load the model, set up the pipeline and train the parser."""
```

```
if model is not None:
    nlp = spacy.load(model)  # load existing spaCy model
    print("Loaded model '%s'" % model)
else:
    nlp = spacy.blank('en')  # create blank Language class
    print("Created blank 'en' model")
# We'll use the built-in dependency parser class, but we want to create
# a fresh instance - just in case.
if 'parser' in nlp.pipe_names:
    nlp.remove_pipe('parser')
parser = nlp.create_pipe('parser')
nlp.add_pipe(parser, first=True)

for text, annotations in TRAIN_DATA:
    for dep in annotations.get('deps', []):
        parser.add_label(dep)
```

The training examples remain the only real change; we can see that this step mirrors the previous training example.

```
other_pipes = [pipe for pipe in nlp.pipe_names if pipe != 'parser']
with nlp.disable_pipes(*other_pipes):  # only train parser
    optimizer = nlp.begin_training()
    for itn in range(n_iter):
        random.shuffle(TRAIN_DATA)
        losses = {}
        for text, annotations in TRAIN_DATA:
            nlp.update([text], [annotations], sgd=optimizer,
                        losses=losses)
        print(losses)
# test the trained model
test_model(nlp)
# save model to output directory
if output_dir is not None:
    output_dir = Path(output_dir)
    if not output_dir.exists():
        output_dir.mkdir()
    nlp.to_disk(output_dir)
    print("Saved model to", output_dir)
# test the saved model
    print("Loading from", output_dir)
    nlp2 = spacy.load(output_dir)
    test_model(nlp2)


def test_model(nlp):
    texts = ["find a hotel with good wifi",
            "find me the cheapest gym near work",
```

```
                "show me the best hotel in berlin"]
    docs = nlp.pipe(texts)
    for doc in docs:
        print(doc.text)
        print([(t.text, t.dep_, t.head.text) for t in doc
            if t.dep_ != '-'])


if __name__ == '__main__':
    plac.call(main)
```

The rest of the steps follow suit; let's have a look at the result when we run the main module.

```
find a hotel with good wifi
[
    ('find', 'ROOT', 'find'),
    ('hotel', 'PLACE', 'find'),
    ('good', 'QUALITY', 'wifi'),
    ('wifi', 'ATTRIBUTE', 'hotel')
]
find me the cheapest gym near work
[
    ('find', 'ROOT', 'find'),
    ('cheapest', 'QUALITY', 'gym'),
    ('gym', 'PLACE', 'find')
    ('work', 'LOCATION', 'near')
]
show me the best hotel in berlin
[
    ('show', 'ROOT', 'show'),
    ('best', 'QUALITY', 'hotel'),
    ('hotel', 'PLACE', 'show'),
    ('berlin', 'LOCATION', 'hotel')
]
```

And voila, it's what we expect to see!

This example illustrates the real power spaCy has when creating our custom models; we can not only retrain our models with domain-specific data to work better for our specifications, but also train completely new dependencies. Couple that with a very easy to use training API, and it becomes very clear that it leads the pack in all practical NLP applications.

Some useful links which might also be relevant when considering spaCy and dependency parsing:

1. Dependency Tree with spaCy [19]
2. Parsing English in 500 Lines of Python [20]

Summary

This brings us to the end of our chapter on spaCy and dependency parsing. The previous four chapters have illustrated the many powers of spaCy, and how we can harness these powers. Dependency parsing, in particular, remains very important to us as finding semantic or syntactic relationships between words within sentences can have many uses, whether it is simply identifying the most used adjectives or adverbs for a particular word or mapping custom relationships.

In the next chapters, we will move on from computational linguistics-based algorithms to information retrieval-based algorithms to conduct our text analysis. In particular, this will be topic models as well as clustering and classification algorithms.

References

[1] Introduction to Structural Syntax:
http://www.home.uni-osnabrueck.de/bschwisc/archives/tesniere.pdf

[2] Term Logic:
https://plato.stanford.edu/archives/win2016/entries/logic-ancient/

[3] Noam Chomsky:
https://en.wikipedia.org/wiki/Noam_Chomsky

[4] Image link:
https://en.wikipedia.org/wiki/Phrase_structure_grammar#/media/File:Thistreeisil
lustratingtherelation(PSG).png

[5] Phrase Structure Grammar:
https://en.wikipedia.org/wiki/Phrase_structure_grammar

[6] Dependency Grammar and Dependency Parsing:
http://stp.lingfil.uu.se/~nivre/docs/05133.pdf

[7] Dependency Grammar:
https://en.wikipedia.org/wiki/Dependency_grammar

[8] CLEAR style:
http://www.mathcs.emory.edu/~choi/doc/cu-2012-choi.pdf

[9] displaCy:
https://explosion.ai/demos/displacy

[10] spaCy annotation page:
https://spacy.io/api/annotation#dependency-parsing

[11] Stanford Dependency Parser:
https://nlp.stanford.edu/software/nndep.shtml

[12] Stanford Statistical Parser:
https://nlp.stanford.edu/software/lex-parser.shtml

[13] NLTK Dependency Grammars:
http://www.nltk.org/howto/dependency.html

[14] Analysing Sentence Structure:
http://www.nltk.org/book/ch08.html

[15] Configuring Stanford Parser and Stanford NER Tagger with NLTK in Python on Windows and Linux:
https://blog.manash.me/configuring-stanford-parser-and-stanford-ner-tagger-with-nltk-in-python-on-windows-f685483c374a

[16] spaCy dependency parsing:
https://spacy.io/usage/linguistic-features#section-dependency-parse

[17] spaCy train parser:
https://spacy.io/usage/linguistic-features#section-dependency-parse

[18] spaCy train intent parser:
https://github.com/explosion/spacy/blob/master/examples/training/train_intent_parser.py

[19] How to get the dependency tree with spaCy?:
https://stackoverflow.com/questions/36610179/how-to-get-the-dependency-tree-with-spacy

[20] Parsing English in 500 Lines of Python:
https://explosion.ai/blog/parsing-english-in-python

8
Topic Models

Until now, we dealt with computational linguistics algorithms and spaCy, and we understood how to use these computational linguistic algorithms to annotate our data, as well as understand sentence structure. While these algorithms helped us understand the finer details of our text, we still didn't get a big picture of our data - what kind of words appear more often than others in our corpus? Can we group our data or find underlying themes? We will be attempting to answer these questions and more in this chapter. Following are the topics we will cover in this chapter:

- What are topic models?
- Topic models in Gensim
- Topic models in scikit-learn

What are topic models?

We will now make our first foray into probabilistic models and machine learning with text. We did, of course, come across such models earlier on (in Chapter 5, *POS-Tagging and Its Applications*, Chapter 6, *NER-Tagging and Its Applications*, and Chapter 7, *Dependency Parsing*), especially in the *way* we trained our NER and POS taggers, but our goal in the previous chapters was not to come up with a statistical model involving our text data.

What is a topic model? As the name might suggest, it is a probabilistic model which contains information about topics in the text. We now must ask what exactly a *topic* is - we can understand a topic as a theme, or underlying ideas represented in text. For example, if we are working with a corpus of newspaper articles, possible topics would be *weather*, *politics*, *sport*, and so on.

Why would such topic models be important in the world of text processing? Traditionally, information retrieval and searching techniques involved using words to identify similarity or relevance - now, we can instead search and arrange our files more broadly, with topics instead of words. But what exactly are topics? They are a distribution of words - in particular, a probabilistic distribution of words. We can further use this model to describe our documents as the probabilistic distribution of topics. Since we know the words and count of the words in documents, we can use this knowledge to generate these topic models. Once we have our topic model, we can start representing all our documents as topic distributions!

So, this means in our newspaper corpus we discussed before, instead of clustering based on **TF-IDF** or **bag-of-words**, we can now cluster according to the topics. We can also explore the documents in each topic, and further zoom in on these documents to better understand the topics, or themes. Creating topic models for your text corpus is also useful when we want to explore our dataset, to see what kind of documents our corpus contains, by just observing the topics.

By arranging our documents in chronological order, we can further see how documents in a topic evolved over time. Why is this interesting, or useful? When time-arranged documents from the research journal science were topic modeled keeping time-stamps in mind (a technique called **Dynamic Topic Modeling**), the results were particularly fascinating.

The topic that we associated with **atomic physics** started in 1881 with a high chance of finding the word *matter, motion*, and *light*. By the year 1999, these words under the same topic soon became *state, energy*, and *electron*!

You can see how we used a topic model that takes time-stamps into account to see how a topics words evolved over time - topic models allow us to look at and understand our data in ways we could not have done before.

We must keep in mind, however, that a topic is merely a probabilistic distribution of words, and doesn't create its own label, or title. For example, the topic that we would call the *weather* topic in the newspaper corpus would just be a collection of words (such as *sun, temperature, wind, storm*, and *forecast*), with the associated probability of those words appearing in the topic. A topic such as the *weather* topic would contain the words we previously mentioned with a high probability of appearing on that topic. By arranging the words according to probability, we can get an idea of what the topic represents. Of course, in our code, these topics would simply be called topic 0, topic 1, topic 2... topic *n-1*, where *n* is the total number of topics we wish to identify in our corpus. At this point, a human will simply have to assign whatever topic label they would like to the probability distribution collection.

Now that we have documents as a representation of topics instead of words, we are effectively reducing the dimensions of our data (documents or articles), from the total vocabulary size to the number of topics. In fact, one of the earliest IR algorithms, latent semantic analysis [1] does pretty much this, inadvertently, and by reducing the dimensions we get a representation of topics in that corpus.

We've discussed a fair amount about what topic models are - but how do you generate them? There is more than one way to do this, and we will be using Gensim [2] to create our models, which has implementations of **Latent Dirichlet Allocation (LDA)**, **Latent semantic analysis (LSA)**, **Hierarchical Dirichlet Process (HDP)**, and **Dynamic Topic Modelling (DTM)** to help us with this. All of these algorithms have a few things in common - they assume words in documents have underlying probabilistic distributions and attempts to find out these distributions. These distributions end up being our topics. The way we attempt to identify these distributions (which is with mathematical and statistical techniques) is what makes these algorithms different.

As for the mathematical foundation of these topic models, that is beyond the scope of the book, but the paper by Blei et al which describes LDA [3] is a great read. A more casual approach to understanding how this works is Edwin Chen's blog post [4]. This Quora article [5] also has a nice repository of explanations of LDA, which might require a little mathematical background. This paper by Blei, titled *Probabilistic Topic Models* [6] is also a nice resource which sums up all the kinds of topic models that have been developed so far.

Topic models in Gensim

Gensim [2] is arguably the most popular topic modeling toolkit freely available, and it being in Python means that it fits right into our ecosystem. Gensim's popularity is because of its wide variety of topic modeling algorithms, straightforward API, and active community. Of course, we have already introduced Gensim before, in `Chapter 4`, *Gensim - Vectorizing Text and Transformations and n-grams*, on vector spaces. We would be needing to know how to set up our corpus for the topic modeling algorithms we will be using, so now is a good time to brush on the contents of the *Vector transformation in Gensim* section, in `Chapter 4`, *Gensim - Vectorizing Text and Transformations and n-grams*.

All done? Now we can start using the powerful tools that Gensim have to offer. The Jupyter notebook [7] runs us through the same corpus generating techniques we previously discussed, as well as loading the Lee Newspaper corpus, which is found in the Gensim code base. The notebook will be attached at the end of this chapter. The code in the notebook is in Python 2.7 to accommodate all users, and it also works in Python 3. The corpus contains headline texts of about 300 documents from 2000-2001.

More information on this corpus can be found in this research paper, *An Empirical Evaluation of Models of Text Document Similarity* [8].

This corpus will be useful in illustrating how topic models work because it is large enough for us to have coherent topics and isn't too large so as to take long training times.

We won't be focusing as much on the how but more on the what - though it is highly encouraged that you have a look at what's happening under the hood, and we will be linking to the relevant reading material as we describe how to use these algorithms. The reason we choose to ignore the *how* is because of how well Gensim abstracts it for us; also, because it is also challenging to interpret the results - which is the *what* of topic modeling is.

Just to remind ourselves of the kind of data we are dealing with, let's look at what texts and corpus look like. This would be after the 8th and 9th cells in the Jupyter notebook.

```
texts[1][0:10]
[u'indian',
 u'security_force',
 u'shoot_dead',
 u'suspect',
 u'militant',
 u'night',
 u'long',
 u'encounter',
 u'southern',
 u'kashmir']

corpus[1][0:10]
[(51, 1),
 (53, 1),
 (95, 1),
 (108, 1),
 (109, 3),
 (110, 2),
 (111, 1),
 (112, 1),
 (113, 4),
 (114, 1)]
```

Texts contain the tokenized and cleaned version of the original text data and the corpus is our bag of words representation, which we will feed into our machine learning algorithms.

Latent Dirichlet allocation

Let's start with the most popular topic modeling algorithm - latent Dirichlet allocation, or LDA as we called it before. The LDA model was created in 2003 by Blei and others and is described in the paper, *Latent Dirichlet Allocation* [3].

Like we discussed before, LDA helps us model a corpus based on topic distributions, which are in turn made of word distributions. What exactly is a distribution of words? Gensim lets us understand and use this very easily.

Cells 15 and 16 of the Jupyter notebook let you see this.

```
ldamodel = LdaModel(corpus=corpus, num_topics=10, id2word=dictionary)
```

That's how easy it is to create a model - just specify the corpus, the dictionary mapping, and the number of topics we want to use in our model.

Keep in mind that we imported `LdaModel` from `gensim.models` back in the first cell.

Now that we have a trained model, let's look at what topics are hidden in our dataset.

```
ldamodel.show_topics()
```

This gives us the following:

```
[(0,
  u'0.006*"force" + 0.006*"year" + 0.005*"australian" + 0.004*"new" +
0.004*"afghanistan" + 0.004*"people" + 0.004*"official" + 0.004*"area" +
0.004*"fire" + 0.004*"day"'),
 (1,
  u'0.005*"attack" + 0.005*"people" + 0.004*"man" + 0.004*"group" +
0.004*"report" + 0.004*"company" + 0.003*"australia" + 0.003*"force" +
0.003*"kill" + 0.003*"come"'),
 (2,
  u'0.009*"australia" + 0.005*"australian" + 0.005*"government" +
0.004*"day" + 0.003*"new" + 0.003*"united_states" + 0.003*"child" +
0.003*"come" + 0.003*"report" + 0.003*"good"'),
 (3,
  u'0.005*"day" + 0.005*"people" + 0.004*"police" + 0.004*"australian" +
0.004*"australia" + 0.003*"today" + 0.003*"test" + 0.003*"palestinian" +
0.003*"attack" + 0.003*"centre"'),
 (4,
  u'0.008*"australian" + 0.005*"fire" + 0.005*"year" + 0.005*"government" +
0.005*"people" + 0.004*"union" + 0.004*"south" + 0.004*"centre" +
0.003*"company" + 0.003*"day"'),
 (5,
  u'0.008*"israeli" + 0.006*"palestinian" + 0.005*"force" + 0.004*"fire" +
```

```
0.004*"people" + 0.004*"kill" + 0.004*"government" + 0.004*"police" +
0.004*"day" + 0.004*"australia"'),
  (6,
   u'0.008*"australian" + 0.007*"year" + 0.006*"world" + 0.005*"australia" +
0.005*"force" + 0.004*"government" + 0.004*"people" + 0.003*"economy" +
0.003*"metre" + 0.003*"win"'),
  (7,
   u'0.005*"government" + 0.004*"australia" + 0.004*"pakistan" +
0.004*"people" + 0.003*"tell" + 0.003*"force" + 0.003*"israeli" +
0.003*"time" + 0.003*"claim" + 0.003*"company"'),
  (8,
   u'0.005*"day" + 0.004*"good" + 0.004*"year" + 0.003*"new" +
0.003*"australian" + 0.003*"australia" + 0.003*"wicket" + 0.003*"take" +
0.003*"hour" + 0.003*"area"'),
  (9,
   u'0.005*"people" + 0.005*"australia" + 0.005*"man" + 0.004*"arrest" +
0.004*"union" + 0.004*"tell" + 0.004*"india" + 0.004*"pakistan" +
0.003*"claim" + 0.003*"united_states"')]
```

 Topic models are probabilistic, and you might see different results, with different words, probabilities, and topic numbers.

Let's spend some time understanding the nature of this output.

The first value in the tuple is the topic id, which is how we will identify the topic. Let's pick up topic 5 and see what we can understand from this.

```
(5,
   u'0.008*"israeli" + 0.006*"palestinian" + 0.005*"force" + 0.004*"fire" +
0.004*"people" + 0.004*"kill" + 0.004*"government" + 0.004*"police" +
0.004*"day" + 0.004*"australia"')
```

What does this mean? This means topic ID 5 is made up of the words `israeli`, `palestinian`, `force`, `fire`, and so on, and these are the ones with the highest probability in the topic. The number that the word is multiplied with (such as `0.008` with Israeli), is the probability of that word appearing in that topic distribution. We can look at the words with the highest probability to understand the theme of our topic.

It's clear that this topic is about the Israel-Palestine conflict, something which would have definitely been in newspaper headlines in the early 21st century. Briefly going through the other topics tells you that most topics have the word *Australia* in it, which again makes sense because it is an Australian news dataset.

There is a lot we can do with topic models, such as clustering, coloring word documents, and topic model visualization. We will talk about all of these further functionalities of topic models in the next chapter (Chapter 9, *Advanced Topic Models*); let's first check out the other topic models that Gensim has to offer.

Latent semantic indexing

Along with LDA, the other algorithm that was first implemented in Gensim is **Latent Semantic Indexing (LSI)**. Setting up our LSI model simply requires us to import the model from gensim.models and set it up the same way we set up our LDA model.

```
lsimodel = LsiModel(corpus=corpus, num_topics=10, id2word=dictionary)
```

To see what our topics are, use this:

```
lsimodel.show_topics(num_topics=5)  # Showing only the top 5 topics
```

This give us the following:

```
[(0,
  u'-0.216*"israeli" + -0.211*"palestinian" + -0.196*"arafat" +
-0.181*"force" + -0.149*"official" + -0.148*"kill" + -0.142*"people" +
-0.142*"attack" + -0.129*"government" + -0.127*"australian"'),
 (1,
  u'-0.321*"palestinian" + -0.306*"israeli" + -0.299*"arafat" +
0.171*"australia" + 0.166*"australian" + -0.158*"israel" +
0.149*"afghanistan" + -0.137*"sharon" + -0.134*"hamas" +
-0.124*"west_bank"'),
 (2,
  u'-0.266*"afghanistan" + -0.242*"force" + -0.191*"al_qaeda" +
0.180*"fire" + -0.176*"bin_laden" + -0.153*"pakistan" + 0.138*"good" +
0.138*"sydney" + -0.131*"tora_bora" + -0.129*"afghan"'),
 (3,
  u'0.373*"fire" + 0.270*"area" + 0.199*"sydney" + -0.191*"australia" +
0.176*"firefighter" + 0.160*"south" + 0.157*"north" + 0.148*"wind" +
-0.146*"good" + 0.132*"wales"'),
 (4,
  u'-0.238*"company" + -0.221*"union" + 0.199*"test" + -0.187*"qantas" +
-0.152*"australian" + 0.145*"good" + 0.141*"match" + 0.137*"win" +
-0.136*"government" + -0.136*"worker"')]
```

It makes sense to note more or less similar topics as our LDA output. The *Israeli-Palestinian* topic emerges once again! For our use-cases, it is okay to ignore the negative sign before the numbers - it is not easy to interpret the significance of the numbers and is related to the **Singular-value Decomposition (SVD)** [9] performed during LSI being run. SVD is a matrix factorization method to decompose matrices. For more mathematical information on how LSI actually works, the original paper, *Indexing by Latent Semantic Analysis* [10] by Deerwester and others, and the publication, *Probabilistic latent semantic indexing* [11], by Hoffman would serve as a useful resource.

Hierarchical Dirichlet process

The other standard topic modeling algorithm popular in Gensim is **Hierarchical Dirichlet process (HDP)** - it is also a brainchild of Micheal. I. Jordan and David Blei. It is different from LDA and LSI because it is non-parametric - we don't need to mention the number of topics we need.

Again, to use it in Gensim we need to import the model from `gensim.models`.

```
hdpmodel = HdpModel(corpus=corpus, id2word=dictionary)
```

Note that we don't need to specify the number of topics.

```
hdpmodel.show_topics()
```

This will allow us to view the topics:

```
[(0,
  u'0.005*israeli + 0.003*arafat + 0.003*palestinian + 0.003*hit +
0.003*west_bank + 0.003*official + 0.002*sharon + 0.002*force + 0.002*afp +
0.002*arrest + 0.002*militant + 0.002*storm + 0.002*hamas + 0.002*strike +
0.002*come + 0.002*military + 0.002*source + 0.002*group + 0.002*soldier +
0.002*kill'),
  (1,
  u'0.004*company + 0.003*administrator + 0.002*yallourn +
0.002*entitlement + 0.002*traveland + 0.002*staff + 0.002*austar +
0.002*union + 0.002*travel + 0.002*employee + 0.002*end + 0.002*cent +
0.002*government + 0.002*remain + 0.002*go + 0.002*seek + 0.002*leave +
0.002*people + 0.002*agreement + 0.002*$'),
  (2,
  u'0.003*airport + 0.003*taliban + 0.002*kill + 0.002*opposition +
0.002*kandahar + 0.002*force + 0.002*night + 0.002*leave + 0.002*man +
0.002*lali + 0.002*near + 0.002*city + 0.001*wound + 0.001*end + 0.001*agha
+ 0.001*civilian + 0.001*gul + 0.001*people + 0.001*military +
0.001*injure'),
  (3,
```

```
    u'0.002*job + 0.002*australian + 0.002*cent + 0.002*read +
0.002*mysticism + 0.002*drop + 0.002*band + 0.001*survey + 0.001*wales +
0.001*olivier + 0.001*beatle + 0.001*week + 0.001*intensive + 0.001*result
+ 0.001*add + 0.001*alarming + 0.001*harrison + 0.001*cite + 0.001*big +
0.001*song'),
  (4,
    u'0.003*group + 0.003*palestinian + 0.002*government + 0.002*sharon +
0.002*kill + 0.002*choose + 0.002*israeli + 0.002*attack + 0.002*bright +
0.002*call + 0.002*security + 0.002*arafat + 0.002*defend +
0.002*suicide_attack + 0.002*terrorism + 0.002*hamas + 0.001*militant +
0.001*human_right + 0.001*gaza_strip + 0.001*civilian'),
  (5,
    u'0.003*match + 0.003*israeli + 0.002*ask + 0.002*team + 0.002*rafter +
0.002*tennis + 0.002*play + 0.002*not + 0.002*australia + 0.002*guarantee +
0.001*france + 0.001*be + 0.001*role + 0.001*hobart_yacht +
0.001*government + 0.001*kill + 0.001*late + 0.001*attack + 0.001*world +
0.001*topple'),
  (6,
    u'0.003*australian + 0.002*afghanistan + 0.002*state + 0.002*reach +
0.002*day + 0.002*head + 0.001*give + 0.001*go + 0.001*couple + 0.001*view
+ 0.001*plan + 0.001*government + 0.001*crash + 0.001*aware + 0.001*report
+ 0.001*future + 0.001*editor + 0.001*prevent + 0.001*blake +
0.001*party'),
  (7,
    u'0.004*storm + 0.003*tree + 0.002*ses + 0.002*work + 0.002*sydney +
0.002*damage + 0.002*hornsby + 0.002*service + 0.002*area + 0.002*home +
0.002*call + 0.002*bad + 0.001*hit + 0.001*bring + 0.001*australia +
0.001*afternoon + 0.001*power + 0.001*large + 0.001*electricity +
0.001*sutherland'),
  (8,
    u'0.004*arrest + 0.003*indonesia + 0.002*year + 0.002*smuggle +
0.002*howard + 0.002*agreement + 0.002*summit + 0.002*police +
0.002*president + 0.002*australia + 0.002*people + 0.002*megawati +
0.001*meeting + 0.001*palestinian + 0.001*meet + 0.001*council +
0.001*leader + 0.001*loya + 0.001*structure + 0.001*host'),
  (9,
    u'0.004*director + 0.003*friedli + 0.003*india + 0.002*union +
0.002*reply + 0.002*day + 0.002*unwell + 0.002*mistake + 0.002*report +
0.002*ask + 0.002*river + 0.002*sector + 0.001*unforeseeable +
0.001*australia + 0.001*people + 0.001*court + 0.001*trip +
0.001*australians + 0.001*swiss + 0.001*people_die'),
  (10,
    u'0.003*guide + 0.003*adventure_world + 0.002*people + 0.002*canyon +
0.002*interlaken + 0.002*charge + 0.002*year + 0.002*tourist +
0.002*republic + 0.001*swiss + 0.001*tragedy + 0.001*atrocity +
0.001*tomorrow + 0.001*include + 0.001*inexperienced + 0.001*kill +
0.001*change + 0.001*sweep + 0.001*allow + 0.001*court'),
  (11,
```

```
    u'0.002*australian + 0.002*commission + 0.002*company + 0.002*call +
0.002*people + 0.002*collapse + 0.001*  + 0.001*power + 0.001*theatre +
0.001*martin + 0.001*begin + 0.001*dickie + 0.001*wisdom + 0.001*refund +
0.001*national + 0.001*include + 0.001*determine + 0.001*arafat +
0.001*procedural + 0.001*today'),
  (12,
    u'0.002*high + 0.002*lee + 0.001*year + 0.001*inject + 0.001*match +
0.001*lockett + 0.001*passage + 0.001*casa + 0.001*day + 0.001*test +
0.001*compare + 0.001*bond + 0.001*presence + 0.001*outlook + 0.001*osaka +
0.001*canada + 0.001*maintenance_worker + 0.001*china + 0.001*game +
0.001*$'),
  (13,
    u'0.003*krishna + 0.003*ash + 0.002*hare + 0.002*ganges + 0.002*harrison
+ 0.002*ceremony + 0.002*hindu + 0.002*devotee + 0.002*sect + 0.002*hundred
+ 0.002*holy + 0.002*river + 0.002*closely + 0.002*benares + 0.001*task +
0.001*scatter + 0.001*place + 0.001*devout + 0.001*official +
0.001*rescue'),
  (14,
    u'0.003*harrison + 0.002*george + 0.002*beatle + 0.002*die +
0.002*tonight + 0.002*liverpool + 0.002*  + 0.002*memory + 0.002*music +
0.002*seventh + 0.001*decisive + 0.001*percent + 0.001*hold + 0.001*silence
+ 0.001*people + 0.001*tree + 0.001*minute + 0.001*pole + 0.001*stabbing +
0.001*plant'),
  (15,
    u'0.003*strong + 0.003*economy + 0.002*forward + 0.002*australia +
0.002*olympic + 0.002*hoon + 0.002*follow + 0.002*proposal +
0.002*extensive + 0.002*australian + 0.002*year + 0.001*goner +
0.001*mystery + 0.001*haggle + 0.001*constitutional + 0.001*fazalur +
0.001*weekend + 0.001*limit + 0.001*term + 0.001*set'),
  (16,
    u'0.002*tell + 0.002*launceston + 0.002*virgin + 0.002*airline +
0.002*terminal + 0.002*flight + 0.001*daily + 0.001*melbourne +
0.001*morning + 0.001*new + 0.001*second + 0.001*check + 0.001*sherrard +
0.001*administrator + 0.001*shot + 0.001*sabotage + 0.001*unacceptable +
0.001*coroner + 0.001*ansett + 0.001*hayden'),
  (17,
    u'0.002*choose + 0.002*aids + 0.002*hiv + 0.001*official +
0.001*state_emergency + 0.001*reporter + 0.001*europe + 0.001*soviet +
0.001*find + 0.001*late + 0.001*rush + 0.001*double + 0.001*today +
0.001*union + 0.001*number_people + 0.001*service + 0.001*report +
0.001*arabian + 0.001*footing + 0.001*state'),
  (18,
    u'0.003*know + 0.002*accident + 0.002*company + 0.002*carry +
0.002*organise + 0.002*region + 0.002*charge + 0.001*appear + 0.001*loot +
0.001*defunct + 0.001*market + 0.001*question + 0.001*live + 0.001*accuse +
0.001*initially + 0.001*rhino + 0.001*stephan + 0.001*canyoning +
0.001*possibility + 0.001*bayu'),
  (19,
```

```
      u'0.003*afghanistan + 0.003*powell + 0.002*taliban + 0.002*southern +
0.002*want + 0.002*developer + 0.001*face + 0.001*marines + 0.001*officer +
0.001*bin_laden + 0.001*pakistan + 0.001*kilometre + 0.001*united_states +
0.001*kandahar + 0.001*vacate + 0.001*force + 0.001*ground + 0.001*troop +
0.001*time + 0.001*secretary')]
```

Again, we can see how we have similar topics creeping up in our results. HDP is particularly interesting to us because it slightly differs from the two previous methods in being non-parametric, and in offering us the capacity to cluster our topics according to hierarchies. The paper describing HDP was among the proceedings at NIPS [12] and is titled *Sharing Clusters Among Related Groups: Hierarchical Dirichlet Processes* [13].

Dynamic topic models

While our previous topic models focused on identifying topics across the whole corpus, the next topic model that we introduce also takes into account the time frame in which the document exists. Using this additional information, we can then model our topics in each time frame and try to understand how these topics evolve over time.

The nature of the topics are fixed in the first time-frame - we are not likely to see the introduction of a new topic as time passes, but can rather see how these topics changed over time - in particular, we can see which words replaced which. We gave an example of this in our introductory section, *What are topic models?*, where we talked about the *Atomic Physics* topic.

The Jupyter notebook I've written for Gensim covers large parts of the theory, as well as all possible uses of the dynamic topic model. The notebook is included in the appendix, and you can also find it on GitHub in the Gensim repository [14].

Topic models in scikit-learn

Gensim isn't the only package offering us the ability to topic model: scikit-learn, while not dedicated for text, still offers fast implementations of LDA and **Non-negative Matrix Factorization (NMF)**, which can help us identify topics.

We already discussed how LDA works, and the only difference between the Gensim and scikit-learn implementations are as follows:

1. The perplexity bounds are not expected to agree exactly here because the bound is calculated differently in Gensim versus sklearn. These bounds are ways we calculate how topics converge in topic modeling algorithms.
2. Sklearn uses cython which creates numerical 6th decimal point differences.

Non-negative matrix factorization (NMF) [15], unlike LDA, is not a method mostly limited to text mining (though interestingly, LDA's variants also have been used in genetics and image processing). NMF [16] is a linear algebra method that involves reconstructing a single matrix V into two matrices, W and H. These matrices when multiplied with each other, approximately reconstruct V. W and H are then used to identify our topics as they best represent the original matrix, V. Here the matrix V is the document-term matrix that contains information about which words are in which documents.

Another key aspect of NMF is that the matrix must have no negative elements. This non-negativity makes the resulting matrices easier to inspect Also, in applications such as processing of audio spectrograms or text processing, non-negativity is inherent to the data being considered. Since the problem is not exactly solvable in general, it is commonly approximated numerically, using various distance norms to do this. Euclidean distance, which we commonly use in 2-dimensional is one such norm, and the **Kullback-Leibler** divergence [17] is another more complex metric. This factorization can be used for example for dimensionality reduction, source separation, or topic extraction. In our example, we use the generalized Kullback-Leibler divergence, which is equivalent to **Probabilistic Latent Semantic Indexing (PLSI)** [1] [11].

Scikit-learn has a very straightforward API which makes it appealing to use, also because of the high-level of consistency it achieves across all of its models - most of which have fit, transform, and predict methods based on the model's purpose. In our case, since they are decomposition models, we will only be using the fit method and using the model's components to print our topics. Let's look at some code that trains two models and prints the topics.

```
from sklearn.decomposition import NMF, LatentDirichletAllocation

no_topic = 10

nmf = NMF(n_components=no_topic).fit(tfidf_corpus)

lda = LatentDirichletAllocation(n_topics=no_topics).fit(tf_corpus)
```

Here, `tfidf_corpus` and `tf_corpus` are the `tfidf` and `tf` transformed corpuses; you can do this either with Gensim or with scikit-learn. Here, `tf_feature_names` and `tfidf_feature_names` are the lists that contain the entire vocabulary arranged alphabetically; you could use Gensim's dictionary method here with equal effect.

Let's now write a small function, which will help us print the topics:

```
def display_topics(model, feature_names, no_top_words):
    for topic_idx, topic in enumerate(model.components_):
        print "Topic %d:" % (topic_idx)
        print " ".join([feature_names[i]
                        for i in topic.argsort()[:-no_top_words - 1:-1]])
```

The `model.components_` objects are the variational parameters for topic word distribution. Since the complete conditional for topic word distribution is a Dirichlet, `components_[i, j]` can be viewed as a pseudo count that represents the number of times the word `j` was assigned to the topic `i`.

Let's run this:

```
no_top_words = 10

display_topics(nmf, tfidf_feature_names, no_top_words)
```

We get the following:

```
Topic 0:
afghanistan bin laden qaeda al force taliban tora bora afghan

Topic 1:
palestinian arafat israeli israel hamas gaza attack suicide sharon militant

Topic 2:
qantas union worker industrial maintenance dispute wage freeze action
relations

Topic 3:
test africa south match day waugh bowler wicket cricket lee

Topic 4:
river guide adventure canyon court trip interlaken australians swiss
accident

Topic 5:
detainee centre woomera detention facility department damage overnight visa
night
```

Topic 6:
hollingworth dr governor abuse general anglican child school allegation
statement

Topic 7:
new year australia south government people sydney australian wales state

Topic 8:
harrison beatle cancer george krishna lord lung know ceremony life

Topic 9:
commission hih royal collapse hearing company report union martin evidence

Now let's run this:

```
display_topics(lda, tf_feature_names, no_top_words)
```

We get the following:

Topic 0:
space station shuttle endeavour russian crew ice vaughan centre launch

Topic 1:
test south day australia match lee africa wicket waugh cricket

Topic 2:
afghanistan force taliban government laden bin president australian united
al

Topic 3:
russian people christmas authority security cause economy drop america
kilometre

Topic 4:
union qantas worker industrial action company maintenance dispute pay
relations

Topic 5:
palestinian israeli arafat attack hamas suicide Gaza sharon israel kill

Topic 6:
win metre good year race event world new australia australian

Topic 7:
year company commission people australian report world director royal child

Topic 8:
new australia south people government sydney state australian storm year

```
Topic 9:
flight virgin disease airline melbourne blue tell second ansett japan
```

Let's briefly inspect the topics - may be to find our Israel and Palestine topics again? And yes! Topic id 1 from NMF and topic id 5 from LDA describes the same topic we saw in all our previous topic modeling experiments with Gensim!

By running the Jupyter notebook based on `Chapter 8`, *Topic Models*, you should be able to reproduce the same results.

And there we have it - we can now use topics to describe our textual data, and in two different Python machine learning frameworks. So far, we've only really seen how to identify and print topics in the text; but there is a lot more we can do with topic models, particularly with the way we can explore documents. We will explore additional topic modeling techniques and also ways to better train our topic models in the next chapter.

Summary

In this chapter, we saw our first usage of Gensim's machine learning algorithms, and in particular, topic models. Topic models are a great way for us to work with unlabeled data, and they help us find underlying structures in text. There are multiple ways for us to identify topics in the text, with LDA, LSI, HDP, and NNMF being the most popular methods, and we have discussed ways to use all these methods in both scikit-learn and Gensim.

In the next chapter, we will move into advanced operations using topic models.

References

[1] Latent Semantic Analysis:
https://en.wikipedia.org/wiki/Latent_semantic_analysis#Latent_semantic_indexing

[2] Gensim:
https://radimrehurek.com/gensim/

[3] Latent Dirichlet Allocation:
http://www.jmlr.org/papers/volume3/blei03a/blei03a.pdf

[4] Introduction to LDA:
http://blog.echen.me/2011/08/22/introduction-to-latent-dirichlet-allocation/

[5] Explanation of LDA:
https://www.quora.com/What-is-a-good-explanation-of-Latent-Dirichlet-Allocation

[6] Probabilistic Topic Models:
http://www.cs.columbia.edu/~blei/papers/Blei2012.pdf

[7] Jupyter Notebook:
https://github.com/bhargavvader/personal/blob/master/notebooks/text_analysis_tutorial/topic_modelling.ipynb

[8] An Empirical Evaluation of Models of Text Document Similarity:
http://www.socsci.uci.edu/~mdlee/lee_pincombe_welsh_document.PDF

[9] Singular-Value Decomposition:
https://en.wikipedia.org/wiki/Singular-value_decomposition

[10] Indexing by Latent Semantic Analysis:
https://search.proquest.com/openview/a1907164bd88dfc38a4875b73a3f7b3d/1?pq-origsite=gscholar&cbl=1818555

[11] Probabilistic Latent Semantic Indexing:
https://dl.acm.org/citation.cfm?id=312649

[12] NIPS:
https://nips.cc/

[13] Sharing Clusters Among Related Groups: Hierarchical Dirichlet Processes:
http://papers.nips.cc/paper/2698-sharing-clusters-among-related-groups-hierarchical-dirichlet-processes.pdf

[14] Dynamic Topic Models:
https://github.com/RaRe-Technologies/gensim/blob/develop/docs/notebooks/ldaseqmodel.ipynb

[15] NNMF:
https://en.wikipedia.org/wiki/Non-negative_matrix_factorization

[16] Algorithms for NNMF:
http://papers.nips.cc/paper/1861-algorithms-for-non-negative-matrix-factorization

[17] On information and sufficiency:
https://projecteuclid.org/euclid.aoms/1177729694

Advanced Topic Modeling **9**

We saw in the previous chapter the power of topic modeling, and how intuitive a way it can be to understand our data, as well as explore it. In this chapter, we will further explore the utility of these topic models, and also on how to create more useful topic models which better encapsulates the topics which may be present in a corpus. Since topic modeling is a way to understand the documents of a corpus, it also means we can analyze documents in ways we have not done before.

In this chapter, we will cover the following topics:

- Advanced training tips
- Exploring documents
- Topic coherence and evaluating topic models
- Visualizing topic models

Advanced training tips

In `Chapter 8`, *Topic Models*, we explored what topic models are, and how to set them up with both Gensim and scikit-learn. But just setting up a topic model isn't sufficient - a poorly trained topic model would not offer us any useful information.

We've already talked about the most important *pre-training* tip - preprocessing. It would be quite clear now that garbage in is garbage out, but sometimes even after ensuring it isn't garbage you're putting in, we still get nonsense outputs. In this section, we will briefly discuss what else it is you can do to polish your results.

It would be wise to re-look at `Chapter 3`, *SpaCy's Language Model*, and `Chapter 4`, *Gensim - Vectorizing Text and Transformations and n-grams*, now - they introduce the methods used in preprocessing, which is usually the first *advanced* training tip given. It is worth noting that some of these preprocessing tips are geared more towards generating topic models than other forms of text analysis algorithms. For example, using lemmatizing instead of stemming is a practice which especially pays off in topic modeling because lemmatized words tend to be more human-readable than stemming. Similarly, using bi-grams or tri-grams as part of your corpus before applying the topic modeling algorithm means our results would be further human interpretable.

Since our purpose with topic models is to explore the corpus, it makes sense that we work towards getting results which are more understandable by humans. This would be slightly different than clustering documents for example, where we would be more focused on having a higher accuracy than on having anything *human interpretable*. Keeping this in mind is important while preprocessing our documents, and also means we are free to add our own preprocessing steps along the way to help us with our results.

It is highly unlikely that we get very *useful* results the first time we attempt to topic model our data - successful topic modeling requires multiple runs of cleaning the data, reading the results, adjusting the preprocessing accordingly and trying again. For example, we might want to add new stop words to our stop-word list after viewing our first topic model. It's more often than not that based on the domain you are conducting your text analysis; the stop words would be quite different.

In the Jupyter notebook we first looked at in `Chapter 8`, *Topic Models*, we were working on the Lee Newspaper corpus. On the first few topic modeling runs, the results weren't the most useful - the word `say` would come up a disproportionately high number of times in the topics. This made sense, of course - in a corpus containing newspaper articles, the words `said` or `saying` would come up often, and these would get lemmatized to `say`. But even though it made sense, it still meant that our topic model was not the most useful. In this case, the solution was clear - remove variations of the word `say` from the corpus so that it does not show up in our topic models.

With spacy, this would be done like this:

```
my_stop_words = [u'say', u'\'s', u'Mr', u'be', u'said', u'says', u'saying']
for stopword in my_stop_words:
    lexeme = nlp.vocab[stopword]
    lexeme.is_stop = True
```

So, what exactly is going on here? For every word that we wish to add as a stop word, we change the `is_stop` attribute for that `lexeme` class. Lexemes are not case sensitive, so we can ignore case here. To add more stop words, we simply add the words to the `my_stop_words` list.

This is just the way spaCy handles stop words - a more common way to remove stop words is to put all our stop words in one list and simply remove all occurrences of those words from the corpus. If you're using NLTK, it would be something like this:

```
from nltk.corpus import stopwords
stopword_list = stopwords.words("english")
```

Here, `stopword_list` is a list, so adding new words to our list is as simple as appending words to the list.

> We will be using spaCy throughout for any kind of preprocessing, so that is the stop-word removal method we should really concern yourself with; that being said, you can technically use any method to remove stop-words.

Another way to prune out unwanted words is to use the Gensim `Dictionary` class. Consider this example:

```
filter_n_most_frequent(remove_n)
```

This filters out the `remove_n` most frequent tokens that appear in the documents.

This quick example from the Gensim `Dictionary` documentation [1] illustrates this:

```
from gensim.corpora import Dictionary
corpus = [["máma", "mele", "maso"], ["ema", "má", "máma"]]
dct = Dictionary(corpus)
len(dct)
5

dct.filter_n_most_frequent(2)
len(dct)
3
```

This process of generating a topic model, manually inspecting it and appropriately changing our preprocessing steps is a common exercise in almost all machine learning or data science projects - in text analysis, the difference is the human interpretable nature of the results.

When do we stop this process of cycles of preprocessing and generating topic models? Pretty much when we are satisfied with the results we see - since we're not attempting to get higher accuracy values when we topic model, we can stop when we think our topic model is finally *useful*. Of course, there are also more objective ways to measure how *useful* a topic model is, and we will discuss these techniques in our *Topic Coherence and evaluating topic models* section.

Now, all of these tips involved what we do *before* we start our topic modeling. There's also a fair amount of tuning we can do even when we are creating our topic models. While these training options are different for Gensim and scikit-learn, one thing is common - how many topics do we choose for the most optimal topic model?

There's no real answer to this question, and again, a measure for the best number of topics really depends on the kind of corpus you are using, the size of the corpus, and the number of topics you might expect to see - maybe a 100 topics for a large corpus and 10 for a smaller one. If we have no prior knowledge about the dataset, running a model with 5 topics, and then 10, and so on and so forth in steps of 10 is actually a reasonable enough approach, though there are also more quantitative methods to measure this, which we will soon discuss in the section on topic coherence.

In all machine learning algorithms, we have various parameters that affect the results of the algorithm. The process of changing these parameters to achieve different results is called parameter tuning, and these parameters are also colloquially referred to as **tuning** parameters.

Some important tuning parameters, at least for Gensim include the following:

1. `chunksize`: This controls how many documents are processed at a time in the training algorithm. Increasing chunksize will speed up training, at least as long as the chunk of documents easily fit into memory (RAM).
2. `passes`: This controls how often we train the model on the entire corpus. Another word for passes might be **epochs**.
3. `iterations`: This controls how often we repeat a particular loop over each document. It is important to set the number of **passes** and **iterations** high enough.

You can see the other parameters for `LdaModel here` [2] - you can recall us using `LdaModel` in `Chapter 8`, *Topic Models*. For scikit-learn, `these` [3] are the parameters for their LDA implementation, for a quick comparison. These are useful to understand what *kind* of parameters we can play around with. Hyperparameters are a word to describe parameters of a machine learning algorithm which are set *before* the machine learning algorithm begins.

In machine learning, we often refer to the result of our algorithm as a model - in the context of topic modeling, an LDA model, HDP model, or LSI model is simply a probabilistic model that describes the documents in the corpus. When we talk about topic models or an LDA model, for example, we refer to this trained model.

In general, an LDA algorithm would have two hyperparameters:

1. **Alpha**: This represents the document-topic density. Higher the value of alpha, documents are composed of more topics and lower the value of alpha, documents contain fewer topics.
2. **Beta**: This represents the topic-word density. If the value of beta is high, topics are composed of a large number of words in the corpus, and with the lower value of beta, they are composed of few words.
3. **Number of topics**: The number of topics we wish to model.

During the training process, for more information, it makes sense to turn on logging, as Gensim doesn't print training information by default.

This can be done with:

```
import logging
logging.basicConfig(filename='logfile.log', format='%(asctime)s :
                    %(levelname)s : %(message)s', level=logging.INFO)
```

This blog post by Chris Tufts also serves as a useful resource for training your LDA model [4]. The Gensim FAQ and recipes page is also worth going through [5].

Once we are sufficiently happy with the model we have trained, we can play around more - and you will see we can do more than just looking at what kind of topics exist in a corpus.

Exploring documents

Once we have our topic model of choice set up, we can use it to analyze our corpus, and also get some more insight into the nature of our topic models. While it is certainly useful to know what kind of topics are present in our dataset, to go one step further we should be able to, for example, cluster or classify our documents based on what topics they are made out of.

In our Jupyter notebook example from Chapter 8, *Topic Models*, let's start looking at document-topic proportions. What exactly are these? When we were looking at topics in the previous chapter, we were observing topic-word proportions - what are the odds of certain words appearing in certain topics. We previously mentioned that we assumed that documents are *generated* from topics - by identifying document-topic proportions, we can see exactly how the topics generated the documents.

So, do we do this Gensim? It's particularly straightforward:

```
ldamodel[document]
```

Is all you need to get the document-topic proportions. Document here is the vector representation of the document which we wish to analyze.

 This does not need to be a document that was used to train the LDA model - it can be an unseen document, so long as the words in the document are within the same vocabulary of the LDA model.

Let's try this with the context of the Lee Newspaper corpus:

```
ldamodel[corpus[0]]
```

This gives us the following:

```
[(1, 0.99395897621183538)]
```

What does this mean? The list contains tuples with the topic number and the corresponding probability of that topic appearing in that topic - above a certain cutoff-probability. Since we only have one tuple in our list, this means that the contributions of the other topics to this document are negligible. Let's verify this.

What is topic 1?

```
ldamodel.show_topics()[1]

(1, u'0.008*"area" + 0.007*"fire" + 0.006*"people" + 0.005*"sydney" +
0.005*"force" + 0.004*"pakistan" + 0.004*"new" + 0.004*"afghan" +
0.004*"new_south" + 0.004*"wales"')
```

It seems to represent two themes - of the Afghan-Pakistan conflict and of a possible fire or accident in New South Wales or Sydney. Let's see if our first document has any of these themes coming up.

Let's now have a look at a few words of our first document and see if the topic assignment makes any sense:

```
texts[0][:15]
```

```
[u'hundred',
 u'people',
 u'force',
 u'vacate',
 u'home',
 u'southern',
 u'highlands',
 u'new_south',
 u'wales',
 u'strong',
 u'wind',
 u'today',
 u'push',
 u'huge',
 u'bushfire']
```

We see that it certainly does match one of the themes of the topic and that our topic model is indeed useful. We can further use this information to cluster documents into each topic based on the document-topic proportions.

One very important point to note: you may be seeing different topics, different proportions, and different words - topic models are probabilistic, and we do not get the same results every time.

It is important to note now that a representation where we have the document-topic proportions is also a vector representation such as TF-IDF; instead of our vector length spanning over the vocabulary, it is the size of the number of topics.

Gensim doesn't just stop here and has further methods to help us analyze the topic proportions of both documents and words.

We will be using this Jupyter notebook [6] I have written for Gensim to illustrate the methods that Gensim has to offer.

Let's quickly have a look at the corpus we will be using to illustrate the methods:

```
texts = [['bank','river','shore','water'],
        ['river','water','flow','fast','tree'],
        ['bank','water','fall','flow'],
        ['bank','bank','water','rain','river'],
        ['river','water','mud','tree'],
```

```
['money','transaction','bank','finance'],
['bank','borrow','money'],
['bank','finance'],
['finance','money','sell','bank'],
['borrow','sell'],
['bank','loan','sell']]
```

Some quick notes about this corpus - it contains sentences that have two distinct topics - one to do with finance, and the other to do with rivers. You should also notice that the word bank repeats itself in both the contexts - this allows us to do some more experiments with words.

Let's look at the topics generated from this corpus:

```
model.show_topics()

[(0, u'0.164*"bank" + 0.142*"water" + 0.108*"river" + 0.076*"flow" +
0.067*"borrow" + 0.063*"sell" + 0.060*"tree" + 0.048*"money" + 0.046*"fast"
+ 0.044*"rain"'),
(1, u'0.196*"bank" + 0.120*"finance" + 0.100*"money" + 0.082*"sell" +
0.067*"river" + 0.065*"water" + 0.056*"transaction" + 0.049*"loan" +
0.046*"tree" + 0.040*"mud"')]
```

We can see that as expected, one topic is to do with river banks, while the other topic is to do with financial banks.

Within documents, it is possible to find the odds of a particular word belonging to a particular topic. This is done with the `get_term_topics()` method. Let's look at a few examples:

```
model.get_term_topics('water')

[(0, 0.12821234071249418), (1, 0.047247458568794511)]
```

This makes sense; the value for it belonging to topic_0 is a lot more.

```
model.get_term_topics('finance')

[(0, 0.017179349495865623), (1, 0.10331511184214655)]
```

As expected, the `finance` word has a much higher probability of being within the second topic. We leave it to the reader to figure out what the result might look like if we ran the same method for the word *bank*.

This method concerned itself with particular words in a corpus - let's now see how to find topic proportions for entire documents. The `get_document_topics` method is the Gensim functionality that uses the inference function to get the sufficient statistics and figure out the topic distribution of the document.

Let's test this with two different documents which have the word bank in it, one in the finance context and one in the river context.

The `get_document_topics` method returns (along with the standard document topic proportion) the word_type followed by a list sorted with the most likely topic ids when `per_word_topics` is set as true.

Have a look at this excerpt from the notebook:

```
bow_water = ['bank','water','bank']
bow_finance = ['bank','finance','bank']

bow = model.id2word.doc2bow(bow_water) # convert to bag of words format
first
doc_topics, word_topics, phi_values = model.get_document_topics(bow,
per_word_topics=True)


word_topics

[(0, [0, 1]), (3, [0, 1])]
```

Now, what does that output mean? It means that like word_type 1, our word_type 3, which is the word `bank`, is more likely to be in topic_0 than topic_1. A reminder here that the numbers 0, 1, and 3 refer to the id or index of that word. Word 1 is the word in the dictionary with id 1, and topic 0 is the first topic.

You must have noticed that while we unpacked into `doc_topics` and `word_topics`, there is another variable - `phi_values`. Phi is essentially the probability of that word in that document belonging to a particular topic. Like the name suggests, `phi_values` contains the phi values for each topic for that particular word, scaled by feature length. The next few lines should illustrate this:

```
phi_values

[(0, [(0, 0.92486455564294345), (1, 0.075135444357056574)]),
 (3, [(0, 1.5817120973072454), (1, 0.41828790269275457)])]
```

This means that word_type 0 has the following `phi_values` for each of the topics. What is interesting to note is word_type 3 - because it has 2 occurrences (that is, the word bank appears twice in the bow), we can see that the scaling by feature length is very evident. The sum of `phi_values` is 2, and not 1.

Now that we know exactly what `get_document_topics` does, let's now do the same with our second document, `bow_finance`.

```
bow = model.id2word.doc2bow(bow_finance) # convert to bag of words format
first
doc_topics, word_topics, phi_values = model.get_document_topics(bow,
per_word_topics=True)

word_topics
```

```
[(3, [1, 0]), (12, [1, 0])]
```

And lo and behold, because the word bank is now used in the financial context, it immediately swaps to be more likely associated with topic_1.

We've seen quite clearly that based on the context, the most likely topic associated with a word can change. This differs from our previous method, `get_term_topics`, where it is a *static* topic distribution.

It must also be noted that because the Gensim implementation of LDA uses **Variational Bayes sampling**, a word_type in a document is only given one topic distribution. For example, the sentence *the bank by the river bank* is likely to be assigned to topic_0, and each of the bank word instances has the same distribution.

Using these two methods we see how we can infer further information from using our topic models. Having the document - topic distributions means we can also use this information to do some cool stuff - for example, coloring all the words in a document based on which topic it belongs to, or using distance metrics to infer how close or far away two topics or documents are.

The following Jupyter notebooks that I've contributed to Gensim exactly tell us how to do the following tasks - it is highly recommended that you have a look and run the notebooks before moving to the next section.

- Coloring Words in a Document - notebook 1 [6]
- Distance Metrics - notebook 2 [7]

Scikit-learn similarly has further caveats you can explore - the blog post [8] would be a good place to start!

We are now going over to a crucial part of topic models - understanding quantitatively how well a topic model performs.

Topic coherence and evaluating topic models

In the previous sections, we spoke extensively about how topic models, in general, are rather qualitative in nature - it's difficult to put a number on how useful a topic model is. Despite this, there is a need to evaluate topic models, and the most popular method out there is topic coherence - and lucky for us, Gensim has quite an extensive suite of topic coherence methods for us to try out.

What exactly is topic coherence? Briefly put, it is a measure of how interpretable topics are for human beings. There are multiple coherence measures in topic modeling literature, and we won't be going through the theory for these, but the following links should walk you through the theory and intuition, if interested:

1. What is topic coherence? [9]
2. Exploring the Space of Topic Coherence Measures [10]

The first link is a Gensim blog post, and the second is a research paper and goes into further theoretical details.

All we need to know to proceed is that we now have a *quantitative* measure of how well our topic model is. This opens up a lot of possibilities for us - we can now compare between two differently trained (with a different number of iterations or passes, for example) LDA models, or between an HDP model and an LSI model, or even between similarly trained models with a different number of topics. This means that we now also have a quantitative way to even measure the optimal number of topics for a corpus, as well as a way to compare between completely different classes of models.

Of course, we can still use qualitative methods to get an understanding how well our topic model performs. Visualizing topic models are one way to do this - we've already explored one such method in the previous section, where the Jupyter notebook walks us through coloring words in a document. By quickly glancing at the colored words in a document, we can get an idea of how well the topic model understands which words belong to which topic. Using more advanced topic visualization tools, we can further analyze how efficient our topic model is. We'll talk about these tools extensively in the next section - for now, let's look at Gensim's topic coherence pipeline!

Before topic coherence, perplexity was used to measure how well a topic model was fit - indeed, even now Gensim allows us to hold out a testing set and measure perplexity while training our model. You can read more about perplexity and topic models over here [11].

Gensim has a very straightforward API to perform topic coherence:

If for example, we wish to check the coherence value of the three models in our Lee Newspaper corpus data-set, we simply run. Note that these examples are from the Jupyter notebook attached at the end of Chapter 8, *Topic Models*.

```
lsi_coherence = CoherenceModel(topics=lsitopics[:10], texts=texts,
dictionary=dictionary, window_size=10)

hdp_coherence = CoherenceModel(topics=hdptopics[:10], texts=texts,
dictionary=dictionary, window_size=10)

lda_coherence = CoherenceModel(topics=ldatopics, texts=texts,
dictionary=dictionary, window_size=10)
```

Here, topics are just the list of the top *n* words for each topic. Since the topics are all different, we pass the list of the top *word* instead of passing the model itself. We can then print the values of coherence for each of the models to get the comparative coherence values - this exercise has been completed in the Jupyter notebook [12] and we urge the reader to explore this comparison.

In cases when we are, for example, just comparing between two different kinds of LdaModel objects, we can also pass the models. Here, goodLdaModel and badLdaModel are just placeholder variable names for a good and bad model- you are expected to pass whichever models you wish to.

```
goodcm = CoherenceModel(model=goodLdaModel, texts=texts,
dictionary=dictionary, coherence='c_v')
badcm = CoherenceModel(model=badLdaModel, texts=texts,
dictionary=dictionary, coherence='c_v')
```

We notice here that in both the examples, we pass texts - here texts is the original corpus before we convert it into its vector form. You can have a look at the texts list in the notebook to confirm the contents of it.

Once we have our coherence models trained, we simply have to run get_coherence() to get the value of coherence. Note that coherence values on their own have no meaning - it is only when compared to another coherence value with the same corpus that it is of any meaning - and higher the value of coherence, better the model.

In the *bad* and *good* LdaModel example, the bad LdaModel object was trained with only 1 iteration, and the good LdaModel object was trained with 50 iterations. When we attempt to print the values of coherence:

```
print(goodcm.get_coherence())
print(badcm.get_coherence())
```

```
-13.8029561191-14.1531313765
```

We can see that the good LdaModel object has a higher value of coherence, which confirms our hypothesis that a model trained with more iterations would perform better. A note: these are sample coherence values based on any sets of models where one is more trained than the other. The user should attempt to train his or her own good and bad models and experiment with the results.

Like we mentioned before, we can also use coherence measures to see what the optimal number of topics for a corpus are. The following is an example of a simple for loop which would do the same:

```
c_v = []
limit = 10
for num_topics in range(1, limit):
        lm = LdaModel(corpus=corpus, num_topics=num_topics,
                        id2word=dictionary)
        cm = CoherenceModel(model=lm, texts=texts, dictionary=dictionary,
                                coherence='c_v')
        c_v.append(cm.get_coherence())
```

Printing c_v would give us a list of the corresponding coherence values for each topic number - the highest coherence value would be a way to identify the number of topics which are most human-comprehensible.

We can also print the top topics from an LDA model, depending on which coherence measure we intend to use. The `top_topics` method helps perform this and uses the coherence model to generate the top topics. While we have covered most of the functionalities of coherence models in this section, there are multiple Gensim Jupyter notebooks which go into more detail into the different functionalities which coherence models can offer:

1. Coherence Model pipeline [13]
2. News Classification with Gensim [14]
3. Topic Coherence on Movies Dataset [15]
4. Topic Coherence Introduction [16]
5. Topic Coherence Use Cases [17]
6. Topic Coherence Model Selection [18]

Now that we have our models set up, as well as analyzed, we can go ahead to visualizing them.

Visualizing topic models

Like we have said before, the purpose of topic models is to better understand our textual data - and visualizations are one of the best ways to understand and look at our data. There are multiple ways and techniques to visualize topic models - we will be focusing on the methods implemented and compatible with Gensim, but like we have done throughout the book, we will be providing links and documentation to the other popular topic modeling visualization tools.

One of the most popular topic modeling visualization libraries is `LDAvis` - an R library build largely on D3, it has been ported to Python as `pyLDAvis` and is just as nifty in Python and is very well integrated with Gensim as well. It is based on the original paper (*LDAvis: A method for visualizing and interpreting topics* [19]) by Carson Sievert and Kenneth E. Shirley.

The `pyLDAvis` library is agnostic to how your model is trained - this means we are not restricted to Gensim or even LDA for that matter. All we need are the topic-term distributions and the document-topic distributions - and basic information about the corpus which was trained on.

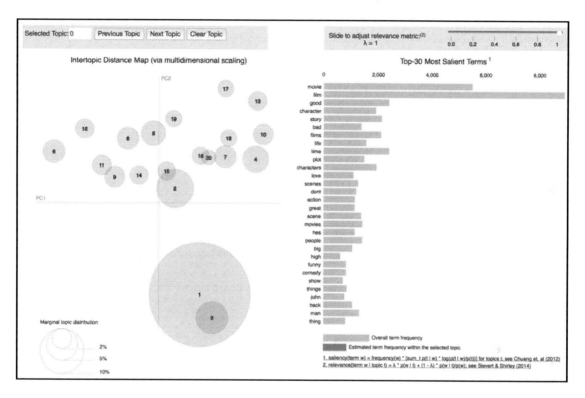

Fig 9.1 pyLDAvis

It's even easier if we are using a Gensim based model. All we need to do is this:

```
import pyLDAvis.gensim
pyLDAvis.gensim.prepare(model, corpus, dictionary)
```

Here the model is a placeholder variable, and we can pass any of our trained lda models.

We are then able to visualize a lot of information about our topics all at once - something which is a lot easier than manually inspecting topics printed out on your console. In the preceding figure, we can see each topic represented as a circle in a 2-dimensional space - this space is generated by finding the distance between the topics. The words on the right refer to the words in a topic and is a quick and useful way to see how words are spread out among topics. The original paper referred to in reference no 19 further details the visual elements.

The `pyLDAvis` library itself has a few more options you can tinker around with it, and it is highly recommended to check out the Jupyter notebook [20] tutorial which walks you through the details.

Now, this visualization is *after* we are done training - what if we want to visualize the progress during training? Gensim has newly added features to help with just this.

We previously discussed coherence and perplexity as measures to check how well a model is fit - we are able to see the progression of these models as it is being trained.

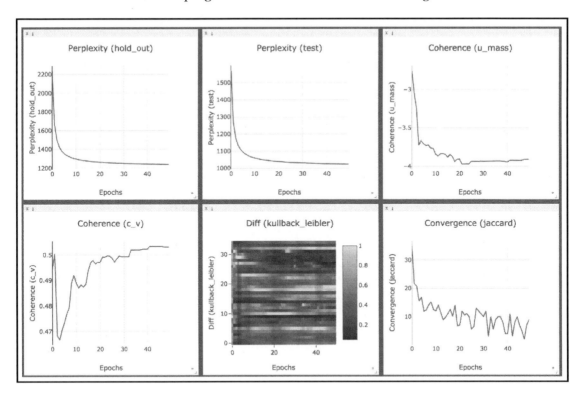

Fig 9.2 Visualizing coherence, perplexity, topic difference, and convergence

We can also measure the topic difference - it calculates the distance between two topic models, using one of the many distance metrics implemented in Gensim. Another metric we can watch is convergence - this is the sum of the difference between all the identical topics from two consecutive epochs.

It is fairly easy to set this up using Gensim, though we also need the **visdom** [21] server to do this. A visdom server is a Python-based server which is specifically built to aid in visualizing data. Since we are visualizing a live training process, we will be needing a server. The instructions to both set-up the server and the visualizations are explained clearly in the Jupyter notebook [22].

Topic models can be further viewed as clusters - for example, by using the machine learning algorithm **T-distributed Stochastic Neighbor Embedding (T-SNE)** [23] we can use the document-topic proportions to cluster our corpus.

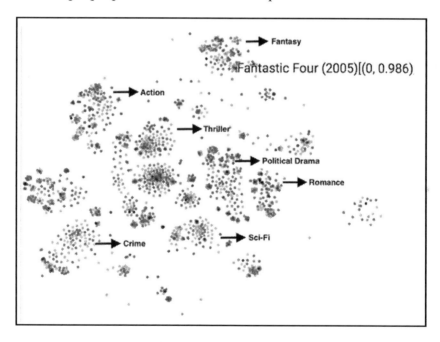

Fig 9.3 LDA document clusters based on topics and T-SNE

It is also possible to cluster using Word2Vec - the details for this kind of clustering is given in the Jupyter notebook [24].

Using Gensim and scipy we can also do cool things such as creating dendrograms of how our topics are related - the Jupyter notebook [25] goes over the details.

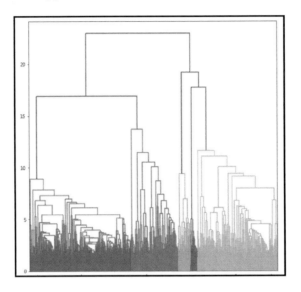

Fig 9.4 Topic dendograms

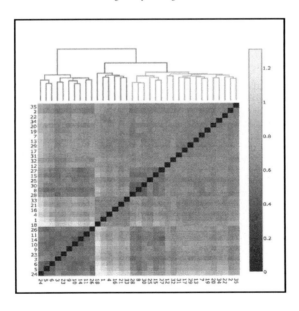

Fig 9.5 Topic dendrogram with heat-maps

A dendrogram is a tree-structured graph that can be used to visualize the result of any kind of hierarchical clustering. Hierarchical clustering puts individual data points into similarity groups, with some groups on *top* of each other based on the content of the groups. For example, if we are modeling a corpus with various kinds of industries, the *Mercedes* topic might come below the *cars* topic. We can use it to explore the topic models and see how the topics are connected to each other in a sequence of successive fusions or divisions that occur in the clustering process.

All of these visualizations are based on Gensim, and the Jupyter notebooks linked to are all from the Gensim documentation - it is worth taking the time to run the Jupyter notebooks and have a look at the visualizations yourself.

There are also some neat visualizations out there which are not officially Gensim but allow us to look at our data in interesting ways. We will link to the pages so that the reader can have a look:

- Visualizing Trends [26]
- Topic Modeling and t-SNE Visualization [27]
- Visualizing Topic Shares [28]
- David Blei - Visualizing Topic Models [29]

Summary

With `Chapter 8`, *Topic Models* and `Chapter 9`, *Advanced Topic Modelling*, we are now equipped with the tools and knowledge of applying topic models to our textual data. Topic modelling is a largely data exploratory tool, but we can also carry out some more targeted analysis, like seeing the topics which make up a document, or which words in a document belong to which topic. Gensim gives us the functionality to carry out these tasks quite easily, with its API constructed so that we can access the mathematical information behind topic models without a hassle.

In the next chapter, we will carry our more targeted text analysis tasks, such as clustering or classification. Clustering and classification algorithms are largely used in text analysis to group similar documents together and are machine learning algorithms. We will explain the intuition behind these methods as well as illustrate code examples.

References

[1] Gensim Dictionary class:
https://radimrehurek.com/gensim/corpora/dictionary.html

[2] Gensim LdaModel Class:
https://radimrehurek.com/gensim/models/ldamodel.html

[3] Scikit-Learn LDA Class:
http://scikit-learn.org/stable/modules/generated/sklearn.decomposition.LatentDirichletAllocation.html

[4] Gensim LDA: Tips and Tricks:
https://miningthedetails.com/blog/python/lda/GensimLDA/

[5] Recipes and FAQ:
https://github.com/RaRe-Technologies/gensim/wiki/Recipes-&-FAQ

[6] Term Topics Jupyter notebook:
https://github.com/RaRe-Technologies/gensim/blob/develop/docs/notebooks/topic_methods.ipynb

[7] Distance Metrics:
https://github.com/RaRe-Technologies/gensim/blob/develop/docs/notebooks/distance_metrics.ipynb

[8] Interpretation of Topic Models:
https://towardsdatascience.com/improving-the-interpretation-of-topic-models-87fd2ee3847d

[9] What is Topic Coherence:
https://rare-technologies.com/what-is-topic-coherence/

[10] Exploring the space of Topic Coherence Measures:
https://svn.aksw.org/papers/2015/WSDM_Topic_Evaluation/public.pdf

[11] Perplexity in Topic Models:
http://qpleple.com/perplexity-to-evaluate-topic-models/

[12] Topic Modelling Notebook:
https://github.com/bhargavvader/personal/blob/master/notebooks/text_analysis_tutorial/topic_modelling.ipynb

[13] Coherence Model pipeline:
https://radimrehurek.com/gensim/models/coherencemodel.html

[14] News Classification with Gensim:
https://github.com/RaRe-Technologies/gensim/blob/develop/docs/notebooks/gensim_news_classification.ipynb

[15] Topic Coherence on Movies Dataset:
https://github.com/RaRe-Technologies/gensim/blob/develop/docs/notebooks/topic_coherence-movies.ipynb

[16] Topic Coherence Introduction:
https://github.com/RaRe-Technologies/gensim/blob/develop/docs/notebooks/topic_coherence_tutorial.ipynb

[17] Topic Coherence Use Cases:
https://gist.github.com/dsquareindia/ac9d3bf57579d02302f9655db8dfdd55

[18] Topic Coherence Model Selection:
https://github.com/RaRe-Technologies/gensim/blob/develop/docs/notebooks/topic_coherence_model_selection.ipynb

[19] LDAvis: A method for visualizing and interpreting topics:
https://nlp.stanford.edu/events/illvi2014/papers/sievert-illvi2014.pdf

[20] pyLDAvis:
http://nbviewer.jupyter.org/github/bmabey/pyLDAvis/blob/master/notebooks/pyLDAvis_overview.ipynb

[21] visdom:
https://github.com/facebookresearch/visdom

[22] LDA training visualization:
https://github.com/parulsethi/gensim/blob/tensorboard_logs/docs/notebooks/Training_visualizations.ipynb

[23] t-SNE:
https://en.wikipedia.org/wiki/T-distributed_stochastic_neighbor_embedding

[24] TensorBoard Visualizations:
https://github.com/RaRe-Technologies/gensim/blob/develop/docs/notebooks/Tensorboard_visualizations.ipynb

[25] Topic Dendrograms:
https://github.com/RaRe-Technologies/gensim/blob/develop/docs/notebooks/Topic_dendrogram.ipynb

[26] Visualizing Trends:
https://de.dariah.eu/tatom/visualizing_trends.html

[27] Topic Modeling and t-SNE Visualization:
https://shuaiw.github.io/2016/12/22/topic-modeling-and-tsne-visualzation.html

[28] Visualizing Topic Shares:
https://de.dariah.eu/tatom/topic_model_visualization.html

[29] David Blei - Visualizing Topic Models:
https://www.aaai.org/ocs/index.php/ICWSM/ICWSM12/paper/viewFile/4645/5021

Clustering and Classifying Text 10

In the last chapter we studied topic models and how they can help us in organizing and better understanding our documents and its sub-structure. We will now move on to our next set of machine learning algorithms, and for two particular tasks — clustering and classification. We will learn what the intuitive reasoning of these two tasks is, as well as how to perform these tasks using the popular Python machine learning library, scikit-learn:

- Clustering text
- Classifying text

Clustering text

So far we looked at analyzing text to understand better what the text or corpus consists of. When we tried to POS-tag or NER-tag, we were interested in knowing what *kind* of words were presented in our documents, and when we topic-modeled, we wanted to know the underlying topics which could be hidden in our texts. Sure, we could use our topic models to attempt to cluster articles, but that isn't its purpose; we would be silly to expect great results if we tried this, too. Remember that since the purpose of topic modeling is to find hidden themes in a corpus and not to group documents together, our methods are not optimized for the task. For example, after we perform topic modeling, a document can be made of 30% topic 1, 30% topic 2, and 40% topic 3. In such a case, we cannot use this information to cluster.

Let us now start exploring how to use machine learning methods to move on to tasks which are more quantitative in nature: **clustering** and **classification**. Clustering is a popular machine learning task, and the techniques used in classical clustering tasks can be used for text as well. As the name suggests, clustering is the task of grouping together or clustering data points in the same group, where points in the same group are more similar to each other than points in other groups. In our context, data points can be thought of as documents, or in some cases, words. Clustering is an unsupervised learning problem. We are not aware of the clusters or groups before we start assigning our data points to them (though we might have an idea of what we might find).

Classification is a similar task and is the problem of identifying to which of a set of categories (sub-populations) a new observation belongs, by a training set of data containing observations (or instances) whose category membership is known. An example would be assigning a given email into *spam* or *non-spam* classes, or the task of assigning newspaper articles to predetermined classes or groups.

An example of a famous clustering or classifying task could be the Iris flower dataset [1], where we attempt to find out which class a flower belongs to based on its petal length. Another popular dataset used for these purposes is the MNIST dataset [2], which contains handwritten digits that are meant to be classified under the number it is supposed to represent.

Clustering text follows most of the principles which standard clustering problems follow, but we have to keep one thing in mind: the high number of dimensions in text analysis. In the Iris dataset, for example, there are only four features which we use to identify our classes or clusters. However, in the case of text, we have to deal with the entire vocabulary size when setting up our problem. Of course, we will do our best to reduce our dimensions using some of the techniques like SVD, LDA, and LSI, which we discussed before.

While we largely used Gensim before to carry out our quantitative tasks, and spaCy for computational linguistics, we will move on to a more traditional machine learning library, scikit-learn. Indeed, we have already introduced scikit-learn earlier on in the book, but from this chapter onward we can expect an increased use of the same.

While we perform our clustering and classifying tasks, you might often come across both Word2Vec and Doc2Vec, two ways of representing words and documents as vectors. We have to remember that it is just another vector representation of words and documents, albeit in a more sophisticated manner than which we have explored so far. We will explore Word2Vec and Doc2Vec in detail in `Chapter 12`, *Word2Vec, Doc2Vec, and Gensim*, and revisit clustering and classifying using them, but for now, it is enough to understand them as a way we can provide more curated information to our clustering or classifying algorithms.

Starting clustering

Like every other text analysis algorithm we applied before, the most important step remains the pre-processing step — getting rid of our stop words and lemmatizing words.

Once we're done with this, the next step is to convert our document into a vector representation we are most comfortable with.

Since we're dealing with scikit-learn's implementations for clustering and classification, let us use scikit-learn for our pre-processing. We should also use this opportunity to decide which dataset we intend to use for our experiments. While there are lots of solid options, we will stick with the popular 20 Newsgroups [3] dataset. Since the dataset comes bundled with scikit-learn, loading it and using it becomes an easy task as well.

You can follow the Jupyter notebook [4] on clustering and classification for the full details; we will be using code snippets from there to explain the process.

To start accessing our dataset, we run:

```
from sklearn.datasets import fetch_20newsgroups


categories = [
    'alt.atheism',
    'talk.religion.misc',
    'comp.graphics',
    'sci.space',
]

dataset = fetch_20newsgroups(subset='all', categories=categories,
shuffle=True, random_state=42)

labels = dataset.target
true_k = np.unique(labels).shape[0]
data = dataset.data
```

Let's have a brief look at what we have done so far. The `import` statement allowed us to easily access the 20NG dataset, and for the sake of the example, we have decided to pick up only 4 categories. Following [3] will give you the full list of categories. We create our dataset by choosing all the subsets, while also shuffling the dataset, but with a random-state set. As always, we have to now convert our textual data to a form which machine learning algorithms can understand — vectors.

We will be using scikit-learn's in-built `TfidfVectorizer` to make our job easy:

```
from sklearn.feature_extraction.text import TfidfVectorizer

vectorizer = TfidfVectorizer(max_df=0.5, min_df=2, stop_words='english',
use_idf=True)

X = vectorizer.fit_transform(data)
```

The X object is now our input vector which contains the TF-IDF representation of our dataset. We have to remember that we are still dealing with rather high-dimensional data when we do a TF-IDF transformation. To better understand the nature of the data, it is useful to visualize it. We can do this by doing a Principal Component Analysis [5] on our data-set to reduce the number of dimensions to 2. PCA is an algorithm which looks for unrelated (mathematically, these are referred to as *linearly uncorrelated*) components from a dataset. By identifying these unrelated components from a high-dimensional dataset, we are effectively performing dimension reduction. Note that we are *only* doing this for the purpose of visualization; for the clustering problem we will attempt other dimensionality reduction techniques:

```
from sklearn.decomposition import PCA
from sklearn.pipeline import Pipeline


newsgroups_train = fetch_20newsgroups(subset='train',
categories=['alt.atheism', 'sci.space'])
pipeline = Pipeline([
    ('vect', CountVectorizer()),
    ('tfidf', TfidfTransformer()),
])
X_visualise = pipeline.fit_transform(newsgroups_train.data).todense()

pca = PCA(n_components=2).fit(X_visualise)
data2D = pca.transform(X_visualise)
plt.scatter(data2D[:,0], data2D[:,1], c=newsgroups_train.target)
```

Let's briefly discuss this code. We loaded the data again, but with only two categories (the ones we want to visualize). We ran a count-vectorizer and a TF-IDF transformation on this and fit a PCA model where we want only two key components. On plotting this, we have an idea of how the clusters in the dataset might be separated:

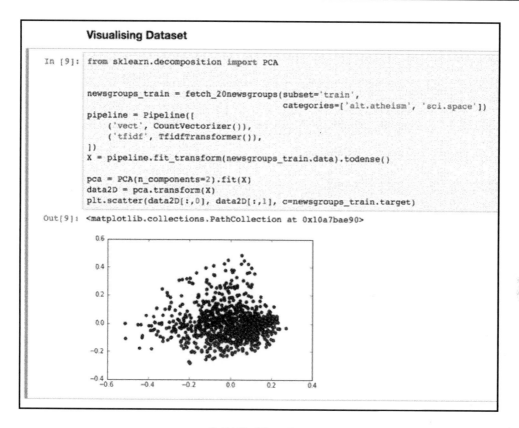

```
In [9]:  from sklearn.decomposition import PCA


         newsgroups_train = fetch_20newsgroups(subset='train',
                                     categories=['alt.atheism', 'sci.space'])
         pipeline = Pipeline([
             ('vect', CountVectorizer()),
             ('tfidf', TfidfTransformer()),
         ])
         X = pipeline.fit_transform(newsgroups_train.data).todense()

         pca = PCA(n_components=2).fit(X)
         data2D = pca.transform(X)
         plt.scatter(data2D[:,0], data2D[:,1], c=newsgroups_train.target)

Out[9]:  <matplotlib.collections.PathCollection at 0x10a7bae90>
```

Fig 10.1: Visualizing our dataset

It is important to note that the axis here simply represents two components which were discovered by PCA.

Let's now get back to our original vector, X, and set it up to be ready for clustering. When discussing topic models, we discussed how they could also work as a dimensionality reduction technique. Let us use **Singular Value Decomposition (SVD)** and **Latent Semantic Analysis (LSA/LSI)** (we came across these methods in Chapter 8, *Topic Models*, on topic modelling) to do our dimensionality reduction for this example.

Note: We have to re-normalize after we run our SVD on the dataset.

```
from sklearn.decomposition import TruncatedSVD
from sklearn.preprocessing import Normalizer
```

```
n_components = 5
svd = TruncatedSVD(n_components)
normalizer = Normalizer(copy=False)
lsa = make_pipeline(svd, normalizer)
X = lsa.fit_transform(X)
```

The final X is the input which we will be using. It has been cleaned, TF-IDF transformed, and further had its dimensions reduced. It is now ready to have clustering techniques run on it!

K-means

K-means [6] is a classical machine learning algorithm for clustering. It is intuitively easy to understand. Based on a predetermined number of clusters the user decides, it attempts to create clusters. This is done by reducing the distance of points from the respective centroid the point is assigned to. It is an iterative algorithm and keeps doing the process until the centroids and points assigned don't change. It is worth one's time to go through the theory behind the algorithm, though it isn't necessary for us to proceed.

Using K-means with scikit-learn is very easy, and scikit-learn offers two implementations [7] which we can use – either in mini-batches or without. In our code, we allow the user to toggle between which option to use:

```
minibatch = True
if minibatch:
    km = MiniBatchKMeans(n_clusters=true_k, init='k-means++', n_init=1,
                        init_size=1000, batch_size=1000)
else:
    km = KMeans(n_clusters=true_k, init='k-means++', max_iter=100,
                n_init=1)
km.fit(X)
```

And voila! We have a *fit* model now which has four different clusters. Instead of visualizing this, let's try and find what the top words per cluster are:

```
original_space_centroids = svd.inverse_transform(km.cluster_centers_)
order_centroids = original_space_centroids.argsort()[:, ::-1]
```

The preceding bit of code is necessary because of our LSI transformation.

```
terms = vectorizer.get_feature_names()

for i in range(true_k):
    print("Cluster %d:" % i)
    for ind in order_centroids[i, :10]:
        print(' %s' % terms[ind])
```

```
Cluster 0:
 graphics
 space
 image
 com
 university
 nasa
 images
 ac
 programposting
Cluster 1:
 god
 people
 com
 jesus
 don
 say
 believe
 think
 bible
 just
Cluster 2:
 space
 henry
 toronto
 nasa
 access
 com
 digex
 pat
 gov
 alaska
Cluster 3:
 sgi
 livesey
 keith
 solntze
 wpd
 jon
 com
 caltech
```

```
morality
moral
```

 Note: You might see different results, as machine learning algorithms do not produce the exact same results each time.

We can see how each of the four clusters represents the four categories we initially chose – our clustering has turned out just fine! We can further use our fit model to predict which cluster a new document belongs to; just remember to run the same pre-processing steps for the new document as well. This is as simple as:

```
km.predict(X_test)
```

So what did we do over here? We loaded our dataset, chose four categories, ran pre-processing steps, visualized our data, trained a K-means model, and printed the top words per cluster to see if they made sense—and they did just fine. Since we knew there were four categories, we choose our K-means cluster to have four clusters, that is, *K=4*.

We are free to play around more with the pre-processing and can expect different kinds of results with different steps. Let's now explore another form of clustering.

Hierarchical clustering

Before we dive into hierarchical clustering, it would be a very handy exercise to go through the scikit-learn documentation on clustering [8]. We have to remember that using a different model in scikit-learn is very easy, and that almost all the other steps in the process of clustering remain the same throughout.

We will use Ward's algorithm/method [9] to attempt hierarchical clustering. The algorithm is based on the idea of reducing the variance within each cluster and uses distance measures to do this. Ward's method is one of the earliest methods used in various hierarchical clustering algorithms, which are based on building clusters and arranging them in a hierarchy. In our examples, we will use dendrograms [10] to represent our hierarchical clusters.

To set up our dataset for this method we must first create a matrix with pair-wise distances. We can do this very easily with scikit-learn like this:

```
from sklearn.metrics.pairwise import cosine_similarity
dist = 1 - cosine_similarity(X)
```

Now that we have our distance matrix ready, we will use SciPy's `ward` and `dendrogram` functions:

```
from scipy.cluster.hierarchy import ward, dendrogram

linkage_matrix = ward(dist)
fig, ax = plt.subplots(figsize=(10, 15)) # set size
ax = dendrogram(linkage_matrix, orientation="right")
```

And that's it! SciPy does all the hard work for us and presents us with this pretty diagram. The dendrogram gives us an idea of the clusters the documents can be arranged in. The x-axis mentions the name or indices of the documents, but those cannot be seen now because there happen to be too many documents. The y-axis refers to the distance between each hierarchy of clusters:

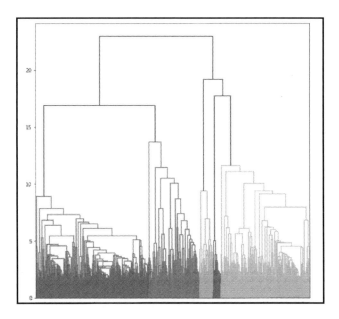

Fig 10.2 An example of a dendrogram generated as a result of text clustering using Ward's algorithm in SciPy

We can see, in this particular case, this might not be the best method to cluster, mainly because of the number of documents. It is tougher to look at the relationship between the documents and what the clusters represent. Trying this for a smaller corpus might prove very handy, though!

The following tutorials (links in the References section) also illustrate the methods we have tried but on different datasets:

- Brandon Rose - Clustering [11]
- Working with Text [12]

We would like to stress again about using different dimensionality reduction and vector representations before feeding our corpus to the clustering algorithm. Both Word2vec and Doc2Vec offer very interesting ways to do this, and Gensim has ready implementations for this very purpose! The blog post at https://towardsdatascience.com/automatic-topic-clustering-using-doc2vec-e1cea88449c [13] on clustering with Word2Vec attempts to explain this as well.

We will now move on to classifying text documents, another popular usage of machine learning algorithms in the text.

Classifying text

In our previous section, we discussed cluster, which was an unsupervised learning algorithm. Classification, on the other hand, is a supervised learning algorithm. What does supervised and unsupervised mean? In our previous example, we had the *labels* or the truth values. This is information about which class or label a document actually belongs to. But you would have also noticed we never used this information. When we trained our model, we never used the labels. This kind of learning is called unsupervised learning, and clustering is a popular example of an unsupervised learning task.

In classification problems, we are aware of the classes which we want to assign documents or data points to, and we use this information to train our model. In fact, as we are going to see very soon - there is hardly any change in our approach to clustering and classification, apart from the fact that we will be paying attention to our labels, and that we will be using a different machine or model to train on.

Like we've been stressing throughout the book, it is important to make sure our text is cleaned and vectorized before we start feeding it into any machine learning pipeline. Our steps will remain the same as before, though we do have the liberty to change things around a bit until we get the accuracy or performance we are looking for.

We will use the Naive Bayes classifier [14] and a Support Vector Machine [15] classifier to help us with our classification tasks. While the mathematical nature of these machines is beyond our scope, the scikit-learn documentation for them (NB [16], SVM [17]) provides for some intuitive reading:

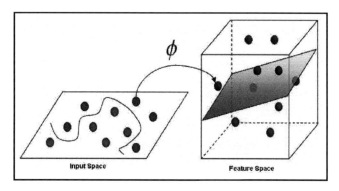

Fig 10.3: Using kernels to transform the input space - SVM. Source: Quora, What does support vector machine (SVM) mean in layman's terms? [19]

Support Vector Machines work by using kernels [18] to *transform* the input space so that we can best draw a line (or in higher dimensions, as is the case with text - a plane) to separate the classes. Kernels are mathematical functions which help us in transforming our dimension space.

Briefly, the **Naive Bayes Classifier** works by applying Bayes' theorem with the *naive* assumption of independence between every pair of features; we can predict which category a document may belong to. One must note that independence is normally assumed. When this case does not hold true, it is called *naïve*. The prior probability of whether a document belongs to a certain class is calculated using the labels. Essentially, we attempt to figure out which words predict which class. The code itself is very straightforward: the only difference being that we use the labels to train our machine as well. This is what the code snippet would look like, but you might want to refer to the notebook once again in case you stumble upon any errors. Do not forget to transform your data before training the model, and to run X = X.toarray() if it is a sparse array:

```
from sklearn.naive_bayes import GaussianNB
gnb = GaussianNB()
gnb.fit(X, labels)

from sklearn.svm import SVC
svm = SVC()
svm.fit(X, labels)
```

And there we have it!

The models `gnb` and `svm` can use their `predict()` method to classify unknown documents into the classes.

For example, with Naive Bayes:

```
gnb.predict(X_test)
```

Would give us an array with all the predicted classes. There are four classes in our dataset, and this is the result we see:

```
array([0, 3, 3, ..., 3, 3, 3])
```

Similarly with SVM, we run:

```
svm.predict(X_test)
```

And our result is:

```
array([0, 3, 3, ..., 3, 3, 3])
```

While clustering tends to also be a more explanatory process, during classification, we tend to want to increase our accuracy or our success rate of predicting the right class. The `GridSearchCV` [21] is a scikit-learn function that lets us choose optimal parameters for a classifier object, and we can check our performance of the classifier with the `classificaiton_report` object.

For an idea of how to do this, the scikit-learn documentation page (http://scikit-learn. org/stable/modules/generated/sklearn.metrics.classification_report.html) linked to gives us a brief example:

```
from sklearn import svm, datasets
from sklearn.model_selection import GridSearchCV
iris = datasets.load_iris()
parameters = {'kernel':('linear', 'rbf'), 'C':[1, 10]}
svc = svm.SVC()
clf = GridSearchCV(svc, parameters)
clf.fit(iris.data, iris.target)
```

In the preceding example, we are doing the grid search for SVM and choose between `linear` and `rbf` kernels, and two different values of C.

The code at `http://scikit-learn.org/stable/auto_examples/text/document_classification_20newsgroups.html` [20] runs us through the process of choosing multiple classifiers of scikit-learn, and you will notice the approach is quite similar to the code you have seen so far. The link is worth visiting to see what other classifiers scikit-learn has to offer, and on how to compare the results of these classifiers. You can see the following image which illustrates this, where the classifiers are compared against each other in terms of relative performance and time.

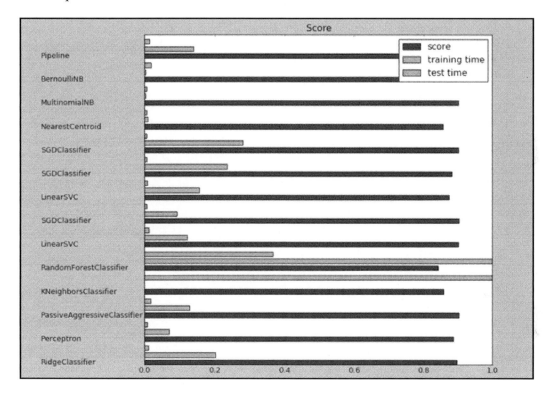

Fig 10.4 Performance of different classifiers on the 20NG dataset. Note that these are for classifiers we have not explored ourselves; link 21 describes the code and the classifiers to generate this image.

For those curious to use even more powerful machine learning tools, the `blog post` at `http://nadbordrozd.github.io/blog/2016/05/20/text-classification-with-word2vec/` [22] tells us how to classify documents using Word2Vec. We will be going over this process in detail ourselves on the chapter on Word2Vec and Doc2Vec.

Summary

And that sums it up! You can now build basic classifiers yourself - the classic problem of classifying emails as spam and not-spam is now something you can replicate yourself. We have seen various clustering algorithms such as k-means, and hierarchal clustering algorithms. We discussed what supervised and unsupervised learning algorithms are, and saw examples of how to run both using scikit-learn.

You can also explore your text data in all sorts of ways with the clustering and topic modeling tools we have. Let's attempt to go one step further in the next chapter - and build a basic information retrieval machine which can search for similar documents.

References

[1] Iris Flower Dataset:
https://en.wikipedia.org/wiki/Iris_flower_data_set

[2] MNIST Digit Data Set:
http://yann.lecun.com/exdb/mnist/

[3] 20 NG Dataset:
http://qwone.com/~jason/20Newsgroups/

[4] Clustering and Classification Notebook:
https://github.com/bhargavvader/personal/blob/master/notebooks/clustering_class
ing.ipynb

[5] Principal Component Analysis:
https://en.wikipedia.org/wiki/Principal_component_analysis

[6] K-Means Clustering:
https://en.wikipedia.org/wiki/K-means_clustering

[7] scikit-learn k-means:
http://scikit-learn.org/stable/modules/clustering.html#k-means

[8] scikit-learn clustering:
http://scikit-learn.org/stable/modules/clustering.html

[9] Ward's Method:
https://en.wikipedia.org/wiki/Ward's_method

[10] Dendrogram:
https://en.wikipedia.org/wiki/Dendrogram#Clustering_example

[11] Document Clustering:
http://brandonrose.org/clustering

[12] Working with Text:
https://de.dariah.eu/tatom/working_with_text.html

[13] Automatic Topic Clustering using Doc2Vec:
https://towardsdatascience.com/automatic-topic-clustering-using-doc2vec-e1cea88
449c

[14] Naive Bayes:
https://en.wikipedia.org/wiki/Naive_Bayes_classifier

[15] Support Vector Machines:
https://en.wikipedia.org/wiki/Support_vector_machine

[16] Naive Bayes Scikit-Learn:
http://scikit-learn.org/stable/modules/naive_bayes.html

[17] Support Vector Machine Scikit-Learn:
http://scikit-learn.org/dev/modules/svm.html

[18] Kernel Method:
https://en.wikipedia.org/wiki/Kernel_method

[19] What does SVM mean in Layman's terms?:
https://www.quora.com/What-does-support-vector-machine-SVM-mean-in-laymans-term
s

[20] Classification of text documents scikit-learn:
http://scikit-learn.org/stable/auto_examples/text/document_classification_20new
sgroups.html

[21] GridSearchCV:
http://scikit-learn.org/stable/modules/generated/sklearn.model_selection.GridSe
archCV.html

[22] Text Classification with Word2Vec:
http://nadbordrozd.github.io/blog/2016/05/20/text-classification-with-word2vec/

11
Similarity Queries and Summarization

Once we have begun to represent text documents in the form of vector representations, it is possible to start finding the similarity or distance between documents, and that is exactly what we will learn about in this chapter. We are now aware of a variety of different vector representations, from standard bag-of-words or TF-IDF to topic model representations of text documents. We will also learn about a very useful feature implemented in Gensim and how to use it—summarization and keyword extraction. Here's a summary of what we'll learn from this chapter:

- Similarity metrics
- Similarity queries
- Text summarization

Similarity metrics

Similarity metrics [1] are a mathematical construct which is particularly useful in natural language processing—especially in information retrieval. Let's first try to understand what a metric is. We can understand a metric as a function that defines a distance between each pair of elements of a set, or vector. It's clear how this would be useful to us - we can compare between how similar two documents would be based on the distance. A low value returned by the distance function would mean that the two documents are similar, and a high value would mean they are quite different.

While we mention documents in the example, we can technically compare any two elements in a set – this also means we can compare between two sets of topics created by a topic model, for example. We can check between the TF-IDF representations of documents and between LSI or LDA representations of documents.

Most of us would be aware of one distance or similarity metric already – the **Euclidean metric**. It is one of the first distance metrics we come across in high school mathematics, and we would have likely seen it being used to calculate the distance between two points in a 2-dimensional space (XY). While we won't get into the mathematical details of metrics, it is worthwhile knowing the four characteristics of a distance metric.

d(x,y) >= 0
This must be non-negative.

d(x,y) = 0 <=> x = y
Here, if x and y are the same, the distance must be zero.

d(x,y) = d(y,x)
This must be symmetric.

d(x,z) <= d(x,y) + d(y,z)
This must obey the triangle inequality law.

A **metric** on a set X is a function (called the *distance function* or simply **distance**)

$$d : X \times X \to [0, \infty),$$

where $[0, \infty)$ is the set of non-negative real numbers and for all $x, y, z \in X$, the following conditions are satisfied:

1. $d(x, y) \geq 0$ non-negativity or separation axiom
2. $d(x, y) = 0 \Leftrightarrow x = y$ identity of indiscernibles
3. $d(x, y) = d(y, x)$ symmetry
4. $d(x, z) \leq d(x, y) + d(y, z)$ subadditivity or triangle inequality

Fig 11.1 The four mathematical prerequisites for a function to be a metric

Gensim (and scikit-learn, and most other machine learning or scientific computing packages) recognize the importance of distance metrics and have them implemented as part of the package, which means it's easy to use them in the context of documents or topics.

Let's now discuss how we can actually use these – we will be following this tutorial I wrote for Gensim, which you can find over `here` in the link [2]. Note that the Gensim notebook does not have TfIdf models, those were added in this chapter to further help illustrate distances.

Let's first remind ourselves of exactly what distances we will be calculating – two vector representations of documents. Let's set up our corpus and the documents we will be comparing. We've used this version of the corpus before in the Chapter 9, *Advanced Topic Modeling* to illustrate the examples on document-word topics.

```
texts = [['bank','river','shore','water'],
        ['river','water','flow','fast','tree'],
        ['bank','water','fall','flow'],
        ['bank','bank','water','rain','river'],
        ['river','water','mud','tree'],
        ['money','transaction','bank','finance'],
        ['bank','borrow','money'],
        ['bank','finance'],
        ['finance','money','sell','bank'],
        ['borrow','sell'],
        ['bank','loan','sell']]

dictionary = Dictionary(texts)
corpus = [dictionary.doc2bow(text) for text in texts]
```

Creating TF-IDF and LDA models for the following corpus will help us illustrate our distance metrics.

```
from gensim.models import ldamodel
from gensim.models import TfidfModel

tfidf = TfidfModel(corpus)
model = ldamodel.LdaModel(corpus, id2word=dictionary, num_topics=2)
```

Note that now that a representation of TF-IDF would have as many features as the size of the vocabulary, and an LDA model representation would have as many features as the number of topics. We will be using both these models later to compare distances.

Now, what do our topics look like?

```
model.show_topics()

[(0, u'0.164*"bank" + 0.142*"water" + 0.108*"river" + 0.076*"flow" +
0.067*"borrow" + 0.063*"sell" + 0.060*"tree" + 0.048*"money" + 0.046*"fast"
+ 0.044*"rain"'),
(1, u'0.196*"bank" + 0.120*"finance" + 0.100*"money" + 0.082*"sell" +
0.067*"river" + 0.065*"water" + 0.056*"transaction" + 0.049*"loan" +
0.046*"tree" + 0.040*"mud"')]
```

Let's use three documents to compare – a document to do with river banks, one to do with financial banks, and one that has the context of both (maybe a financial bank on the bank of a river?).

```
doc_water = ['river', 'water', 'shore']
doc_finance = ['finance', 'money', 'sell']
doc_bank = ['finance', 'bank', 'tree', 'water']
```

Once we have our documents, we quickly convert these into a bag of words, TF-IDF, and LdaModel representations.

```
bow_water = model.id2word.doc2bow(doc_water)
bow_finance = model.id2word.doc2bow(doc_finance)
bow_bank = model.id2word.doc2bow(doc_bank)

lda_bow_water = model[bow_water]
lda_bow_finance = model[bow_finance]
lda_bow_bank = model[bow_bank]

tfidf_bow_water = tfidf[bow_water]
tfidf_bow_finance = tfidf[bow_finance]
tfidf_bow_bank = tfidf[bow_bank]
```

Let's have a look at `lda_bow_water` and see what it looks like:

```
[(0, 0.8225102558524345), (1, 0.17748974414756546)]
```

This makes sense – the document contained words to do with river banks, and its proportion of topic_0 is 82%. The `lda_bow_finance` variable should be roughly the opposite – let's test this:

```
[(0, 0.14753674420005805), (1, 0.852463255799942)]
```

And voila, as we expected – the LDA representations of the two documents are quite different, which we could see even when we constructed the documents. This means that their distance would also be quite high, as they are not similar documents.

Let's have a quick peek at `lda_bow_bank` as well:

```
[(0, 0.4415339545450870797), (1, 0.558466045491292)]
```

This is a well-balanced document with respect to the topics (as expected).

Let's import our distance functions which we will be using – the **Hellinger metric** [3], the **Kullback-Leibler divergence** function [4], and the **Jaccard index** [5]. The Hellinger and KL-Divergence are two distance metrics that help us identify how similar or different two probability distributions are. Links 3, 4, and 5 explain the mathematical basis behind these metrics; what we should keep in mind is that there is no one perfect metric to choose when deciding to compare two documents, and to give both methods a shot, which is why we include examples of both. The Jaccard index is a more traditional metric primarily used to compare between two sets.

```
from gensim.matutils import kullback_leibler, jaccard, hellinger
```

Let's find the distances between our documents:

```
hellinger(lda_bow_water, lda_bow_finance)
0.5125119977875359

hellinger(lda_bow_finance, lda_bow_bank)
0.2340730527221049

hellinger(lda_bow_bank, lda_bow_water)
0.28728176544255285
```

Interpreting these results are very straightforward – we find the largest Hellinger distance returned for the documents to do with finance and water – they don't have much in common, so this is a good result. The bank document, which contains both the finance and water contexts, is equally distant from both the water and the finance documents – but seems to be further from the water document (0.287 opposed to 0.234). These are relative values that range from 0 to 1, where 0 means no distance, 0.5 could be intuitively understood as being *in-between*, and 1 is when they are equal. This again makes sense – when we looked at `lda_bow_bank`, it leaned more towards finance than water.

 Try this: A small exercise for the reader would be to identify why the bank document tend toward the finance topic – is the word bank in the document associated with finance or water? Doing a document word coloring would be a way to identify this!

So as we can see, using these distance metrics we can identify how far or close certain documents are. Its usefulness might not be as apparent in a small corpus and small documents, but this becomes invaluable as we continue. We can similarly do the same experiments with the KL function and Jaccard function. A subtle point to remember; in the strictest sense, the Kullback-Leibler function is not a metric. This is because it isn't symmetric. This means that `kullback_leibler(lda_bow_finance, lda_bow_bank)` is not equal to `kullback_leibler(lda_bow_bank, lda_bow_finance)`, for example.

Let's illustrate this; we already calculated the Hellinger distance between the water and finance documents. Calculating the distance by swapping the finance and water documents should return the same value got before because the Hellinger metric is a mathematical distance metric.

```
hellinger(lda_bow_finance, lda_bow_water)
0.5125119977875359
```

As we expected, we got the same value as before, and this confirms what we already know about Hellinger – it is a symmetrical distance function. Let's try the same exercise with the KL function.

```
kullback_leibler(lda_bow_water, lda_bow_bank)
0.30823547

kullback_leibler(lda_bow_bank, lda_bow_water)
0.36547804
```

The values aren't terribly far apart, but they aren't the same; this means that while the KL function can give us an intuition of how far or close two probability distributions are, it isn't a strict mathematical distance metric. This doesn't discount its usefulness, however – values closer to 0 are still considered similar and values that are close to 1 are not similar.

Our last distance function is the popular Jaccard metric. Unlike the other distance functions, the Jaccard method also works on a bag of words.

```
jaccard(bow_water, bow_bank)
0.8571428571428572

jaccard(doc_water, doc_bank)
0.8333333333333334

jaccard(['word'], ['word'])
0.0
```

The preceding three examples feature two different input methods.

In the first case, we present to `jaccard` document vectors already in the bag of words format. The distance can be defined as 1 minus the size of the intersection upon the size of the union of the vectors. We can see (on manual inspection as well), that the distance is likely to be high – and it is. The last two examples illustrate the ability for `jaccard` to accept even lists (that is, documents) as inputs. In the last case, because they are the same vectors, the value returned is 0 – this means the distance is 0 and they are very similar.

We can also use these distance functions to find how close or far apart topics themselves are. While it is more useful to attempt doing this with larger corpuses and larger vocabularies, we will still give this a shot. First, we must make appropriate changes to the way we display topics so that we can pass it into our distance functions.

```
def make_topics_bow(topic):
    # takes the string returned by model.show_topics()
    # split on strings to get topics and the probabilities
    topic = topic.split('+')
    # list to store topic bows
    topic_bow = []
    for word in topic:
        # split probability and word
        prob, word = word.split('*')
        # get rid of spaces
        word = word.replace(" ","")
        # convert to word_type
        word = model.id2word.doc2bow([word])[0][0]
        topic_bow.append((word, float(prob)))
    return topic_bow
```

On passing the results of model.show_topics() to these, we can create appropriate representations.

```
topic_water, topic_finance = model.show_topics()
finance_distribution = make_topics_bow(topic_finance[1])
water_distribution = make_topics_bow(topic_water[1])
```

Let's look at what finance_distribution would look like, for example.

```
[(3, 0.196),
 (12, 0.12),
 (10, 0.1),
 (14, 0.082),
 (2, 0.067),
 (0, 0.065),
 (11, 0.056),
 (15, 0.049),
 (5, 0.046),
 (9, 0.04)]
```

This basically maps the ID of the word and its proportion in the topic.

Let's now run the following:

```
hellinger(water_distribution, finance_distribution)
0.36453028040240248
```

A small corpus and overlap of the word bank in the topics mean that the distance doesn't seem as large as we expect – an interesting experiment is to generate more topics with a larger corpus and rank topic pairs on how similar they are – this would better illustrate the distance metrics we have been working with.

That pretty much sums up using distance functions in the context of documents and topics – but we should remember that we can compare between any two vector representations of topic distributions, so this is a useful function to have in our arsenal.

For a few more details on using the distance metrics, it is recommended that you run the Jupyter notebook [2] which illustrates these examples.

We can now move on to making queries and using these distance metrics for more sophisticated purposes!

Similarity queries

Now that we have the capability to compare between two documents, it is possible for us to set up our algorithms to extract out the most similar documents for an input query – simply index each of the documents, then search for the lowest distance value returned between the corpus and the query, and return the documents with the lowest distance values – these would be most similar. Luckily for us, however, Gensim has in-built structures to do this document similarity task!

We will be using the similarities module to construct this structure.

```
from gensim import similarities
```

We previously mentioned creating an index – we can do this far faster with the similarities module. As mentioned in the Gensim documentation for the `Similarity` class – the `Similarity` class splits the index into several smaller sub-indexes (**shards**), which are disk-based. If your entire index fits in memory (hundreds of thousands of documents for 1 GB of RAM), you can also use the `MatrixSimilarity` or `SparseMatrixSimilarity` classes directly. These are more simple but do not scale as well (they keep the entire index in RAM, no sharding).

Since we have a small corpus, we can use the `MatrixSimilarity` class to create our indexing.

```
index = similarities.MatrixSimilarity(model[corpus])
```

We created our index based on the similarities created by the LDA transformation of our corpus. We can create the same index using TF-IDF, or even bag of words, but we can expect better performance when using topics. We should also keep in mind that our queries should be in the same input space as the representation in which we created our index.

Now that we've created our index, we can query to find the most similar documents in the corpus. Let's use the same `lda_bow_finance` document and find which articles are most similar.

```
sims = index[lda_bow_finance]
```

Sims now contains the similar documents; let's have a better look at what's inside.

```
print(list(enumerate(sims)))

[(0, 0.36124918),
 (1, 0.27387184),
 (2, 0.30807066),
 (3, 0.30388257),
 (4, 0.33108047),
 (5, 0.99913883),
 (6, 0.8764254),
 (7, 0.9970802),
 (8, 0.99956596),
 (9, 0.5114244),
 (10, 0.9995375)]
```

And there we go! We now have a list with each document and the corresponding similarity values. Keep in mind that these values were generated using cosine similarities – Gensim doesn't have the functionality to plug in our own similarity metrics, so until then we must stick to using the cosine similarity – or create our own indexing method.

Let's look at which documents were actually picked up, and sort them according to how similar they are.

```
sims = sorted(enumerate(sims), key=lambda item: -item[1])

for doc_id, similarity in sims:
    print(texts[doc_id], similarity)

['finance', 'money', 'sell', 'bank'] 0.99956596
['bank', 'loan', 'sell'] 0.9995375
['money', 'transaction', 'bank', 'finance'] 0.99913883
['bank', 'finance'] 0.9970802
['bank', 'borrow', 'money'] 0.8764254
['borrow', 'sell'] 0.5114244
```

```
['bank', 'river', 'shore', 'water'] 0.36124918
['river', 'water', 'mud', 'tree'] 0.33108047
['bank', 'water', 'fall', 'flow'] 0.30807066
['bank', 'bank', 'water', 'rain', 'river'] 0.30388257
['river', 'water', 'flow', 'fast', 'tree'] 0.27387184
```

Quite nifty, eh? By simply sorting `sims` we have an ordered list of each document similarity – we then print the original documents. Our query was the LDA representation of a finance-related document, and the similarity query returned all finance-related documents as most similar while the documents to do with trees and rivers were least similar - just as we would expect.

The tutorial [6] on the Gensim website performs a similar experiment, but on the Wikipedia corpus – it is a useful demonstration on how to conduct similarity queries on much larger corpuses and is worth checking if you are dealing with a very large corpus.

A Gensim-related project, **simserver** [7] contains more dedicated similarity querying functionalities, but this project is no longer maintained as open source – with that being said, the tutorial [8] might still be relevant, and the GitHub source code [9] could inspire you in your similarity querying efforts.

What have we seen in the last two sections? We can now effectively compare between two probability distributions, which means we can compare both topics and documents. This means that we are one step closer to creating our own search engine – and with the similarities module, the heavy lifting is done for us, and we have a ready-made API to conduct basic queries!

In the examples, we used LDA models for both distance calculation and to generate the index for the similarities. We can, however, use any vector representation of documents to generate this – it's up to us to decide which one would be most effective for our use case.

Summarizing text

Often in text analysis, it is useful to summarize large bodies of text – either to have a brief overlook of the text before deeply analyzing it or identifying the keywords in a text. It is also often the end game – a text analysis task of its own. We will not be working on building our own text summarization pipeline, but rather focus on using the built-in summarization API which Gensim offers us.

It is important to remember that the algorithms included in Gensim do not create its own sentences, but rather extracts the key sentences from the text which we run the algorithm on. This summarizer is based on the **TextRank** algorithm, from an article by Mihalcea and others, called *TextRank* [10]. This algorithm was later improved upon by Barrios and others in another article, *Variations of the Similarity Function of TextRank for Automated Summarization* [11], by introducing a **BM25 ranking function** [12].

It must be noted that unlike all the other algorithms discussed so far, as of Gensim version 3.4.0 [13], the text summarization module in Gensim only works in English – it doesn't allow you to preprocess the text as well or add your own stop words.

To illustrate the summarization module, we will use a story from the *Harry Potter and the Philosopher's Stone* movie.

```
from gensim.summarization import summarize
```

We can now simply use the summarization module to create the summarized text.

```
print(summarize(text))
```

Remember to copy the text you wish to summarize and store it in the `text` variable. In our example, we will be using the following text.

Eleven-year-old Harry Potter has been living an ordinary life, constantly abused by his surly and cold uncle and aunt, Vernon and Petunia Dursley, and bullied by their spoiled son, Dudley.

Hagrid explains Harry's hidden past as the wizard son of James and Lily Potter, who are a wizard and witch, respectively, and how they were murdered by the most evil and powerful dark wizard in history, Lord Voldemort, which resulted in the one-year-old Harry being sent to live with his aunt and uncle.

There, Harry also makes an enemy of yet another first-year, Draco Malfoy, who prejudices against Hermione due to her being the daughter of Muggles, a term used by wizards and witches, which describes ordinary humans with no magical ability.

He winds up in Gryffindor instead with Ron and Hermione while Draco is sorted into Slytherin, like his whole family before him. As classes begin at Hogwarts, Harry discovers his innate talent for flying on broomsticks despite no prior experience and is recruited into his House's Quidditch (a competitive wizards' sport, played in the air) team as a Seeker, which is said to be the most difficult role.

When the school's headmaster Albus Dumbledore is lured from Hogwarts under false pretenses, Harry, Hermione, and Ron fear that the theft is imminent and descend through the trapdoor themselves.

The eventful school year ends at the final feast, during which Gryffindor wins the House Cup. Harry returns to Privet Drive for the summer, neglecting to tell them that the use of spells is forbidden by under-aged wizards and witches and thus anticipating some fun and peace over the holidays.

A quick glance tells us this pretty much covers the important parts of the book (further examination of the original Wikipedia text can help with this). Of course, it isn't a perfect summarization of the story – a little more fine-tuning is required.

If we would just like the top sentences picked up from the paragraph and returned as a list, we can use the `split` option, which returns a list of strings instead of a single string.

We can also adjust how much text the summarizer outputs via the `ratio` parameter or the `word_count` parameter. Using the `ratio` parameter, you specify what fraction of sentences in the original text should be returned as output. The default is 20%.

Now, let's run the following:

```
print (summarize(text, word_count=50))
```

We get this:

```
He winds up in Gryffindor instead with Ron and Hermione while Draco is
sorted into Slytherin, like his whole family before him. As classes begin
at Hogwarts, Harry discovers his innate talent for flying on broomsticks
despite no prior experience and is recruited into his House's Quidditch (a
competitive wizards' sport played in the air) team as a Seeker, which is
said to be the most difficult role.
```

What's been done here is what is considered the top-ranked sentence, which is chosen, as with a word limit of 50 only one sentence could make the cut – we see here that it is not always the best algorithm for very short summaries if the sentences are long.

 An interesting experiment for the reader – try using the same summarization technique on the IMDB synopsis of the plot of the *Harry Potter and the Philosopher's Stone* movie and compare the results!

As mentioned earlier, this module also supports keyword extraction. Keyword extraction works in the same way as a summary generation (that is, sentence extraction), in that the algorithm tries to find words that are important or seem representative of the entire text. The keywords are not always single words; in the case of multi-word keywords, they are typically all nouns.

```
from gensim.summarization import keywords
print(keywords(text))
```

```
harry
wizard
wizarding
wizards
school
hagridhermione
year
named
powerful dark
slytherin
burns
burning
life constantly
hogwarts
magical
final
son
quirrell
magic like
corridor
cloak
grubby
report
owl
earlier
railway
voldemort
powers
power
london
```

```
desires come
comes
hidden
dog standing
stand
protect
protective
events
eventful
despite
explains
houses
house
ron
gryffindor
instead
game
source
requires unique skills possessed
ordinary
master
```

A quick run-through of the words tells us that they are indeed the keywords from the synopsis.

For your information, the other parameters involved in the keywords module are as follows:

- `text (str)`: Input text
- `ratio (float, optional)`: If no `words` option is selected, the number of sentences is reduced by the provided ratio, else, the ratio is ignored
- `words (int, optional)`: Number of returned words
- `split (bool, optional)`: Whether split keywords if True
- `scores (bool, optional)`: Whether score of the keyword
- `pos_filter (tuple, optional)`: Part of speech filters
- `lemmatize (bool, optional)`: If True – lemmatize words
- `deacc (bool, optional)`: If True – remove accentuation

An excerpt from the Gensim tutorial tells us a little bit about the complexity and time taken for the algorithm:

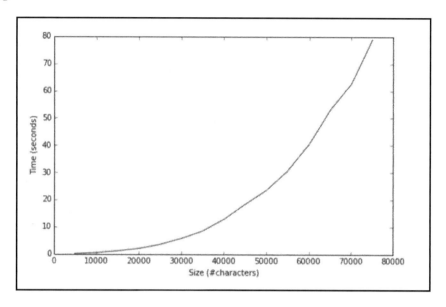

Fig 11.2 A figure describing the running time versus size of the corpus

In the preceding plot, we see the running times together with the sizes of the datasets. To create datasets of different sizes, we have simply taken prefixes of text; in other words, we take the first n characters of the book. The algorithm seems to be quadratic in time, so one needs to be careful before plugging a large dataset into the summarizer. One reason for this difference in running times is the data structure that is used. The algorithm represents the data using a graph, where vertices (nodes) are sentences and then constructs weighted edges between the vertices that represent how the sentences relate to each other. This means that every piece of text will have a different graph, thus making the running times different. The size of this data structure is quadratic in the worst case (the worst case is when each vertex has an edge to every other vertex).

Gensim has another way to extract keywords: the Montemurro and Zanette's entropy-based keyword extraction algorithm. The paper – *Towards the quantification of the semantic information encoded in written language* [14] describes the algorithm, which uses the entropy of each word's distribution among the blocks to pick keywords.

```
from gensim.summarization import mz_keywords

mz_keywords(text, scores=True, weighted=False, threshold=1.0)

[(u'had', 0.002358350743193241),
 (u'from', 0.002039753203785301),
 (u'hagrid', 0.002039753203785301),
 (u'hermione', 0.002039753203785301),
 (u'into', 0.002039753203785301),
 (u'hogwarts', 0.0017206396372542237),
 (u'an', 0.001400618744466898),
 (u'first', 0.001400618744466898),
 (u'ron', 0.001400618744466898),
 (u'slytherin', 0.001400618744466898),
 (u'trapdoor', 0.001400618744466898),
 (u'is', 0.00111564319627375),
 (u'dark', 0.0010787207994767374),
 (u'instead', 0.0010787207994767374),
 (u'snape', 0.0010787207994767374),
 (u'wizard', 0.0010787207994767374)]
```

The **MZ keyword** extraction algorithm tends to perform better for larger corpuses. The complexity of the algorithm is $O(Nw)$, where N is the number of words in the document and w is the number of unique words. The parameters for this algorithm are as follows:

- `text (str)`: Document for summarization.
- `blocksize (int, optional)`: Size of blocks to use in analysis.
- `scores (bool, optional)`: Whether to return score with keywords.
- `split (bool, optional)`: Whether to return results as list.
- `weighted (bool, optional)`: Whether to weight scores by word frequency. False can useful for shorter texts and allows automatic thresholding.
- `threshold (float or 'auto', optional)`: Minimum score for returned keywords, `auto` calculates the threshold as *n_blocks / (n_blocks + 1.0) + 1e-8*, use `auto` with `weighted=False`.

With text similarity and text summarization, we can now build more sophisticated text analysis pipelines. In the next few chapters, we will be working on more advanced machine learning techniques for text, such as deep learning.

Summary

Throughout this chapter, we saw how basic mathematical and information retrieval methods can be used to help identify how similar or dissimilar two text documents are. We also saw how we can extend these methods to any probabilistic distribution as well, such as topic models themselves – this can be particularly handy especially when we are working with more topics than we can analyze with the human eye. Summarization is also another useful tool we are now exposed to – since it works on the principle of which keywords provide the most information in a passage, we can use this knowledge of keywords to further aid us in building natural language processing pipelines.

We will now move on to more advanced topics involving neural networks and deep learning for textual data. These include methods such as Word2Vec and Doc2Vec, as well as shallow and deep neural networks. We will explore the Python packages, the theory, and the application of these deep learning methods in the text.

References

[1] Similarity Metrics:
https://en.wikipedia.org/wiki/Metric_(mathematics)

[2] Distance Metrics ipynb:
https://github.com/RaRe-Technologies/gensim/blob/develop/docs/notebooks/distance_metrics.ipynb

[3] Hellinger Distance:
https://en.wikipedia.org/wiki/Hellinger_distance

[4] KL- divergence:
https://en.wikipedia.org/wiki/Kullback%E2%80%93Leibler_divergence

[5] Jaccard:
https://en.wikipedia.org/wiki/Jaccard_index

[6] Gensim wikipedia example:
https://radimrehurek.com/topic_modeling_tutorial/3%20-%20Indexing%20and%20Retrieval.html

[7] Simserver:
https://pypi.org/project/simserver/#description

[8] Doc Similarity Server:
https://radimrehurek.com/gensim/simserver.html

[9] Gensim SimServer GitHub:
https://github.com/RaRe-Technologies/gensim-simserver

[10] textRank:
http://web.eecs.umich.edu/~mihalcea/papers/mihalcea.emnlp04.pdf

[11] Variations of the Similarity Function of TextRank for Automated Summarization:
https://arxiv.org/pdf/1602.03606.pdf

[12] BM25:
https://en.wikipedia.org/wiki/Okapi_BM25

[13] Gensim:
https://pypi.org/project/gensim/#description

[14] Towards the quantification of the semantic information encoded in written language:
https://arxiv.org/abs/0907.1558

12

Word2Vec, Doc2Vec, and Gensim

We have previously talked about vectors a lot throughout the book – they are used to understand and represent our textual data in a mathematical form, and the basis of all the machine learning methods we use rely on these representations. We will be taking this one step further, and *use* machine learning techniques to generate vector representations of words that better encapsulate the meaning of a word. This technique is generally referred to as **word embeddings**, and Word2Vec and Doc2Vec are two popular variations of these.

- Word2Vec
- Doc2Vec
- Other word embeddings

Word2Vec

Arguably the most important application of machine learning in text analysis, the Word2Vec algorithm is both a fascinating and very useful tool. As the name suggests, it creates a vector representation of words based on the corpus we are using. But the magic of Word2Vec is in how it manages to capture the semantic representation of words in a vector. The papers, *Efficient Estimation of Word Representations in Vector Space* [1] [Mikolov and others, 2013], *Distributed Representations of Words and Phrases and their Compositionality* [2] [Mikolov and others, 2013], and *Linguistic Regularities in Continuous Space Word Representations* [3] [Mikolov and others, 2013] lay the foundations for Word2Vec and describe their uses.

We've mentioned that these word vectors help represent the semantics of words – what exactly does this mean? Well for starters, it means we could use vector reasoning for these words – one of the most famous examples is from Mikolov's paper, where we see that if we use the word vectors and perform (here, we use V(word) to represent the vector representation of the word) **V(King)** - **V(Man)** + **V(Woman)**, and the resulting vector is closest to **V(Queen)**. It is easy to see why this is remarkable – our intuitive understanding of these words is reflected in the learned vector representations of the words!

This gives us the ability to add more of a punch in our text analysis pipelines – having an intuitive semantic representation of vectors (and by extension, documents – but we'll get to that later) will come in handy more than once.

Finding word-pair relationships is one such interesting use – if we define a relationship between two words such as France : Paris, using the appropriate vector difference we can identify other similar relationships – Italy : Rome, Japan : Tokyo are two such examples which are found using Word2Vec. We can continue to play with these vectors like any other vectors – by adding two vectors, we can attempt to get what we would consider the *addition* of two words. For example, **V(Vietnam) + V(Capital)** is closest to the vector representation of **V(Hanoi)**.

How exactly does this technique result in such an understanding of words? Word2Vec works by understanding context – in particular, what of words tend to appear in certain words? We choose a sliding window size, and based on this window size, attempt to identify the conditional probability of observing the output word based on the surrounding words. For example, if the sentence is *The personal nature of text data always adds an extra bit of* ***motivation****, and it also likely means we are aware of the nature of the data, and what kind of results to expect.*, and our target word is the word in bold, motivation, we try and figure out what are the odds of finding the word *motivation* if the context is *always adds an extra bit of* on the left-hand side of the window and *and it also likely means* on the right. Of course, this is just an illustrative example – the exact training procedure requires us to choose a window size and the number of dimensions among other details.

There are two main methods to perform Word2Vec training, which are the **Continuous Bag of Words** model (**CBOW**) and the **Skip Gram** model. The underlying architecture of these models is described in the original research paper, but both of these methods involve in understanding the context which we talked about before. The papers written by Mikolov and others provide further details of the training process, and since the code is public, it means we actually know what's going on under the hood!

The blog post [4], *Word2Vec Tutorial - The Skip-Gram Model*, by Chris McCormick explains some of the mathematical intuition behind the skip-gram word2vec model, and the post [5], *The amazing power of word vectors*, by Adrian Colyer talks about the some of the things we can do with word2vec. The links are useful if you wish to dig a little deeper into the mathematical details of Word2Vec, a topic we will *not* be covering in this chapter. The resources page [6] contains theory and code resources for Word2Vec and is also useful in case you wish to look up the original material or other implementation details.

While Word2Vec remains the most popular word vector implementation, this is not the first time it has been attempted, and certainly not the last either – we will discuss some of the other word embeddings techniques in the last section of this chapter. Right now, let's jump into using these word vectors ourselves.

Gensim comes to our assistance again and is arguably the most reliable open source implementation of the algorithm, and we will explore how to use it.

Using Word2Vec with Gensim

While the original C code [7] released by Google does an impressive job, Gensims' implementation is a case where an open source implementation is *more* efficient than the original.

The Gensim implementation was coded up back in 2013 around the time the original algorithm was released – the blog post by Radim Řehůřek [8] chronicles some of the thoughts and problems encountered in implementing the same for Gensim, and is worth reading if you would like to know the process of coding word2vec in Python. The interactive web tutorial [9] involving Word2Vec is quite fun and illustrates some of the examples of Word2Vec we previously talked about. It is worth looking at if you're interested in running Gensim Word2Vec code online, and can also serve as a quick tutorial of using Word2Vec in Gensim.

We will now get into actually training our own Word2Vec model. The first step, like all the other Gensim models we used, involved importing the appropriate model.

```
from gensim.models import word2vec
```

At this point, it is important to go through the documentation for the `word2vec` class, as well as the `KeyedVector` class, which we will both use a lot. From the documentation page, we list the parameters for the `word2vec.Word2Vec` class.

1. `sg`: This defines the training algorithm. By default (sg=0), CBOW is used. Otherwise (sg=1), skip-gram is employed.

2. `size`: This is the dimensionality of the feature vectors.

3. `window`: This is the maximum distance between the current and predicted word within a sentence.

4. `alpha`: This is the initial learning rate (will linearly drop to `min_alpha` as training progresses).

5. `seed`: This is used for the random number generator. Initial vectors for each word are seeded with a hash of the concatenation of word + `str(seed)`. Note that for a fully deterministically reproducible run, you must also limit the model to a single worker thread, to eliminate ordering jitter from OS thread scheduling. (In Python 3, reproducibility between interpreter launches also requires the use of the PYTHONHASHSEED environment variable to control hash randomization.)

6. `min_count`: Ignore all words with a total frequency lower than this.

7. `max_vocab_size`: Limit RAM during vocabulary building; if there are more unique words than this, then prune the infrequent ones. Every 10 million word types need about 1 GB of RAM. Set to `None` for no limit (default).

8. `sample`: This is the threshold for configuring which higher-frequency words are randomly downsampled; default is 1e-3, the useful range is (0, 1e-5).

9. `workers`: Use this many worker threads to train the model (faster training with multicore machines).

10. `hs`: If 1, hierarchical softmax will be used for model training. If set to 0 (default), and negative is non-zero, negative sampling will be used.

11. `negative`: If > 0, negative sampling will be used, the int for negative specifies how many *noise words* should be drawn (usually between 5-20). The default is 5. If set to 0, no negative sampling is used.

12. `cbow_mean`: If 0, use the sum of the context word vectors. If 1 (default), use the mean. Only applies when CBOW is used.

13. `hashfxn`: This is the hash function to use to randomly initialize weights, for increased training reproducibility. The default is Python's rudimentary built-in hash function.

14. `iter`: This is the number of iterations (epochs) over the corpus. The default is 5.

15. `trim_rule`: The vocabulary trimming rule specifies whether certain words should remain in the vocabulary, be trimmed away, or handled using the default (discard if word count < `min_count`). This can be None (`min_count` will be used), or a callable that accepts parameters (`word`, `count`, and `min_count`) and returns either `utils.RULE_DISCARD`, `utils.RULE_KEEP`, or `utils.RULE_DEFAULT`. Note that the rule, if given, is only used to prune vocabulary during `build_vocab()` and is not stored as part of the model.

16. `sorted_vocab`: If 1 (default), sort the vocabulary by descending frequency before assigning word indexes.

17. `batch_words`: This is the target size (in words) for batches of examples passed to worker threads (and thus cython routines). The default is 10000. (Larger batches will be passed if individual texts are longer than 10000 words, but the standard cython code truncates to that maximum).

We won't be using or exploring all of these parameters in our examples, but they're still important to have an idea of - fine-tuning your model would heavily rely on this. When training our model, we can use our own corpus or more generic ones – since we wish to not train on a particular topic or domain, we will use the Text8 corpus [10] which contains textual data extracted from Wikipedia. Be sure to download the data first - we do this by finding the link `text8.zip` under the *Experimental Procedure* section.

We will be more or less following the Jupyter notebook attached at the end of this chapter, which can also be found here [13].

```
sentences = word2vec.Text8Corpus('text8')
model = word2vec.Word2Vec(sentences, size=200, hs=1)
```

Our model will use hierarchical **softmax** for training and will have 200 features. This means that it has a hierarchical output and uses the softmax function in its final layers. The softmax function is a generalization of the logistic function that *squashes* a K-dimensional vector z of arbitrary real values to a K-dimensional vector of real values, where each entry is in the range (0, 1), and all the entries add up to 1. We don't need to understand the mathematical foundation at this point, but if interested, links [1] to [3] go into more details about this.

Printing our model tells us this:

```
print(model)
```

Word2Vec(vocab=71290, size=200, alpha=0.025)

Now that we have our trained model, let's give the famous *King - Man + Woman* example a try:

```
model.wv.most_similar(positive=['woman', 'king'], negative=['man'],
topn=1)[0]
```

Here, we are adding `king` and `woman` (they are positive parameters), and subtracting `man` (it is a negative parameter), and choosing only the first value in the tuple.

(u'queen')

And voila! As we expected, `queen` is the closest word vector when we search for the word most similar to `woman` and `king`, but far away from man. Note that since this is a probabilistic training process, there is a slight chance you might get a different word - but still relevant to the context of the words. For example, words like throne or empire might come up.

We can also use the `most_similar_cosmul` method – the Gensim documentation [11] describes this as being slightly different to the traditional similarity function by instead using an implementation described by Omer Levy and Yoav Goldberg in their paper [12] *Linguistic Regularities in Sparse and Explicit Word Representations*. Positive words still contribute positively toward the similarity, negative words negatively, but with less susceptibility to one large distance dominating the calculation. Consider this example:

```
model.wv.most_similar_cosmul(positive=['woman', 'king'], negative=['man'])
```

```
[(u'queen', 0.8473771810531616),
 (u'matilda', 0.8126628994941711),
 (u'throne', 0.8048466444015503),
 (u'prince', 0.8044915795326233),
 (u'empress', 0.803791880607605),
 (u'consort', 0.8026778697967529),
 (u'dowager', 0.7984940409660339),
 (u'princess', 0.7976254224777222),
 (u'heir', 0.7949869632720947),
 (u'monarch', 0.7940317392349243)]
```

If we wish to look up the vector representation of a word, all we need to do is this:

```
model.wv['computer']
model.save("text8_model")
```

We won't display the output here, but we can expect to see a 200-dimension array, which is what we specified as our size.

If we wish to save our model to disk and reuse it again, we can do this using the save and load functionalities. This is particularly useful – we can save and retrain models, or further train on models adapted to a certain domain.

```
model.save("text8_model")
model = word2vec.Word2Vec.load("text8_model")
```

The magic of Gensim remains in the fact that it doesn't just give us the ability to train a model – like we have been seeing so far, it's API, which means we don't have to worry much about the mathematical workings, but can focus on using the full potential of these word vectors. Let's check out some other nifty functionalities the Word2Vec model offers:

Using word vectors we can identify which word in a list is the farthest away from the other words. Gensim implements this functionality with the doesnt_match method, which we illustrate here:

```
model.wv.doesnt_match("breakfast cereal dinner lunch".split())
```

'cereal'

As expected, the one word which didn't match the others on the list is picked out – here, it is cereal. We can also use the model to understand how similar or different words are in a corpus:

```
model.wv.similarity('woman', 'man')
```

0.6416034158543054

```
model.wv.similarity('woman', 'cereal')
```

0.04408454181286298

```
model.wv.distance('man', 'woman')
```

0.35839658414569464

The results are quite self-explanatory in this case, and as expected, the words woman and cereal are not similar. Here, distance is merely 1 - similarity.

We can continue training our Word2Vec model using the train method – just remember to explicitly pass an epochs argument, as this is a suggested way to avoid common mistakes around the model's ability to do multiple training passes itself. The Gensim notebook tutorial [14] walks one through how to perform online training with Word2Vec. Briefly, it requires performing the following tasks - building a new vocabulary and then running the train function again.

Once we're done training our model, it is recommended that you start only using the model's keyed vectors. You might have noticed so far that we've been using the keyed vectors (which is simply a `Gensim` class to store vectors) to perform most of our tasks – `model.wv` represents this. To free up some RAM space, we can run the following:

```
word_vectors = model.wv
del model
```

We can now perform all the tasks we did before using the word vectors. Keep in mind that this is not just for Word2Vec but even for all word embeddings.

To evaluate how well our model has done, we can test it on data-sets that are loaded when we install Gensim.

```
model.wv.evaluate_word_pairs(os.path.join(module_path,
'test_data','wordsim353.tsv'))

((0.6230957719715976, 3.90029813472169e-39),
SpearmanrResult(correlation=0.645315618985209,
pvalue=1.0038208415351643e-42), 0.56657223796034)
```

Here, to make sure that we find our file, we have to specify the module path – this is the path for the `gensim/test` folder, which is where the files exist. We can also test our model on finding word pairs and relationships by running the following code.

```
model.wv.accuracy(os.path.join(module_path, 'test_data', 'questions-
words.txt'))
```

In our examples so far, we used a model which we trained ourselves – this can be quite a time-consuming exercise sometimes, and it is handy to know how to load pretrained vector models. Gensim allows for an easy interface to load the original Google news trained Word2Vec model (you can download this file from link [9]), for example.

```
from gensim.models import KeyedVectors
# load the google word2vec model

filename = 'GoogleNews-vectors-negative300.bin'
model = KeyedVectors.load_word2vec_format(filename, binary=True)
```

Our model now uses a 300-dimension word vector model, and we can run all the previous code examples we ran before, again – the results won't be too different, but we can expect a more sophisticated model.

Gensim also allows similar interfaces to download models using other word embeddings – we'll go over this in the last section. We're now equipped to train models, load models, and use these word embeddings to conduct experiments!

Doc2Vec

We know how important vector representation of documents are – for example, in all kinds of clustering or classification tasks, we have to represent our document as a vector. In fact, in most of this book, we have looked at techniques either using vector representations or worked on using these vector representations – topic modeling, TF-IDF, and a bag of words were some of the representations we previously looked at.

Building on Word2Vec, the kind researchers have also implemented a vector representation of documents or paragraphs, popularly called Doc2Vec. This means that we can now use the power of the semantic understanding of Word2Vec to describe documents as well, and in whatever dimension we would like to train it in!

Previous methods of using word2vec information for documents involved simply averaging the word vectors of that document, but that did not provide a nuanced enough understanding. To implement document vectors, Mikilov and Le simply added another vector as part of the training process – one which they called the paragraph id. Similar to word2vec, there are two primary training methods - **Distributed Memory** version of paragraph vector (**PV-DM**) and **Words** version of paragraph vector (**PV-DBOW**). They are variations of the **CBOW** and **Skip Gram** models, which were used to train Word2Vec, and we can understand it as extending the idea of context to paragraphs by adding a label or an ID. The paper [15] by Mikolov and Le, *Distributed Representations of Sentences and Documents*, describes the algorithm in detail, and if you take the effort to read the Word2Vec papers – this is definitely worth a shot!

For an easier reading into the inner workings of Doc2Vec, the blog post, *A gentle introduction to Doc2Vec* [16] also helps. The blog post walks us through the training methods we discussed before, namely SkipGram and CBOW.

As usual, we are less interested in the theory and more interested in the practical applications of these algorithms – so let's jump right into using Gensim for Doc2Vec!

The one major difference about Gensim's Doc2Vec implementation is that it doesn't expect a simple corpus as input – the algorithm expects tags or labels, and we are also expected to provide this as part of our input. Gensim helps us do this with.

```
gensim.models.doc2vec.LabeledSentence
```

Alternately, we can use this:

```
gensim.models.doc2vec.TaggedDocument

sentence = LabeledSentence(words=[u'some', u'words', u'here'],
labels=[u'SENT_1'])
```

In case of any errors, also try the following:

```
sentence = TaggedDocument(words=[u'some', u'words', u'here'],
tags=[u'SENT_1'])
```

Here, `sentence` is an example of what our input is going to be like. For our illustrative example, we will be using the Lee news corpus, and more or less follow the Lee tutorial [17] – we are familiar with this corpus, having previously worked with it during our topic modeling exercises. It should be noted that similar to Word2Vec, the more varied and larger the corpus, the better we can expect our training results to be. We load the corpus the same way we did before:

```
test_data_dir = '{}'.format(os.sep).join([gensim.__path__[0],
                'test', 'test_data'])
lee_train_file = test_data_dir + os.sep + 'lee_background.cor'
lee_test_file = test_data_dir + os.sep + 'lee.cor'
```

To construct our corpus, we will use the `TaggedDocument` class.

```
def read_corpus(file_name, tokens_only=False):
    with smart_open.smart_open(file_name, encoding="iso-8859-1") as f:
        for i, line in enumerate(f):
            if tokens_only:
                yield gensim.utils.simple_preprocess(line)
            else:
                # For training data, add tags
                yield gensim.models.doc2vec.TaggedDocument(
                gensim.utils.simple_preprocess(line), [i])
```

Here, we are simply adding the document number as our label – if we have further, more useful information about our data, we are welcome to add this information. In our function we defined to read the Lee corpus, we added a parameter to only read the tokens – this is for testing purposes.

```
train_corpus = list(read_corpus(lee_train_file))
test_corpus = list(read_corpus(lee_test_file, tokens_only=True))
```

From here onwards, Gensim's simple API remains the same, and to define and train our model we run this:

```
model = gensim.models.doc2vec.Doc2Vec(vector_size=50, min_count=2,
epochs=100)
```

Again, we will list out all the parameters from the `Doc2Vec` class. The original documentation can be found `here` [18].

1. `dm`: This defines the training algorithm. By default (dm=1), distributed memory (PV-DM) is used. Otherwise, a distributed bag of words (PV-DBOW) is employed.

2. `size`: This is the dimensionality of the feature vectors.

3. `window`: This is the maximum distance between the predicted word and context words used for prediction within a document.

4. `alpha`: This is the initial learning rate (will linearly drop to `min_alpha` as training progresses).

5. `seed`: This is used for the random number generator. Note that for a fully deterministically reproducible run, you must also limit the model to a single worker thread, to eliminate ordering jitter from OS thread scheduling. (In Python 3, reproducibility between interpreter launches also requires the use of the PYTHONHASHSEED environment variable to control hash randomization.)

6. `min_count`: Ignore all words with a total frequency lower than this.

7. `max_vocab_size`: Limit RAM during vocabulary building; if there are more unique words than this, then prune the infrequent ones. Every 10 million word types need about 1 GB of RAM. Set to None for no limit (default).

8. `sample`: Threshold for configuring which higher-frequency words are randomly downsampled.

9. `default`: This is 1e-3, values of 1e-5 (or lower) may also be useful, set to 0.0 to disable downsampling.

10. `workers`: Use this many worker threads to train the model (faster training with multicore machines).

11. `iter`: Number of iterations (epochs) over the corpus. The default inherited from Word2Vec is 5, but values of 10 or 20 are common in published *paragraph vector* experiments.

12. `hs`: If 1, hierarchical softmax will be used for model training. If set to 0 (default), and negative is non-zero, negative sampling will be used.

13. `negative`: if > 0, negative sampling will be used, the int for negative specifies how many noise words should be drawn (usually between 5-20). The default is 5. If set to 0, no negative sampling is used.

14. `dm_mean`: If 0 (default), use the sum of the context word vectors. If 1, use the mean. Only applies when `dm` is used in non-concatenative mode.

15. `dm_concat`: If 1, use concatenation of context vectors rather than sum/average; default is 0 (off). Note concatenation results in a much-larger model, as the input is no longer the size of one (sampled or arithmetically combined) word vector, but the size of the tag(s) and all words in the context strung together.

16. `dm_tag_count`: This is the expected constant number of document tags per document, when using the `dm_concat` mode; default is 1.

17. `dbow_words`: If set to 1 trains word-vectors (in skip-gram fashion) simultaneous with DBOW doc-vector training; default is 0 (faster training of doc-vectors only).

18. `trim_rule`: The vocabulary trimming rule specifies whether certain words should remain in the vocabulary, be trimmed away, or handled using the default (discard if word count < `min_count`). This can be `None` (`min_count` will be used), or a callable that accepts parameters (`word`, `count`, and `min_count`) and returns either `util.RULE_DISCARD`, `util.RULE_KEEP`, or `util.RULE_DEFAULT`. Note that the rule, if given, is only used prune vocabulary during `build_vocab()` and is not stored as part of the model.

We have a fairly small corpus in our case, so we decide on 50 dimensions, a minimum count of 2 to ignore low information words, and 100 iterations of our training algorithm.

```
model.build_vocab(train_corpus)
model.train(train_corpus, total_examples=model.corpus_count,
        epochs=model.epochs)
```

And there we go! With this, we have our Doc2Vec model trained. This is just to illustrate *how* to go about setting up the corpus and training a model – evaluating, assessing, and fine-tuning our model is a more nuanced process and depends on our use case as well – we could see how this was done with Word2Vec, by attempting to assess question-answer pairs or semantic pairs. For a more detailed example of evaluating Doc2Vec, as well as code examples, the Gensim notebook [19] on using IMDB to train the vectors is worth a look.

In the paper on Doc2Vec, the authors recommend using both the PV-DBOW training method, as well as the PV-DM method to train the model. We can do this using the following:

```
from gensim.models import Doc2Vec

models = [
    # PV-DBOW
    Doc2Vec(dm=0, dbow_words=1, vector_size=200, window=8, min_count=10,
epochs=50),
```

```
# PV-DM w/average
Doc2Vec(dm=1, dm_mean=1, vector_size=200, window=8, min_count=10,
epochs=50),
]
```

We then build the vocabularies before we start with our training. Just a note here: documents are any tagged document and are a placeholder variable, we can use train_corpus or provide different documents of our choice.

```
models[0].build_vocab(documents)
models[1].reset_from(models[0])

for model in models:
    model.train(documents, total_examples=model.corpus_count,
                epochs=model.epochs)
```

This leaves us with two trained models, and we can evaluate these how we would like. The ConcatenatedDoc2Vec class helps us here.

You may need to run pip install testfixtures before running this code.

```
from gensim.test.test_doc2vec import ConcatenatedDoc2Vec
new_model = ConcatenatedDoc2Vec((models[0], models[1]))
```

As for what we can do with a Doc2Vec model, inferring a vector and searching for similar vectors are the more obvious applications. We can see this for ourselves with the Lee dataset from link [17] or the Jupyter notebook:

```
inferred_vector = model.infer_vector(train_corpus[0].words)
sims = model.docvecs.most_similar([inferred_vector])
print(sims)

[(0, 0.9216967225074768),
 (48, 0.822547435760498),
 (255, 0.7833435535430908),
 (40, 0.7805585861206055),
 (8, 0.7584196925163269),
 (33, 0.7528027892112732),
 (272, 0.7409536838531494),
 (9, 0.7000102400779724),
 (264, 0.6848353743553162),
 (10, 0.6837587356567383)]
```

Note that in practical cases, we will not be testing for most similar vectors on the training set – this is to simply illustrate how to use the methods.

We can see that in the list of documents most similar to document 0, ID 0 shows up first – this is obvious (and redundant information). However, things get interesting when we check the 48th or 255th document. Let's see what document 0 contains:

"hundreds of people have been forced to vacate their homes in the southern highlands of new south wales as strong winds today pushed huge bushfire towards the town of hill top new blaze near goulburn south west of sydney has forced the closure of the hume highway at about pm aedt marked deterioration in the weather as storm cell moved east across the blue mountains forced authorities to make decision to evacuate people from homes in outlying streets at hill top in the new south wales southern highlands an estimated residents have left their homes for nearby mittagong the new south wales rural fire service says the weather conditions which caused the fire to burn in finger formation have now eased and about fire units in and around hill top are optimistic of defending all properties as more than blazes burn on new year eve in new south wales fire crews have been called to new fire at gunning south of goulburn while few details are available at this stage fire authorities says it has closed the hume highway in both directions meanwhile new fire in sydney west is no longer threatening properties in the cranebrook area rain has fallen in some parts of the illawarra sydney the hunter valley and the north coast but the bureau of meteorology claire richards says the rain has done little to ease any of the hundred fires still burning across the state the falls have been quite isolated in those areas and generally the falls have been less than about five millimetres she said in some places really not significant at all less than millimetre so there hasn't been much relief as far as rain is concerned in fact they ve probably hampered the efforts of the firefighters more because of the wind gusts that are associated with those thunderstorms"

A brief run through can tell us it contains information about a fire and the response of the fire-fighters. As for document 48:

"thousands of firefighters remain on the ground across new south wales this morning as they assess the extent of fires burning around sydney and on the state south coast firefighters are battling fire band stretching from around campbelltown south west of sydney to the royal national park hundreds of people have been evacuated from small villages to the south and south west of sydney authorities estimate more than properties have been destroyed in the greater sydney area fourteen homes have been destroyed in the hawkesbury area north of sydney and properties have been ruined at jervis bay john winter from the new south wales rural fire service says firefighters main concern is the fire band from campbelltown through to the coast that is going to be very difficult area today we do expect that the royal national park is likely to be impacted by fire later in the morning he said certainly in terms of population risk and threat to property that band is going to be our area of greatest concern in the act it appears the worst of the fire danger may have passed though strong winds are expected to keep firefighters busy today the fires have burned more than hectares over the past two days yesterday winds of up to kilometres an hour fanned blazes in dozen areas including queanbeyan connor mount wanniassa red hill and black mountain strong winds are again predicted for today but fire authorities are confident they have the resources to contain any further blazes total fire ban is in force in the act today and tomorrow emergency services minister ted quinlan has paid tribute to the efforts of firefighters there has just been the whole body of people that have been magnificent in sacrificing their christmas for the benefit of the community he said."

We can see very clearly that the context has been captured perfectly by Doc2Vec! We just searched up the most similar document – imagine the power Doc2Vec can bring if used in tandem with clustering and classifying documents. We urge the reader to retry some of the problems from Chapter 10, *Clustering and Classifying Text*, using Doc2Vec instead of TF-IDF or topic models as representation.

We now have the ability to vectorize (with semantic understanding!) both our words and documents. While word2vec and doc2vec remain the most popular vectorizing algorithms, these are not the only ones – let's explore how to use some of the alternate algorithms in the next section.

Other word embeddings

There is a wealth of word embeddings which we can choose from for our vectorization tasks – the original implementations of these methods are scattered around in different languages, hosting websites, binaries, and repositories – but luckily for us, Gensim comes to the rescue again, with implementations or well-documented wrappers for most (if not all) of other word embeddings.

Gensim has wrappers for WordRank, VarEmbed, and FastText, as well as native implementations for **Poincare Embeddings** and FastText. Gensim also has a neat script to use **GloVe embeddings** as well, which comes in handy when comparing between different kinds of embeddings.

Gensim's KeyedVectors class means that we have a base class to use all our word embeddings. The documentation page [21] covers most of the information you need to know (though we have already used these vectors in our examples for Word2Vec).

All we need to know is that after we are finished training our model, it's more prudent to run this:

```
word_vectors = model.wv
```

Also, continue using `word_vectors` for all our other tasks – for most similar words, most dissimilar, as well as running tests for word embeddings. It's worth having a look at the code of the `KeyedVectors.py` [22] file to see what's going on under the hood!

Once we're aware of how to use word vectors, we can have a look at how to get the other word embeddings up and running using Python.

GloVe

GloVe is a word vector representation method where the training is performed on aggregated global word-word co-occurrence statistics from a corpus. This means that like Word2Vec, it uses context to understand and create the word representations. The GloVe method was developed by the Natural language processing lab at Stanford University – you can find more information about their project on their website. The research paper describing the method is called *GloVe: Global Vectors for Word Representation* [23] and is well worth a read as it describes some of the drawbacks of LSA and Word2Vec before describing their own method.

There are multiple implementations of GloVe out there, and even multiple implementations in Python – but we will only stick to *using* these vectors, and not training them. Of course, if one wishes to train their own GloVe vectors this can be done with either `glove_python` [24] or just `glove` [25]. You can also have a look at the original Stanford code over here [26].

As usual, we will be using Gensim to load these vectors. Our first step is to download (or train) our GloVe vectors. Once we have them saved, we convert the GloVe vector format to the Word2Vec format so that we can continue using them with the Gensim API. Remember to download the GloVe input file from link [22].

```
from gensim.scripts.glove2word2vec import glove2word2vec

glove_input_file = 'glove.6B.100d.txt'
word2vec_output_file = 'glove.6B.100d.txt.word2vec'
glove2word2vec(glove_input_file, word2vec_output_file)
```

Here, we have loaded the glove vectors and converted it into the word2vec format, and further saved it to disk. We load this the same way we would load any saved vector file.

```
from gensim.models import KeyedVectors
filename = 'glove.6B.100d.txt.word2vec'
model = KeyedVectors.load_word2vec_format(filename, binary=False)
```

Our model should now work the same way our word2vec models – albeit slightly better if we go by the results which the GloVe paper describe. Let's give our go-to example a shot:

```
model.most_similar(positive=['woman', 'king'], negative=['man'], topn=1)
```

```
[(u'queen', 0.7698540687561035)]
```

And like clockwork, we have our expected result!

FastText

FastText is a vector representation technique developed at Facebook AI research. As its name suggests, it is a fast and efficient method to perform the same task – and because of the nature of its training method, it ends up learning morphological details as well. FastText is unique because it can derive word vectors for unknown words or out of vocabulary words – this is because by taking morphological characteristics of words into account, it can *create* the word vector for an unknown word.

This becomes particularly interesting in languages where the morphological structure is important – Turkish and Finnish are two such examples. It also means that with a limited vocabulary it is still possible to make sufficiently intelligent word embeddings. In the case of English, for example, it means it is able to understand what the *ly* represents in words like *charmingly* or *strangely*. We can further extend this to say that according to FastText, *embedding(strange) - embedding(strangely) ~= embedding(charming) - embedding(charmingly)*.

We see that FastText more or less captures this in practice, and does this by character level analysis of using words such as Word2Vec or GloVe. We test the performance of word embeddings either by measuring how well the vectors perform in semantic tasks and syntactic tasks. Since morphology refers to the structure or syntax of words, FastText tends to perform better for such tasks, and Word2Vec performs better for semantic tasks.

The original paper describing the method is titled *Enriching Word Vectors with Subword Information*, and can be found on arxiv [27]. The implementation by Facebook can be found in their GitHub repo [28]. We will be using Gensim to use FastText, which contains both a native implementation as well as a wrapper. The blog post [29] covers some of the comparisons between FastText and Word2Vec, which we discussed before, while the notebook [30] has code examples for the same. The blog post is part of the official Gensim blog and compares it using Gensim as a common interface.

Training is similar to the other gensim models we have dealt with. To use and train the native Gensim implementation [31], we can run the following code, where data is a placeholder variable for the textual data you wish to train the model on.

```
from gensim.models.fasttext import FastText

ft_model = FastText(size=100)
ft_model.build_vocab(data)

ft_model.train(data, total_examples=ft_model.corpus_count,
               epochs=ft_model.iter)
```

We can also use the original C++ code through a **wrapper** [32], though this requires us to first download the code.

```
from gensim.models.wrappers.fasttext import FastText

# Set FastText home to the path to the FastText executable
ft_home = '/home/bhargav/Gensim/fastText/fasttext'

# train the model
model_wrapper = FastText.train(ft_home, train_file)
```

Using the vectors generated from FastText are similar to all the word vectors operations we covered before, so we will not explain how to use them – for a simple illustration the following Jupyter notebooks help – notebook 1 [33], notebook 2 [30].

One interesting exercise to try out with FastText is to see how it evaluates words not present in the vocabulary. Consider this example:

```
print('dog' in ft_model.wv.vocab)
print('dogs' in ft_model.wv.vocab)

True
False
```

But, we can still generate word vectors for both dog and dogs despite dogs not being in the training vocabulary! A quick observation of the vectors also tells us that they are quite similar as we would expect. We can further verify this:

```
print('dog' in model)
print('dogs' in model)
```

True
True

We leave it to the user to test the other method provided by Gensim, using FastText.

WordRank

WordRank, as the name suggests, attempts to solve embeddings as a ranking problem. The idea behind it remains similar to GloVe, where we used global co-occurrences of words to generate the word embeddings. The code can be downloaded off bitbucket [34], and the GitHub [35] can also be used. The original paper describing the method is titled *WordRank: Learning Word Embeddings via Robust Ranking,* and can also be found on arxiv [36].

Again, we will be using Gensim's wrapper to access and use WordRank. Here, data is a variable which holds the path to your personal Gensim installation followed by the data. Remember how we did this for the Lee corpus – we used gensim.__path__[0].

```
from gensim.models.wrappers import Wordrank

wordrank_path = 'wordrank' # path to Wordrank directory
out_dir = 'model' # name of output directory to save data to
data = '../../gensim/test/test_data/lee.cor' # sample corpus

model = Wordrank.train(wordrank_path, data, out_dir, iter=21,
                       dump_period=10)
```

In this particular case, we are using the same Lee corpus to run our training and testing.

We need to be aware of two parameters, dump_period and iter, which need to be synchronized as it dumps the embedding file with the start of next iteration. For example, if you want results after 20 iterations, we set iter=21, and dump_period can be any multiple after which there is no remainder – for 20, this could be 2, 4, 5, or 10.

The Gensim documentation [37] can be found here, as well look at a basic tutorial [38].

Some caveats – a window size of 15 performed with optimum results, and 100 epochs is a better idea than 500 epochs, as training time can be quite long. Again, as with the other embeddings, we use the `KeyedVectors` class that contains the same methods throughout all word vectors. For a comparison between FastText, word2vec, and WordRank, the blog-post [39] and Jupyter notebook [40] will walk you through.

Varembed

Varembed is the 4th-word embedding method we will discuss, and like FastText, it takes advantage of morphological information to generate word vectors. The original paper describing the method is titled *Morphological Priors for Probabilistic Neural Word Embeddings*, and can be found on arxiv [41].

Similar to our GloVe vectors, we cannot update our model with new words and would need to train a new model. Information on training our own models can be found on the original [42] containing the code.

Gensim comes with Varembed word embeddings trained on the Lee dataset, so we will take advantage of this to illustrate setting up a model. You can find the documentation for Varembed [43]. Here, Varembed is a variable that holds the path to your personal Gensim installation and the test data. Remember how we did this for the Lee corpus – we used `gensim.__path__[0]`.

```
from gensim.models.wrappers import varembed

varembed_vectors =
'../../gensim/test/test_data/varembed_leecorpus_vectors.pkl'

model = varembed.VarEmbed.load_varembed_format(vectors=varembed_vectors)
```

We previously mentioned how Varembed uses morphological information – we can adjust our vectors accordingly by also adding this information. Again, Gensim comes with this morphological information.

```
morfessors = '../../gensim/test/test_data/varembed_leecorpus_morfessor.bin'
model = varembed.VarEmbed.load_varembed_format(vectors=varembed_vectors,
morfessor_model=morfessors)
```

Once our model is loaded, we use its methods similar to our other word embeddings.

Poincare

The last word embedding technique we will look at is Poincare embeddings, also developed by the good folks over at Facebook AI research. The general idea is to use a graphical representation of words to better understand the relationship between words and to generate the word embeddings. Poincare embeddings can also capture hierarchical information using this graphical representation – in the original paper [44], titled *Poincaré Embeddings for Learning Hierarchical Representations*, this hierarchical information is learned by using **WordNet** noun hierarchy. This information is calculated in the hyperbolic space, and not the traditional euclidean space – allowing for us to better capture the notions of hierarchy.

Gensim's notebook directory contains data required to train these embeddings. We can access this using the following:

```
import os

poincare_directory = os.path.join(os.getcwd(), 'docs', 'notebooks',
                                    'poincare')
data_directory = os.path.join(poincare_directory, 'data')
wordnet_mammal_file = os.path.join(data_directory,
                                    'wordnet_mammal_hypernyms.tsv')
```

To use this data to train our model, we run this:

```
from gensim.models.poincare import PoincareModel, PoincareKeyedVectors,
PoincareRelations
relations = PoincareRelations(file_path=wordnet_mammal_file, delimiter='t')
model = PoincareModel(train_data=relations, size=2, burn_in=0)
                    model.train(epochs=1, print_every=500)
```

We can also use our own iterable of relations to train our model. In such a case, each *relation* is just a pair of nodes. Gensim also has pre-trained models we can use the following:

```
models_directory = os.path.join(poincare_directory, 'models')
test_model_path = os.path.join(models_directory,
'gensim_model_batch_size_10_burn_in_0_epochs_50_neg_20_dim_50')
                    model = PoincareModel.load(test_model_path)
```

We can use the standard word embeddings methods with our Poincare model, as well as use graph related information, such as closest_child, closest_parent, and norm.

For more information about the model refer to the following:

Documentation [45]: https://radimrehurek.com/gensim/models/poincare.html

Evaluation [46]: `https://github.com/RaRe-Technologies/gensim/blob/develop/docs/notebooks/Poincare%20Evaluation.ipynb`

Training [47]: `https://github.com/RaRe-Technologies/gensim/blob/develop/docs/notebooks/Poincare%20Tutorial.ipynb`

Blog Post [48]: `https://rare-technologies.com/implementing-poincare-embeddings/`

Summary

We explored in this chapter one of the major innovation in text analysis, word embeddings or word vectors. Word vectors are unique in being not only a way for us to represent our documents and our words but to also offer a new *way* of looking at our words. The success of Word2Vec led to an explosion in various word embedding methods, each with its own quirks, advantages, and disadvantages. We not only learned about the popular Word2Vec and Doc2Vec implementations but also five other word embedding methods – all of them are supported well in the Gensim eco-system making them easy to use.

References

[1] *Efficient Estimation of Word Representations in Vector Space* [Mikolov et al. 2013]:
`https://arxiv.org/pdf/1301.3781.pdf`

[2] *Distributed Representations of Words and Phrases and their Compositionality* [Mikolov et al. 2013]:
`https://papers.nips.cc/paper/5021-distributed-representations-of-words-and-phrases-and-their-compositionality.pdf`

[3] *Linguistic Regularities in Continuous Space Word Representations* [Mikolov et al. 2013]:
`http://www.aclweb.org/anthology/N13-1090`

[4] Word2Vec Tutorial - The Skip-Gram Model:
`http://mccormickml.com/2016/04/19/word2vec-tutorial-the-skip-gram-model/`
[5] Amazing power of word vectors:
`https://blog.acolyer.org/2016/04/21/the-amazing-power-of-word-vectors/`

[6] Word2Vec resources:
`http://mccormickml.com/2016/04/27/word2vec-resources/`

[7] Original C Word2Vec code:
https://code.google.com/archive/p/word2vec/

[8] *Deep Learning with Word2Vec and Gensim:*
https://rare-technologies.com/deep-learning-with-word2vec-and-gensim/

[9] Interactive Word2Vec tutorial:
https://rare-technologies.com/word2vec-tutorial/

[10] text8 data file:
http://mattmahoney.net/dc/textdata.html

[11] Word2Vec model:
https://radimrehurek.com/gensim/models/word2vec.html

[12] *Linguistic Regularities in Sparse and Explicit Word Representations:*
http://www.aclweb.org/anthology/W14-1618

[13] Word2Vec/Doc2Vec notebook:
https://github.com/bhargavvader/personal/blob/master/notebooks/text_analysis/word2vec.ipynb

[14] Online word2vec:
https://github.com/RaRe-Technologies/gensim/blob/develop/docs/notebooks/online_w2v_tutorial.ipynb

[15] *Distributed Representations of Sentences and Documents*:
https://cs.stanford.edu/~quocle/paragraph_vector.pdf

[16] A gentle introduction to Doc2Vec:
https://medium.com/scaleabout/a-gentle-introduction-to-doc2vec-db3e8c0cce5e

[17] Doc2Vec Lee tutorial:
https://github.com/RaRe-Technologies/gensim/blob/develop/docs/notebooks/doc2vec-lee.ipynb

[18] Doc2Vec Gensim:
https://radimrehurek.com/gensim/models/doc2vec.html

[19] Doc2Vec IMDB:
https://github.com/RaRe-Technologies/gensim/blob/develop/docs/notebooks/doc2vec-IMDB.ipynb

[20] KeyedVectors:
https://radimrehurek.com/gensim/models/keyedvectors.html

[21] KeyedVectors file:
https://github.com/RaRe-Technologies/gensim/blob/develop/gensim/models/keyedvec
tors.py

[22] GloVe:
https://nlp.stanford.edu/projects/glove/

[23] GloVe: Global Vectors for Word Representation:
https://nlp.stanford.edu/pubs/glove.pdf

[24] GloVe Python:
https://github.com/maciejkula/glove-python

[25] GloVe:
https://github.com/JonathanRaiman/glove

[26] Standford GloVe:
https://github.com/stanfordnlp/GloVe

[27] *Enriching Word Vectors with Subword Information:*
https://arxiv.org/pdf/1607.04606.pdf

[28] fastText:
https://github.com/facebookresearch/fastText

[29] *FastText and gensim word embeddings:*
https://rare-technologies.com/fasttext-and-gensim-word-embeddings/

[30] FastText comparison notebook:
https://github.com/RaRe-Technologies/gensim/blob/develop/docs/notebooks/Word2Ve
c_FastText_Comparison.ipynb

[31] Gensim fastText:
https://radimrehurek.com/gensim/models/fasttext.html#module-gensim.models.fastt
ext

[32] fastText wrapper:
https://radimrehurek.com/gensim/models/wrappers/fasttext.html

[33] FastText Gensim notebook:
https://github.com/RaRe-Technologies/gensim/blob/develop/docs/notebooks/FastTex
t_Tutorial.ipynb

[34] WordRank:
https://bitbucket.org/shihaoji/wordrank

[35] WordRank GitHub:
https://github.com/shihaoji/wordrank

[36] *WordRank: Learning Word Embeddings via Robust Ranking:*
https://arxiv.org/pdf/1506.02761.pdf

[37] WordRank Gensim:
https://radimrehurek.com/gensim/models/wrappers/wordrank.html

[38] WordRank tutorial:
https://github.com/RaRe-Technologies/gensim/blob/develop/docs/notebooks/WordRank_wrapper_quickstart.ipynb

[39] WordRank blog-post:
https://rare-technologies.com/wordrank-embedding-crowned-is-most-similar-to-king-not-word2vecs-canute/

[40] WordRank Jupyter notebook:
https://github.com/RaRe-Technologies/gensim/blob/develop/docs/notebooks/Wordrank_comparisons.ipynb

[41] *Morphological Priors for Probabilistic Neural Word Embedding:*
https://arxiv.org/pdf/1608.01056.pdf

[42] GitHub page Varembed:
https://github.com/rguthrie3/MorphologicalPriorsForWordEmbeddings

[43] Varembed:
https://radimrehurek.com/gensim/models/wrappers/varembed.html

[44] Poincare Embeddings:
https://arxiv.org/pdf/1705.08039.pdf

[45] Documentation:
https://radimrehurek.com/gensim/models/poincare.html

[46] Evaluation:
https://github.com/RaRe-Technologies/gensim/blob/develop/docs/notebooks/Poincare%20Evaluation.ipynb

[47] Training:
https://github.com/RaRe-Technologies/gensim/blob/develop/docs/notebooks/Poincare%20Tutorial.ipynb

[48] Blog Post:
https://rare-technologies.com/implementing-poincare-embeddings/

Deep Learning for Text 13

Until now, we have explored the use of machine learning for text in a variety of contexts – topic modeling, clustering, classification, text summarization, and even our POS-taggers and NER-taggers were trained using machine learning. In this chapter, we will begin to explore one of the most cutting-edge forms of machine learning – **Deep Learning**. Deep Learning is a form of ML where we use biologically inspired structures to generate algorithms and architectures to perform various tasks on the text. Some of these tasks are text generation, classification, and word embeddings. In this chapter, we will discuss some of the underpinnings of deep learning as well as how to implement our own deep learning models for text. Following are the topics we will cover in this chapter:

- Deep learning
- Deep learning for text
- Text generation

Deep learning

Throughout this book, we have made use of machine learning techniques, with topic modeling, clustering and classifying algorithms, as well as what we call **shallow learning** – word embeddings. Word embeddings were our first glimpse into neural networks and the kind of semantic information they can learn.

Neural networks can be understood as a computing system or machine learning algorithm whose architecture is vaguely inspired by biological neurons in the brain. We say vaguely here because of the lack of thorough understanding we have of the human brain – through the neural connections and structure of the brain was certainly influential in some of the basic building blocks of neural networks, such as the **perceptron** [1] and **single-layer neural network** [2].

A neural network generally consists of a number of nodes that perform mathematical operations and interact with each other via connections. This model resembles a brain in the sense that the nodes tend to represent neurons and the connections the wiring between these neurons. Different layers can perform a different kind of operations, and there is generally an input layer, multiple hidden layers, and an output layer.

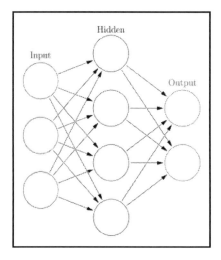

Fig 13.1 An example of the common structure of neural networks [4]

In turn, neural network research has inspired cognitive research, and there was considerable interest in using neural networks to also understand human brains [3]. Neural networks can be used for most of the machine learning tasks we have previously conducted, such as classification, clustering, and as we saw in just the last chapter, in creating vector representations of words and documents.

Outside of the domain of text analysis, neural networks have found considerable success. State-of-the-art results in image classification, computer vision, speech recognition, and medical diagnosis are often achieved by neural networks. We mentioned earlier that we used neural networks to generate word embeddings – after the learning or training was completed, we used the values stored in the hidden layers as our embeddings.

We've been talking extensively about neural networks even though this chapter is titled deep learning – but deep learning is just another way to refer to neural networks with multiple layers. Since most current neural networks tend to use multiple layers in their architecture, we can refer to these techniques as deep learning techniques. There are exceptions to this of course, such as in Word2Vec, where we pick up the weights from only one layer.

Neural networks and deep learning architectures are versatile in their use, and even though we may not have a complete mathematical understanding of neural networks, it is still a very good choice for practical natural language processing, and that is what we will attempt to walk the reader through in this chapter.

Deep learning for text (and more)

We're already aware of the power of neural networks first hand when we used word embeddings. This is one aspect of neural networks – using parts of the architecture itself to get useful information, but neural networks are far from limited to this. When we start using deeper networks, it is not prudent to use the weights to extract useful information – in these cases; we are more interested in the natural output of the neural network. We can train neural networks to perform multiple tasks to do with text analysis – indeed, for some of these tasks, the introduction of neural networks have completely changed how we approach the task.

A popular example here is **Language Translation**, and in particular, Google's **Neural Translation** model. Starting from until September 2016 Google used statistical and rule-based methods and models to perform its language translation, but with the advent of the Google Brain research team, they soon switched over to using neural networks, and a technique now referred to as

zero-shot translation [5]. This means that if the Google translate algorithm intended to translate from Malaysian to Arabic, for example, it would first translate to English as an intermediate step. With its current neural network set-up, models take an input sentence, and its output is a translated sentence – of course, it doesn't just throw the first output, there is usually a scoring mechanism, where grammatical correctness is verified. Instead of breaking up a sentence into multiple parts, performing rule-based translation and rearranging the sentence, we now have a *cleaner* method of attempting a translation. The neural models also tend to be smaller than the statistical models, even if they might need more data or time to perform the initial training. More languages are being released by Google as and when these models outperform the existing models – only recently Google released new models for a number of Indian languages.

Despite the advances made in machine translation, it still remains a difficult task – while we can expect more or less grammatically accurate sentences, it is more meant to provide a general idea to the user about what the input sentence would mean in another language. Like other deep learning fields, one can expect the results of machine translation to only get better.

Word embeddings are another very popular use of neural networks for text – considering how word vectors and document vectors are used in many NLP tasks, it means word embeddings have a home in many machine learning algorithms involving text. In fact, replacing all previous vectors with word embeddings means that we now have a few neural networks in all our algorithms or applications! With its ability to capture context so well, it can help heavily in tasks such as clustering or classification.

Also, speaking of techniques such as clustering or classification, we can also train neural networks to perform these tasks. In fact, more complex text analysis tasks, such as building a chatbot, require one to perform text classification along the way. The task that we refer to as **sentiment analysis** in the text is essentially a classification task where we classify documents as having positive or negative sentiment (or multiple sentiments if that is our job, of course). We can use more complex kinds of neural networks to perform this, such as **Convolutional Neural Networks (CNN)** [6] or **Recurrent Neural Networks (RNN)** [7], but even your vanilla single layer NN tends to do an okay job.

We saw a glimpse of this when we were training our own POS-taggers or NER-taggers - what was going on under the hood was a neural network being trained to identify different *classes* for words – these classes were different parts of speech or a named entity. So, *technically*, we've been using elements of deep learning in all of our applications, just using the spaCy trained POS-taggers!

We will not be going to the mathematical details of neural networks as it is beyond the scope of the book, but when discussing different kinds of neural networks and how we will be using them, we will attempt to discuss the architecture and more importantly – the hyperparameters and best practices of that particular method. Just a reminder: hyper parameters are parameters to a machine learning algorithm which are set *before* starting the algorithm.

When dealing with vanilla neural networks or even convolutional neural networks, our input space and output space is fixed – we decide what the input is. It could be an image, or it could be a sentence, but it is basically a vector input which produces a vector output. In natural language processing, this vector output can be, for example, the probabilities of a document belonging to a certain class. Recurrent neural networks are different with regard to this because of its architecture (information is) - by allowing sequences as inputs, we can do a lot more than just predicting classes. Recurrent neural networks are particularly useful for text because they understand the input data as sequences, and allow us to capture the context of the words in a sentence.

One of the ideas of how neural networks work with text is that generates a probabilistic language model for the body of text. This can be understood as it is a technique where we calculate the probability of the next word (or character!) in a sequence based on the previous inputs. In other words, they attempt to calculate the probability of a word based on its context. Indeed, even before neural networks were regularly used in natural language processing this was a popular method – we have previously used n-grams, which more or less work on the same principle. Based on a corpus or group of texts, it attempts to learn what the odds of two words appearing next to each other based on a particular context - that is, words around it. This is how we start to consider *new_york* as a new addition to our vocabulary, it means that there is a high probability that these two words will appear next to each other, and this probability was calculated through basic conditional probability and chain probability rules.

When using a neural network, we can argue that by learning the odds or probabilities of words or characters appearing, we are using a sequence generator, or that a neural network is now a generative model. Generative models in the context of natural language processing can be particularly interesting – if we can teach a neural network what kind of sentences occur with high probability, we can also attempt to make this neural network output sequences which mimic the text it was trained on.

It's this same thinking which lets us create word embeddings – the odds of the word *blue* appearing after the sentence *the wall is painted* would be similar to the word *red* appearing, and our embeddings learn to encode *blue* and *red* with similar semantics. This kind of semantic understanding is further explored with experiments on shared representations. Shared representations are the idea that different kinds of input sharing the same semantics can map to the same vector space – for example, the English word for *dog* and the Chinese word for *dog* would map to very similar vectors in a shared Chinese-English vector space. But the power of neural networks gets even more impressive – it is possible to train a network to also map images to the same space! Image captioning is also a task performed well by such neural networks.

Using reinforcement learning [8] (where our model learns from its own mistakes through a system of rewards and punishments) neural networks have also been able to beat humans at the game of Go, which was once considered a very tough game for artificial intelligence systems to beat.

One of the first natural language processing tasks was text summarization – the traditional approach to such a problem is to rank the sentences based on which ones provide the most information, and choose a subset of these. We used such an algorithm in our own attempts at text summarization. With deep learning, however, we now have the capacity to generate text, and much like more *human* text summarization attempts, we will not be just choosing important sentences, but rather creating the summary from a probabilistic model. This process is also often referred to as **Natural Language Generation** (**NLG**).

Indeed, when we previously discussed the power of neural networks in language translation, it is through such generative models with which it recreates the sentence in another language. As our first example of using neural networks for text, we will attempt to generate text – in a variety of contexts.

Generating text

In our discussions involving deep learning and natural language processing, we extensively spoke about how it is used in text generation to very convincing results – we are now going to get our hands dirty with a little bit of text generation ourselves.

The neural network architecture we will be using is a recurrent neural network, and in particular, an **LSTM** [9]. LSTM stands for **Long Short Term Memory** and is unique because its architecture allows it to capture both short term and long term context of words in a sentence. The very popular blog post *Understanding LSTM Networks* [11] by deep learning researcher Colah is a great way to further understand LSTMs.

This is the same architecture used in the popular blog post [10] by Andrej Karpathy, *The unreasonable effectiveness of Neural Networks*, though Karpathy wrote his code for his NN in Lua – we will be using Keras, which with its high level of abstraction serves as a perfect choice.

The Python ecosystem for deep learning is certainly thriving now – depending on your use case there are multiple ways we can build a deep learning system. For us, we would like a high level of abstraction, and the ability to easily use text to train our machine. As of now, in 2018, choosing a deep learning framework is no easy task, but we will stick with Keras for our deep learning tasks, but not before briefly discussing what other tools there are out there.

1. **TensorFlow** (https://www.tensorflow.org/): TensorFlow is a neural network library released by Google, and also happens to be the same framework that their artificial intelligence team, Google Brains uses. It is, of course, different from the exact framework used for production, but TensorFlow is nevertheless very well maintained, remains an active community, and has strong GPU support. GPU support is important because it allows us to perform mathematical operations faster than a normal CPU can. Because of its graph-based computation model, it ends up being a natural fit for constructing neural networks. It offers a high level of control and options in terms of how low-level you want the operations to be and is generally a popular choice now in both research and industry.

2. **Theano** (http://deeplearning.net/software/theano/): Arguably one of the first thorough deep learning frameworks, it was built at MILA by Yoshia Bengio, one of the pioneers of deep learning. Focused on using symbolic graphs as the building blocks of neural networks, its API is quite low level, and if used effectively can result in some very powerful deep learning systems. It is not being maintained anymore, but is still worth checking out, even if just for the history! The libraries, `Lasagne` [12] and `Blocks` [13] allow you to use Theano from a higher layer of abstraction.

3. **Caffe** (http://caffe.berkeleyvision.org/) & **Caffe2** (https://caffe2.ai/): Caffe is one of the first dedicated deep learning frameworks, developed at UC Berkeley. It is both fast and modular, if a bit clunky to use because it is not written in native Python and requires you to manage the `.prototxt` files to use the networks in your applications. These `.protoxt` files describe neural networks using a predescribed format you can find `here` [14]. This only adds an extra layer of complexity to our time span coding neural networks, and there are more abstracted libraries which we would rather want to use.

4. **PyTorch** (https://pytorch.org/): The new kid on the block but also a library which is growing rapidly, PyTorch is loosely based on Lua's Torch library. The **Facebook Artificial Intelligence Research** team (**FAIR**) has endorsed PyTorch, and with a healthy mix of low level and high-level APIs also based on dynamic computational graphs, it is definitely worth checking out.

5. **Keras** (https://keras.io/): Keras will be our library of choice - and we are not alone here. With its high level of abstraction and clean API, it remains the best deep learning framework for prototyping and can use either Theano or TensorFlow as the backend for constructing the networks. It is very easy to go from the idea -> execution, as we will see in our text generation example. It has a large and active community, and with TensorFlow announcing they will be shipping with Keras, it means that it will continue to be used for the foreseeable future.

We invite the reader to have a look at the other deep learning frameworks out there – depending on the use case; a different framework might be better for you! Of course, the techniques we will be trying out will remain the same, so apart from syntactic changes we can expect the same logic and process for text generation.

We mentioned before that we would be using a recurrent neural network for our example. A recurrent neural network does one step better than other neural networks because of its ability to remember the context, as each layer in the network is built with information from the previous layer – this additional context allows it to perform better, and also gives it the name *recurrent*.

We will be using a particular variant of an RNN called LSTM, or Long Short-Term Memory – as the name suggests, it has the ability to have a short-term memory which can last for a long period of time. Whenever there is a significant time-lag between inputs, LSTMs tend to perform well - considering the nature of language, where a word which appears later on in a sentence is influenced by the context of the sentence, this property starts becoming more important. We mentioned before it is unique because it can understand the context of words immediately around it while *remembering* words from before.

For a more detailed explanation of the mathematics or intuition behind an LSTM and RNN, the following blog posts can be very useful (we've come across these blog posts earlier on in the chapter).

- Understanding LSTM Networks [11]
- Unreasonable Effectiveness of Recurrent Neural Networks [10]

As usual, we start with our imports – be sure to install Keras and tensorflow using pip or conda before we start!

The code we will be using as a reference is from the Jupyter notebook [15], though there will be some differences.

```
import keras
from keras.models import Sequential
from keras.layers import LSTM, Dense, Dropout
from keras.callbacks import ModelCheckpoint
from keras.utils import np_utils
import numpy as np
```

Here, we use Keras' sequential model where we can add an LSTM structure. The next step is to deal with data organization. We can use any text source as our input, based on what kind of data we would like to generate. This is where we can get creative - do we want our RNN to write like J.K. Rowling, Shakespeare, or even like yourself – if you have enough examples of your writing stored somewhere!

When using Keras to generate text, we need to generate a mapping of all the distinct characters in the book (our LSTM is a character level model). A note – `source_data.txt` here is *your* personal dataset of choice. In the example code which follows, all the other variables depend on what you choose as your dataset of choice, but the code will run fine regardless of any text file you choose.

```
filename     = 'data/source_data.txt'
data         = open(filename).read()
data         = data.lower()
# Find all the unique characters
chars        = sorted(list(set(data)))
char_to_int  = dict((c, i) for i, c in enumerate(chars))
ix_to_char   = dict((i, c) for i, c in enumerate(chars))
vocab_size   = len(chars)
```

Our two dictionaries will help us in both passing characters to our model and in generating text as well. A standard data source will give us results resembling this if we use `print(chars)`, `vocab_size`, and `char_to_int`.

This is a list of unique characters:

```
['n', ' ', '!', '&', "'", '(', ')', ',', '-', '.', '0', '1', '2', '3', '4',
'5', '6', '7', '8', '9', ':', ';', '?', '[', ']', 'a', 'b', 'c', 'd', 'e',
'f', 'g', 'h', 'i', 'j', 'k', 'l', 'm', 'n', 'o', 'p', 'q', 'r', 's', 't',
'u', 'v', 'w', 'x', 'y', 'z']
```

This is a number of unique characters:

```
51
```

The character to integer mapping is as follows:

```
{'n': 0, ' ': 1, '!': 2, '&': 3, "'": 4, '(': 5, ')': 6, ',': 7, '-': 8,
'.': 9, '0': 10, '1': 11, '2': 12, '3': 13, '4': 14, '5': 15, '6': 16, '7':
17, '8': 18, '9': 19, ':': 20, ';': 21, '?': 22, '[': 23, ']': 24, 'a': 25,
'b': 26, 'c': 27, 'd': 28, 'e': 29, 'f': 30, 'g': 31, 'h': 32, 'i': 33,
'j': 34, 'k': 35, 'l': 36, 'm': 37, 'n': 38, 'o': 39, 'p': 40, 'q': 41,
'r': 42, 's': 43, 't': 44, 'u': 45, 'v': 46, 'w': 47, 'x': 48, 'y': 49,
'z': 50}
```

Our RNN accepts sequences of characters as an input and outputs such similar sequences. Let's now break up our data source into such sequences.

```
seq_length = 100
list_X = [ ]
list_Y = [ ]
for i in range(0, len(chars) - seq_length, 1):
    seq_in = raw_text[i:i + seq_length]
    seq_out = raw_text[i + seq_length]
    list_X.append([char_to_int[char] for char in seq_in])
    list_Y.append(char_to_int[seq_out])
n_patterns = len(list_X)
```

We have to do a little bit more to get our input perfectly ready for our model:

```
X = np.reshape(list_X, (n_patterns, seq_length, 1))
# Encode output as one-hot vector
Y = np_utils.to_categorical(list_Y)
```

We do this because we want to predict one character at a time, which means we would want one-shot encoding, which is what the `np_utils.to_categorical` function does. For example, when we want to encode the letter m with the index 37, it would look like this:

```
[ 0. 0. 0. 0. 0. 0. 0. 0. 0. 0. 0. 0. 0. 0. 0. 0. 0. 0.
  0. 0. 0. 0. 0. 0. 0. 0. 0. 0. 0. 0. 0. 0. 0. 0. 0. 0.
  1. 0. 0. 0. 0. 0. 0. 0. 0. 0. 0. 0. 0. 0.]
```

Let's now define our neural network model.

```
model = Sequential()
model.add(LSTM(256, input_shape=(X.shape[1], X.shape[2])))
model.add(Dropout(0.2))
model.add(Dense(y.shape[1], activation='softmax'))
model.compile(loss='categorical_crossentropy', optimizer='adam')
```

In this case, we have defined an LSTM with one layer (which we create with `Dense`), and a Dropout of 0.2, SoftMax activation, and the ADAM optimizer.

Dropout is a value used to control *overfitting* when a neural network only performs well only on one dataset. Activation methods decide at what value we *activate* a neuron in a network, and optimizers are used to reduce the error overtime we navigate back and forth over a neural network.

Indeed, choosing these hyperparameters ends up being a matter of practice and fine-tuning, though we will briefly mention how to choose appropriate parameters for your particular text processing task in the next chapter. For the moment, it is sufficient to treat this a black-box, while understanding the intuition behind it. Note that the hyperparameters used here are the standard parameters for text generation using Keras.

Training our model is easy – like scikit-learn, we run the fit function to do this.

```
filepath="weights-improvement-{epoch:02d}-{loss:.4f}.hdf5"
checkpoint = ModelCheckpoint(filepath, monitor='loss', verbose=1,
save_best_only=True, mode='min')
callbacks_list = [checkpoint]
# fit the model
model.fit(X, y, epochs=20, batch_size=128, callbacks=callbacks_list)
```

The fit function will run the input batchwase n_epochs number of times, and it will save the weights to a file whenever there is an improvement. This is taken care of through the callback.

You should be done with training after running fit – keep in mind that based on the size of the dataset used this could take hours or even days.

Another option is to simply load the weights of an already pretrained model:

```
filename = "weights.hdf5"
model.load_weights(filename)
model.compile(loss='categorical_crossentropy', optimizer='adam')
```

So now, with either our loaded weights or with a trained model, we are ready to generate text character by character!

```
start   = np.random.randint(0, len(X) - 1)
pattern = np.ravel(X[start]).tolist()
```

We wish to start our text generation randomly, so we use numpy to find this character within our range.

```
output = []
for i in range(250):
    x          = np.reshape(pattern, (1, len(pattern), 1))
    x          = x / float(vocab_size)
    prediction = model.predict(x, verbose = 0)
    index      = np.argmax(prediction)
    result     = index
    output.append(result)
    pattern.append(index)
```

```
    pattern = pattern[1 : len(pattern)]
print (""", ''.join([ix_to_char[value] for value in output]), """)
```

What happened here? Based on our input, x, we choose the highest probability for the next character (using argmax, which is a method to return the indie of the maximum value), and then convert that index to a character, and append it to our output list. Based on how many iterations we want to see in our output, we run that many loops.

In the LSTM example, we have just seen, we have not trained a massive network – by stacking further layers on top, we can start seeing even better results. We have already seen in our example that after a few epochs our model starts performing a lot, lot better. Indeed, Andrej Karpathy's blog demonstrates this particularly well, and with a wide variety of inputs, from Shakespeare to the Linux code base!

Further pruning of the input data would give us even better results, as well as increasing the number of epochs. Of course, adding more layers or increasing the number of epochs would increase our training time – if our mission is just to experiment with RNNs and not build a scalable or in the production model, Keras does a very good job.

Summary

We saw the incredible power of deep learning first hand – we could successfully train a neural network to generate text that very much resembles human-produced text, if at least in its syntax and to some extent, grammar and spelling. With more fine-tuning and maybe a little bit of human supervision, we can see how we can create very realistic chatbots with this kind of technology.

While this kind of text analysis may not seem particularly *useful* for us, neural networks find a lot of use in more practical text analysis tasks, such as in text classification or text clustering. We will be exploring these kinds of tasks in our next chapter – in particular, text classification using Keras and using spaCy.

We present the following links to the reader before moving on to the next chapter; they are blog posts discussing effective strategies when dealing with text generation using deep learning.

1. NLP Best Practices [16]
2. Deep Learning and Representations [17]
3. Unreasonable Effectiveness of Neural Networks [10]
4. Best of 2017 for NLP and DL [18]

References

[1] Perceptron:
https://en.wikipedia.org/wiki/Perceptron

[2] Feedforward Neural Network:
https://en.wikipedia.org/wiki/Feedforward_neural_network

[3] Biologically Inspired Computing:
https://en.wikipedia.org/wiki/Bio-inspired_computing

[4] By Glosser.ca - Own work, Derivative of File:Artificial neural network.svg, CC BY-SA 3.0:
https://commons.wikimedia.org/w/index.php?curid=24913461

[5] Zero-Shot Translation with Google's Multilingual Neural Machine Translation System:
https://research.googleblog.com/2016/11/zero-shot-translation-with-googles.html

[6] Convolutional Neural Network:
https://en.wikipedia.org/wiki/Convolutional_neural_network

[7] Recurrent Neural Network:
https://en.wikipedia.org/wiki/Recurrent_neural_network

[8] Reinforcement Learning:
https://en.wikipedia.org/wiki/Reinforcement_learning

[9] LSTM:
https://en.wikipedia.org/wiki/Long_short-term_memory

[10] The Unreasonable Effectiveness of RNNs:
http://karpathy.github.io/2015/05/21/rnn-effectiveness/

[11] Understanding LSTM networks:
http://colah.github.io/posts/2015-08-Understanding-LSTMs/

[12] Lasagne:
https://github.com/Lasagne/Lasagne

[13] Blocks:
https://github.com/mila-udem/blocks

[14] Caffe:
http://caffe.berkeleyvision.org/tutorial/net_layer_blob.html

[15] Text Generation:
`https://github.com/kirit93/Personal/blob/master/text_generation_keras/text_generation.ipynb`

[16] Deep Learning for NLP best practices:
`http://ruder.io/deep-learning-nlp-best-practices/index.html`

[17] Deep Learning, NLP, and Representations:
`http://colah.github.io/posts/2014-07-NLP-RNNs-Representations/`

[18] Deep Learning 2017:
`https://tryolabs.com/blog/2017/12/12/deep-learning-for-nlp-advancements-and-trends-in-2017/`

14
Keras and spaCy for Deep Learning

In the previous chapter we introduced you to deep learning techniques for text, and to get a taste of using neural networks, we attempted to generate text using an RNN. In this chapter, we will take a closer look at deep learning for text, and in particular, how to set up a Keras model that can perform classification, as well as how to incorporate deep learning into spaCy pipelines.

Here are few useful links:

1. Keras Sequential model [1]
2. Keras CNN LSTM [2]
3. Pre-trained word embeddings [3]

Keras and spaCy

In the previous chapter, we already discussed various deep learning frameworks - in this chapter, we will discuss a little more in detail about one, in particular, Keras, while also exploring how we can use deep learning with spaCy.

During our attempts at text generation, we already used Keras, but did not explain the motivation behind using the library, or indeed even how or why we constructed our model the way we did. We will attempt to demystify this, as well as set up a neural network model that will aid us in text classification.

In our brief review of the various deep learning frameworks available in Python, we described Keras as a high-level library which allows us to easily construct neural networks.

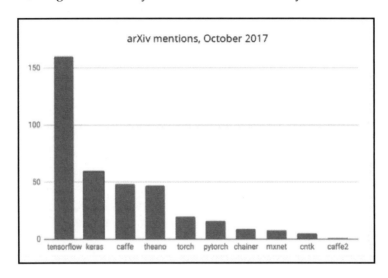

Fig 14.1 The arXiv mentions of Keras. arXiv is a website where researchers upload research papers before it is accepted by a journal. Here, the *x*-axes are the different Python deep learning libraries, and the *y*-axis is the number of references of that library by the papers on arXiv

Keras happens to be all this and much more and offers one of the cleanest APIs for generating very complex learning systems. Only Tensorflow is cited more on arXiv, and even in industry, Keras is widely used. It comes packaged with Tensorflow as `tf.keras`, which means it is backed by Google, and its CNTK [4] backend is supported by Microsoft. CNTK is another backend that can be used to build neural networks, but we will not be using it or going into detail about it, as it is not as supported or widely used as Tensorflow or Theano. Being able to use multiple backends (Theano, Tensorflow, and CNTK) makes it a very flexible framework to adapt. There are a wide user base and active community, which means that getting your problems solved on StackOverflow or GitHub is highly likely, and it is also easy to put your model into production. For example, iOS development is supported by Apple's **CoreML** [5], where Apple provides support for Keras.

But the reason we, as text analysis practitioners, are interested in Keras is how easy it is to perform text analysis tasks with Keras. We have mentioned throughout the book how important preprocessing is when it comes to text analysis - Keras has a class on preprocessing, and even a sub-module [6] more focused on text preprocessing. When cleaning text for deep learning purposes, the context can be slightly different. For example, for text generation, we don't remove stop words or stem words, because we want the model to predict what will look like *real* text. In this chapter, we will focus on classification, where we will follow more or less the same preprocessing we did before.

When we previously mentioned neural networks, we used the terms models, and how these models are made of an input, one or several layers, and an output. These layers consist of neurons (or nodes) that are interconnected in different ways. Different kinds of neural networks have different ways of being connected - for example, a **Convolutional Neural Network** is what is considered a dense network, with multiple connections between the layers and the nodes. A **Recurrent Neural Network**, which we used to generate text in the previous chapter, had resulted from previous nodes and layers appended, to build context. The performance of a neural network heavily depends on its architecture. Luckily for us, the architecture we intend to use for text and document classification is very well researched – we won't have to worry *too* much about our hyperparameters and *how* we intend to set up our neural network, as most of this has already been thoroughly researched (though with that being said, there is still a lot more to understand about neural networks!).

The Keras documentation is thorough, and worth having a look at. We will be describing some of the more important parts of Keras as and when we use it, but before we start with our examples, it is highly recommended for the user to go through the following links involving Keras:

1. **About Keras Models** [7]: This explains the various kinds of neural network models in Keras
2. **About Keras Layers** [8]: This discusses the various kinds of layers you can add to a Keras neural network
3. **Core Layers** (Dense) [9]: This is the documentation of the dense layer in Keras
4. **Keras Datasets** [10]: This is the list explaining and documenting various Keras datasets
5. **LSTMs** [11]: This has more detail about the Keras LSTM module
6. **Convolutional Layers** [12]: This has More detail about the Keras convolutional layer

We will be learning how to classify sequences and documents in this chapter, so some reading about Dense layers, LSTMs, and RNNs from the preceding links will give you the background to breeze through the coming examples.

We will be using Sequential models for our classifier - this simply means that it is a simpler neural net with the layers stacked in order. It is worth having a look at the Keras documentation for sequential models [1] as well.

But before we get into the gritty details and code, let's briefly discuss spaCy and how it is linked to deep learning. While we didn't get into details when we trained custom spaCy models before, it was entirely based on deep learning techniques. We have mentioned before the spaCy's POS-tagger, NER-tagger, and parser. We must credit spaCy's smooth training APIs here - we are allowed to treat the model doing the training as a black box and focus on just the training data or what kind of new information we intend to train. But with that being said, we can *still* play around with the model, with the ability to change various hyperparameters, such as regularizes or the dropout rate. A quick reminder: dropout rate is the hyperparamter that controls overfitting and makes sure that our neural network doesn't perform well only on the training dataset.

From a purely technical point of view, using Doc2Vec to vectorize your documents and then classifying them using a standard statistical classifier (such as the Naive Bayes classifier) can also be considered as a machine learning system employing neural networks/deep learning; however, in this chapter we will attempt to build a classifier system where the final classification task is performed by a neural network.

spaCy allows us to use its built-in `TextCategorizer` component, where we train it in a manner similar to its other components such as POS or NER tagging. It also seamlessly integrates with other word embeddings such as Gensim's Word2Vec or GloVe, as well as allows us to plug in a Keras model if we would like. Using spaCy and Keras in tandem can allow us to leverage a very powerful classification machine - and now that we have the theory and ideas out of the way, let's jump into the code!

Classification with Keras

For our experiments, we will be using the IMDB sentiment classification task. This is quite the small dataset - we are using it for the convenience of loading it and using it, as it is easily available via Keras. It is very important to understand here that for datasets of the size we are using, it is *not* the best idea to use a **Deep Neural Network** for classification - indeed, we might even get better results with a simple bag of words followed by a **Support Vector Machine** (SVM) doing the classification. The purpose of the following examples is to rather allow the user to understand *how* to construct a neural network using Keras, and how to make predictions using it. The fine tuning of the neural network and studying its hyperparameters is a different ball game altogether and is not the focus of this chapter. Another thing to remember when working with text data and neural networks is that in almost all cases, more data is better and that neural networks are far better suited to tackle problems with a lot more data to work with.

We will be following the code and examples from the `Keras/examples` folder [13] to help us - this gives the opportunity for the readers to verify their code or run the examples as a whole. We start with the sequential model you can find `here` [17]:

Let's first set up our imports:

```
from keras.preprocessing import sequence
from keras.models import Sequential
from keras.layers import Dense, Embedding
from keras.layers import LSTM
from keras.datasets import imdb
```

The following are some notes:

1. We are not using the text preprocessing modules in this example because we will be using a dataset which is included in Keras (IMDB).
2. We will be using an LSTM for the classification task, which is a variant of a recurrent neural network. We previously came across this in our text generation tasks.
3. We imported `Sequential` from the model's module. Our LSTM here is merely a layer, and the type of model is a simple sequential model. `Dense` is a layer of regularly connected neurons.

```
max_features = 20000
maxlen = 80  # cut texts after this number of words (among top max_features
most common words)
batch_size = 32
print('Loading data...')
(x_train, y_train), (x_test, y_test) =
imdb.load_data(num_words=max_features)
print(len(x_train), 'train sequences')
print(len(x_test), 'test sequences')
print('Pad sequences (samples x time)')
x_train = sequence.pad_sequences(x_train, maxlen=maxlen)
x_test = sequence.pad_sequences(x_test, maxlen=maxlen)
print('x_train shape:', x_train.shape)
print('x_test shape:', x_test.shape)
```

The `max_features` variable here refers to the top words we wish to use from the dataset - we limit this to `20000` words here. This is similar to getting rid of least used words, a technique we discussed previously during text preprocessing. The `maxlen` variable is used when we are creating our sequences from the dataset - we need to fix the length of sequences as the neural network accepts a fixed length as input. The `batch_size` variable is later used to specify the number of batches during training, which is an empirically measured value. The print statements in the code are for the user to manually inspect the size of the data (we can see it isn't so large!).

We then split our data into training and testing and print the sizes for this.

```
print('Build model...')
model = Sequential()
model.add(Embedding(max_features, 128))
model.add(LSTM(128, dropout=0.2, recurrent_dropout=0.2))
model.add(Dense(1, activation='sigmoid'))
```

And this is it - in 4 lines of code we've built up a neural network! The first line sets up our sequential model, after which we just keep stacking on what we need. In the first layer of stacking, we've put up word embeddings - this means from 20000 features, we've dropped straight down to 128. We'll find out soon that we can also use our own word embeddings, such as Word2Vec or GloVe vectors. Our next layer is the LSTM - we can see the number 128 there, which is our total number of dimensions that the neural network will be dealing with.

Here, the dropout argument is to prevent overfitting - here we use the default value, which happens to be 0.2. Since an LSTM is a recurrent neural network, we have a value for the recurrent dropout too. Our final layer is a standard `Dense` layer, with just one input (which happens to be the output from the LSTM). We use the sigmoid activation for this layer. An *activation* here refers to the activation function [14] used for that particular layer - you can read more about activation layers that Keras provides on their documentation page [15]. We can understand them as the way the neural network decides to accept an input, and what kind of output it provides. That's it then - we've constructed our first neural network!

Of course, it isn't ready for us to start any kind of prediction or classification - we still must compile and fit it before any prediction.

```
# try using different optimizers and different optimizer configs
model.compile(loss='binary_crossentropy',
              optimizer='adam',
              metrics=['accuracy'])
```

```
print('Train...')
model.fit(x_train, y_train,
          batch_size=batch_size,
          epochs=15,
          validation_data=(x_test, y_test))
```

A heads up – this is some intense training you will be doing, and it could take between 30 minutes to an hour if you are running this on a CPU.

And voila! We're done training and fitting our model. This means that we are now ready to predict. You would have noticed when we ran the `compile` method we used `binary_crossentropy` as our loss and `adam` as our optimizer for the same. All neural networks need a loss function and optimizer to learn. We can understand loss here as the way it learns how far away the predictions of the neural network are from the truth and the optimizer as the way it adjusts its weights to get better results.

Let's first test how well our model works – Keras allows us to very easily verify this with the `evaluate` function. Let's have a quick look at how well our model works.

```
score, acc = model.evaluate(x_test, y_test,
                            batch_size=batch_size)

print('Test score:', score)
print('Test accuracy:', acc)
```

For a neural network, we just cooked up in 4 lines, not so bad, eh? We are soon going to see what else we can do with Keras - let's now build a convolutional neural network, which has a little more complexity in it. The neural network we built was trained on the IMDB dataset for text classification, so it is now equipped with the power to classify documents based on sentiment. It was also a sequential neural network - we will now build a convolutional neural network.

For the convolutional neural network, we will need a few more parameters to fine tune our network. We are following the code from this example [18] on the Keras GitHub page.

```
from keras.preprocessing import sequence
from keras.models import Sequential
from keras.layers import Dense, Dropout, Activation
from keras.layers import Embedding
from keras.layers import LSTM
from keras.layers import Conv1D, MaxPooling1D
from keras.datasets import imdb
```

We have some new imports over here which we should keep an eye out for – in particular, separate modules for `Dropout`, `Activation`, and for our convolutional net, `Conv1D`, and `MaxPooling1D`.

```
# Convolution
kernel_size = 5
filters = 64
pool_size = 4
# Embedding
max_features = 20000
maxlen = 100
embedding_size = 128
# LSTM
lstm_output_size = 70
# Training
batch_size = 30
epochs = 2
```

We notice a bunch of new variables right in the start – these are all for the convolutional layer, and at this point, we will have to ask the reader to trust our choice in setting these constants – these variables usually end up affecting the training quite heavily and are empirically derived after experiments. We've come across the other variables/arguments in the previous example.

```
print('Build model...')
model = Sequential()
model.add(Embedding(max_features, embedding_size, input_length=maxlen))
model.add(Dropout(0.25))
model.add(Conv1D(filters,
                 kernel_size,
                 padding='valid',
                 activation='relu',
                 strides=1))
model.add(MaxPooling1D(pool_size=pool_size))
model.add(LSTM(lstm_output_size))
model.add(Dense(1))
model.add(Activation('sigmoid'))
```

We see immediately that this model has a lot more complexity than the previous one. We can understand complexity to be the number of layers, and we have 7 layers added up here. We see there is a separate dropout layer here - again, like previous cases, this is to prevent overfitting. We then add our first convolutional layer - this is where the variables/arguments we mentioned before kick in.

The pooling layer we soon add is also part of our convolutional architecture. The Stanford course on convolutional neural networks describes the function of a pooling layer as - its function is to progressively reduce the spatial size of the representation to reduce the number of parameters and computation in the network, and hence to also control overfitting [16]. The remaining layers we've already seen before, though we also explicitly add an `Activation` function for our network, which like last time, is the `sigmoid` function. This completes the setup of our network - we can now proceed to compiling and training. We use the same loss and optimizer methods as our last neural network.

```
model.compile(loss='binary_crossentropy',
              optimizer='adam',
              metrics=['accuracy'])
print('Train...')
model.fit(x_train, y_train,
          batch_size=batch_size,
          epochs=epochs,
          validation_data=(x_test, y_test))
score, acc = model.evaluate(x_test, y_test, batch_size=batch_size)
print('Test score:', score)
print('Test accuracy:', acc)
```

We can see the extra layers added some punch to our network, didn't it? We can see our improved accuracies. Along with the improved accuracies, we can also see our training time has increased to more than 30 minutes on a CPU.

We previously mentioned how using pretrained word embeddings in a classifier can improve the results - Keras allows us to use these results, and quite easily too. In our chapter on word embeddings (Chapter 12, *Word2Vec, Doc2Vec, and Gensim*), we discussed GloVe word embeddings - if you still have them downloaded, we can get going right away. We will be following the code found in this example [19].

```
BASE_DIR = ''" # you would have to paste the actual directory of where your
GloVe file is over here.
GLOVE_DIR = os.path.join(BASE_DIR, 'glove.6B')
MAX_SEQUENCE_LENGTH = 1000
MAX_NUM_WORDS = 20000
EMBEDDING_DIM = 100
```

We will be using the preceding variables/arguments to help load our word embeddings. Our first step is to access these embeddings from the file and index them.

```
print('Indexing word vectors.')
embeddings_index = {}
with open(os.path.join(GLOVE_DIR, 'glove.6B.100d.txt')) as f:
    for line in f:
```

```
        values = line.split()
        word = values[0]
        coefs = np.asarray(values[1:], dtype='float32')
        embeddings_index[word] = coefs
print('Found %s word vectors.' % len(embeddings_index))
```

A simple loop through the embeddings file was all that was needed to set this up. We now set up a matrix that will help us actually use the embeddings.

```
print('Preparing embedding matrix.')

# prepare embedding matrix
num_words = min(MAX_NUM_WORDS, len(word_index) + 1)
embedding_matrix = np.zeros((num_words, EMBEDDING_DIM))
for word, i in word_index.items():
    if i >= MAX_NUM_WORDS:
        continue
    embedding_vector = embeddings_index.get(word)
    if embedding_vector is not None:
        # words not found in embedding index will be all-zeros.
        embedding_matrix[i] = embedding_vector
```

We are now ready to use our embeddings in our model – it is important to make sure that we set the training argument to false, so we are using the word vectors as is.

```
embedding_layer = Embedding(num_words,
                            EMBEDDING_DIM,
                            weights=[embedding_matrix],
                            input_length=MAX_SEQUENCE_LENGTH,
                            trainable=False)
```

With the embedding layer set up, our model is almost done – we now follow a pattern very similar to what we used before.

```
print('Training model.')

# train a 1D convnet with global maxpooling
sequence_input = Input(shape=(MAX_SEQUENCE_LENGTH,), dtype='int32')
embedded_sequences = embedding_layer(sequence_input)
x = Conv1D(128, 5, activation='relu')(embedded_sequences)
x = MaxPooling1D(5)(x)
x = Conv1D(128, 5, activation='relu')(x)
x = MaxPooling1D(5)(x)
x = Conv1D(128, 5, activation='relu')(x)
x = GlobalMaxPooling1D()(x)
x = Dense(128, activation='relu')(x)
preds = Dense(len(labels_index), activation='softmax')(x)
```

In this example, we stack up our layers slightly differently, with the x variable *holding* each layer. The `preds` variable is our final layer that contains all the previous layers. We set up our model with the `Model` class, and now we are good to go!

```
model = Model(sequence_input, preds)
model.compile(loss='categorical_crossentropy',
              optimizer='rmsprop',
              metrics=['acc'])
model.fit(x_train, y_train,
          batch_size=128,
          epochs=10,
          validation_data=(x_val, y_val))
```

Notice here that we used a different measure for calculating the loss; we encourage the reader to try different loses and optimizers themselves to get a feel for it. We've seen examples of a basic LSTM, a convolutional neural network, and a convolutional neural network which uses pretrained word embeddings. We can also see the progressive increase in the performance of each of these networks. Embeddings are particularly useful to us when we do not have much training data – we have previously read how word embeddings learn context; we use this same context to inject some extra prediction power into our network.

Generally, the convolutional model will perform better than a sequential model, and the model using the word embeddings performs even better. This makes sense; word embeddings add more context to the model and better describes each word from a computational point of view, we have discussed this in Chapter 12, *Word2Vec, Doc2Vec, and Gensim*. As for when to use which model, if we have access to word embeddings trained on a dataset with a context similar to that we are going to classify, and if we have computers powerful enough to train a neural network, we might as well use a convolutional network for our classification tasks. Like any machine learning task, it is also worth training another model which is more simple, such as a support vector machine or a Naive Bayes classifier. After we examine the performance and accuracies, we can choose which model to use in our final pipeline.

Keras gives us the ease of use, flexibility, and power to build neural networks at will. Deep learning papers published on arXiv often link to GitHub repositories with Keras code examples, and having gone through this chapter and the previous one should give you the ability to easily understand how these neural networks are built.

Classification with spaCy

While Keras works especially well in standalone text classification tasks, sometimes it might be useful to use Keras in tandem with spaCy, which works exceedingly well in text analysis. In Chapter 3, *spaCy's Language Models*, Chapter 5, *POS-Tagging and Its Applications*, Chapter 6, *NER-Tagging and Its Applications*, and Chapter 7, *Dependency Parsing*, we already saw how well spaCy works with textual data, and it is no exception when it comes to deep learning – its text oriented approach makes it easy to build a classifier that works well with text. There are two ways to perform text classification with spaCy – one is using its own neural network library, thinc, while the other uses Keras. Both the examples we will explain are from spaCy's documentation, and it is highly recommended that you check out the original examples!

The first example we will be exploring can be found on the spaCy example page, and is titled deep_learning_keras.py [20]. In the example, we use an LSTM for the sentiment classification task. This will be a Keras-trained model. This model is trained to classify sentences, and the scores and then aggregated so that we can then classify documents. It is more difficult to perform this kind of hierarchical aggregation using pure Keras or Tensorflow, so this is a good example to observe the power of spaCy.

```
import plac
import random
import pathlib
import cytoolz
import numpy
from keras.models import Sequential, model_from_json
from keras.layers import LSTM, Dense, Embedding, Bidirectional
from keras.layers import TimeDistributed
from keras.optimizers import Adam
import thinc.extra.datasets
from spacy.compat import pickle
import spacy
```

We should be able to recognize most of these imports, having used them with Keras or spaCy before.

```
class SentimentAnalyser(object):
    @classmethod
    def load(cls, path, nlp, max_length=100):
        with (path / 'config.json').open() as file_:
            model = model_from_json(file_.read())
        with (path / 'model').open('rb') as file_:
            lstm_weights = pickle.load(file_)
        embeddings = get_embeddings(nlp.vocab)
```

```
model.set_weights([embeddings] + lstm_weights)
return cls(model, max_length=max_length)
def __init__(self, model, max_length=100):
    self._model = model
    self.max_length = max_length
def __call__(self, doc):
    X = get_features([doc], self.max_length)
    y = self._model.predict(X)
    self.set_sentiment(doc, y)
```

The first few lines just set up our class and instruct how to load our model and our embedding weights. We then initialize the model, maximum length, and set up instructions to predict. The `load` method returns the loaded model, which we use in the evaluate method to set up our pipeline. We initialize the class with the model and maximum length. The `call` method gets the features and the prediction. We continue our explanation after the next block of code, which is the `pipe` method. Note that it is a not a new code file, but a method of the `SentimentAnalyser` class; do make it a point to look at this link [21] for the entire code!

```
def pipe(self, docs, batch_size=1000, n_threads=2):
    for minibatch in cytoolz.partition_all(batch_size, docs):
        minibatch = list(minibatch)
        sentences = []
        for doc in minibatch:
            sentences.extend(doc.sents)
        Xs = get_features(sentences, self.max_length)
        ys = self._model.predict(Xs)
        for sent, label in zip(sentences, ys):
            sent.doc.sentiment += label - 0.5
        for doc in minibatch:
            yield doc
def set_sentiment(self, doc, y):
    doc.sentiment = float(y[0])
```

The pipe method actually performs the prediction after splitting up our dataset into batches. We can see the `ys = self._model.predict(Xs)` line, which calculates the sentiment value. It also assigns a sentiment value to a document. Now that we have finished writing the `SentimentAnalyser` class, we will start writing methods that will help with our training.

```
def get_labelled_sentences(docs, doc_labels):
    labels = []
    sentences = []
    for doc, y in zip(docs, doc_labels):
        for sent in doc.sents:
            sentences.append(sent)
```

```
                labels.append(y)
            return sentences, numpy.asarray(labels, dtype='int32')
    def get_features(docs, max_length):
        docs = list(docs)
        Xs = numpy.zeros((len(docs), max_length), dtype='int32')
        for i, doc in enumerate(docs):
            j = 0
            for token in doc:
                vector_id = token.vocab.vectors.find(key=token.orth)
                if vector_id >= 0:
                    Xs[i, j] = vector_id
                else:
                    Xs[i, j] = 0
                j += 1
                if j >= max_length:
                    break
        return Xs
```

The methods for getting labeled sentences is fairly straightforward, with it returning
sentences and the appropriate label. The `get_features` method needs a little more
attention paid: you can notice it is where we construct our feature vector for each
document.

```
    def train(train_texts, train_labels, dev_texts, dev_labels,
            lstm_shape, lstm_settings, lstm_optimizer,
            batch_size=100, nb_epoch=5, by_sentence=True):
        nlp = spacy.load('en_vectors_web_lg')
        nlp.add_pipe(nlp.create_pipe('sentencizer'))
        embeddings = get_embeddings(nlp.vocab)
        model = compile_lstm(embeddings, lstm_shape, lstm_settings)
        train_docs = list(nlp.pipe(train_texts))
        dev_docs = list(nlp.pipe(dev_texts))
        if by_sentence:
            train_docs, train_labels =
get_labelled_sentences(train_docs, train_labels)
            dev_docs, dev_labels = get_labelled_sentences(dev_docs,
dev_labels)
        train_X = get_features(train_docs, lstm_shape['max_length'])
        dev_X = get_features(dev_docs, lstm_shape['max_length'])
        model.fit(train_X, train_labels, validation_data=(dev_X,
dev_labels),
                nb_epoch=nb_epoch, batch_size=batch_size)
        return model
```

It is easy to guess that the training method is where all our heavy lifting is happening – some important lines to notice here are the ones involving spaCy's pipeline, where we add a *sentencizer* to it. The lines following the setting up of the pipe involve compiling the LSTM (we will have a look at our model just below), in loading our word embeddings, and then receiving our features from our documents so we can proceed with training.

```python
def compile_lstm(embeddings, shape, settings):
    model = Sequential()
    model.add(
        Embedding(
            embeddings.shape[0],
            embeddings.shape[1],
            input_length=shape['max_length'],
            trainable=False,
            weights=[embeddings],
            mask_zero=True
        )
    )
    model.add(TimeDistributed(Dense(shape['nr_hidden'],
                                    use_bias=False)))
    model.add(Bidirectional(LSTM(shape['nr_hidden'],
                            recurrent_dropout=settings['dropout'],
                            dropout=settings['dropout'])))
    model.add(Dense(shape['nr_class'], activation='sigmoid'))
    model.compile(optimizer=Adam(lr=settings['lr']),
                  loss='binary_crossentropy',metrics=['accuracy'])
    return model
```

This part of the code should look more familiar to us – as we have done in the previous section, we set up each of our layers and stack them up. We can use any Keras model we would like to do this, and in this case, a bidirectional LSTM is used.

```python
def get_embeddings(vocab):
    return vocab.vectors.data
def evaluate(model_dir, texts, labels, max_length=100):
    def create_pipeline(nlp):
        '''
        This could be a lambda, but named functions are easier
        to read in Python.
        '''
        return [nlp.tagger, nlp.parser,
                SentimentAnalyser.load(model_dir, nlp,
                max_length=max_length)]
    nlp = spacy.load('en')
    nlp.pipeline = create_pipeline(nlp)
    correct = 0
    i = 0
```

```
for doc in nlp.pipe(texts, batch_size=1000, n_threads=4):
    correct += bool(doc.sentiment >= 0.5) == bool(labels[i])
    i += 1
return float(correct) / i
```

The evaluate method returns a score of how well our model performed; the code is fairly straightforward and merely checks the assigned sentiment score with the label of the document.

```
def read_data(data_dir, limit=0):
    examples = []
    for subdir, label in (('pos', 1), ('neg', 0)):
        for filename in (data_dir / subdir).iterdir():
            with filename.open() as file_:
                text = file_.read()
            examples.append((text, label))
    random.shuffle(examples)
    if limit >= 1:
        examples = examples[:limit]
    return zip(*examples) # Unzips into two lists
```

We use the IMDB sentiment analysis dataset; this method is an interface to access this data.

```
@plac.annotations(
    train_dir=("Location of training file or directory"),
    dev_dir=("Location of development file or directory"),
    model_dir=("Location of output model directory",),
    is_runtime=("Demonstrate run-time usage", "flag", "r", bool),
    nr_hidden=("Number of hidden units", "option", "H", int),
    max_length=("Maximum sentence length", "option", "L", int),
    dropout=("Dropout", "option", "d", float),
    learn_rate=("Learn rate", "option", "e", float),
    nb_epoch=("Number of training epochs", "option", "i", int),
    batch_size=("Size of minibatches for training LSTM", "option", "b",
int),
    nr_examples=("Limit to N examples", "option", "n", int)
)
```

The preceding annotations set up our options which sets the various model directories, runtime, and the parameters for the model. Let's move on to the main function now.

```
def main(model_dir=None, train_dir=None, dev_dir=None,
         is_runtime=False,
         nr_hidden=64, max_length=100, # Shape
         dropout=0.5, learn_rate=0.001, # General NN config
         nb_epoch=5, batch_size=100, nr_examples=-1):  # Training params
    if model_dir is not None:
        model_dir = pathlib.Path(model_dir)
```

```
        if train_dir is None or dev_dir is None:
            imdb_data = thinc.extra.datasets.imdb()
    if is_runtime:
        if dev_dir is None:
            dev_texts, dev_labels = zip(*imdb_data[1])
        else:
            dev_texts, dev_labels = read_data(dev_dir)
        acc = evaluate(model_dir, dev_texts, dev_labels,
                        max_length=max_length)
        print(acc)
    else:
        if train_dir is None:
            train_texts, train_labels = zip(*imdb_data[0])
        else:
            print("Read data")
            train_texts, train_labels = read_data(train_dir,
                                        limit=nr_examples)
        if dev_dir is None:
            dev_texts, dev_labels = zip(*imdb_data[1])
        else:
            dev_texts, dev_labels = read_data(dev_dir, imdb_data,
                                    limit=nr_examples)
        train_labels = numpy.asarray(train_labels, dtype='int32')
        dev_labels = numpy.asarray(dev_labels, dtype='int32')
        lstm = train(train_texts, train_labels, dev_texts, dev_labels,
                    {'nr_hidden': nr_hidden, 'max_length': max_length,
                     'nr_class': 1},
                    {'dropout': dropout, 'lr': learn_rate},
                    {},
                    nb_epoch=nb_epoch, batch_size=batch_size)
        weights = lstm.get_weights()
        if model_dir is not None:
            with (model_dir / 'model').open('wb') as file_:
                pickle.dump(weights[1:], file_)
            with (model_dir / 'config.json').open('wb') as file_:
                file_.write(lstm.to_json())
if __name__ == '__main__':
    plac.call(main)
```

Don't let the size of the main function scare you – you can notice that the first few lines set up the model folder and will load the dataset. We then check if we wish to print run time information, in which case we run the evaluate method. If not, and training is not complete, we proceed to train our model. The lstm.train() method trains the model and then if the model folder is not undefined, we save our model.

Running, saving and using the model in your own production pipelines is a huge motivation behind using Keras and spaCy in such a way. The key takeaway here is that we are updating the `sentiment` attribute for each doc. How we decide to use this is up to us. One of the main selling points of the spaCy implementation is that it does not remove or truncate the inputs - the writers argue that doing so negatively affects the results because users tend to sum up their review in the last sentence of the document, and a lot of the sentiment can be inferred from this sentence.

So now that we have our trained model, how do we use it? Our model now adds one more attribute to our document, which is the `doc.sentiment` attribute. This value captures the sentiment of the document. The user can verify this by later loading the saved model and running any document through the pipeline the same way we did in Chapter 5, *POS-Tagging and Its Applications,* Chapter 6, *NER-Tagging and Its Applications,* and Chapter 7, *Dependency Parsing:*

```
doc = nlp(document)
```

Here, `nlp` is the pipeline object of the loaded model which we just trained, and the document is any unicode text we wish to analyze. The doc object now contains information about the sentiment.

We can also train a more traditional classifier based on the probability of a document belonging to a particular class. The training is extremely simple to perform - the `update` method which is part of the pipeline is what does the actual training. The example code in the documentation can be found here [21], and the code on GitHub can be found here [22]. We will be walking the reader through the code, and highly encourage the user to run the code and to have a look at what it adds to the pipeline. Note that this file is meant to be ran all at once, and we have only *split-up* the code so that we can explain it. When testing the code, run the file which can be found here [22].

```
import plac
import random
from pathlib import Path
import thinc.extra.datasets
import spacy
from spacy.util import minibatch, compounding
```

These imports are what we are used to seeing, but we do not have Keras here as we will be using the in-built `thinc` library.

```
@plac.annotations(
    model=("Model name. Defaults to blank 'en' model.", "option", "m",
            str),
    output_dir=("Optional output directory", "option", "o", Path),
```

```
    n_texts=("Number of texts to train from", "option", "t", int),
    n_iter=("Number of training iterations", "option", "n", int))
def main(model=None, output_dir=None, n_iter=20, n_texts=2000):
    if model is not None:
        nlp = spacy.load(model)  # load existing spaCy model
        print("Loaded model '%s'" % model)
    else:
        nlp = spacy.blank('en')  # create blank Language class
        print("Created blank 'en' model")
```

We have set up the annotations during printing, as well as loaded the model. If we don't pass a model, we can initiate an empty model.

```
    if 'textcat' not in nlp.pipe_names:
        textcat = nlp.create_pipe('textcat')
        nlp.add_pipe(textcat, last=True)
    # otherwise, get it, so we can add labels to it
    else:
        textcat = nlp.get_pipe('textcat')


    # add label to text classifier
    textcat.add_label('POSITIVE')
```

We now add a text categorizer label to our pipeline if it doesn't already exist – and if it does exist, we get it and add a sample label to it.

```
    print("Loading IMDB data...")
    (train_texts, train_cats), (dev_texts, dev_cats) =
load_data(limit=n_texts)
    print("Using {} examples ({} training, {} evaluation)"
    .format(n_texts, len(train_texts), len(dev_texts)))
    train_data = list(zip(train_texts,
                    [{'cats': cats} for cats in train_cats]))
```

We're now playing with our dataset – we've loaded our dataset, and then stored the training data.

```
        other_pipes = [pipe for pipe in nlp.pipe_names if pipe !=
                'textcat']
```

Before we start any training, we first disable all the other parts of the pipeline.

```
        with nlp.disable_pipes(*other_pipes):
            optimizer = nlp.begin_training()
            print("Training the model...")
            print('{:^5}t{:^5}t{:^5}t{:^5}'.format('LOSS', 'P', 'R', 'F'))
            for i in range(n_iter):
```

```
losses = {}
# batch up the examples using spaCy's minibatch
batches = minibatch(train_data, size=compounding(4., 32.,
                        1.001))
for batch in batches:
    texts, annotations = zip(*batch)
    nlp.update(texts, annotations, sgd=optimizer, drop=0.2,
               losses=losses)
```

We will be using batches to train our data, similar to previous examples. The `nlp.update` method is the heart of all the code and performs the training using the training information and annotations.

```
with textcat.model.use_params(optimizer.averages):
    # evaluate on the dev data split off in load_data()
scores = evaluate(nlp.tokenizer, textcat, dev_texts, dev_cats)
    print('{0:.3f}t{1:.3f}t{2:.3f}t{3:.3f}'
    # print a simple table
        .format(losses['textcat'], scores['textcat_p'],
        scores['textcat_r'], scores['textcat_f']))


if output_dir is not None:
    output_dir = Path(output_dir)
    if not output_dir.exists():
        output_dir.mkdir()
    nlp.to_disk(output_dir)
    print("Saved model to", output_dir)

    # test the saved model
    print("Loading from", output_dir)
    nlp2 = spacy.load(output_dir)
    doc2 = nlp2(test_text)
    print(test_text, doc2.cats)
```

We then test our model with the evaluate method, which calculates precision, recall, and f-score values. The last part of the main function is saving the trained model in an output directory if specified, and in testing the saved model.

```
def load_data(limit=0, split=0.8):
    """Load data from the IMDB dataset."""
    # Partition off part of the train data for evaluation
    train_data, _ = thinc.extra.datasets.imdb()
    random.shuffle(train_data)
    train_data = train_data[-limit:]
    texts, labels = zip(*train_data)
    cats = [{'POSITIVE': bool(y)} for y in labels]
    split = int(len(train_data) * split)
```

```
        return (texts[:split], cats[:split]), (texts[split:], cats[split:])
def evaluate(tokenizer, textcat, texts, cats):
    docs = (tokenizer(text) for text in texts)
    tp = 1e-8   # True positives
    fp = 1e-8   # False positives
    fn = 1e-8   # False negatives
    tn = 1e-8   # True negatives
    for i, doc in enumerate(textcat.pipe(docs)):
        gold = cats[i]
        for label, score in doc.cats.items():
            if label not in gold:
                continue
            if score >= 0.5 and gold[label] >= 0.5:
                tp += 1.
            elif score >= 0.5 and gold[label] < 0.5:
                fp += 1.
            elif score < 0.5 and gold[label] < 0.5:
                tn += 1
            elif score < 0.5 and gold[label] >= 0.5:
                fn += 1
    precision = tp / (tp + fp)
    recall = tp / (tp + fn)
    f_score = 2 * (precision * recall) / (precision + recall)
    return {'textcat_p': precision, 'textcat_r': recall, 'textcat_f':
f_score}
if __name__ == '__main__':
    plac.call(main)
```

We've come across these methods earlier in the main function; one is to load the dataset, and the other to evaluate the performance of our trained model. We use the dataset which comes bundled with `thinc`, and return the data appropriately shuffled and split. The evaluate function simply calculates the true negatives, true positives, false negatives, and false positives to create the measures for recall, precision, and f-measure.

```
test_text = "This movie disappointed me severely"
doc = nlp(test_text)
print(test_text, doc.cats)
```

The `doc.cats` parameter gives us the result of the classification – here, it is negative sentiment and is correctly classified as so.

This would be our final step – to test our model on a sample sentence. It is here we can also see one of the main advantages of using spaCy for deep learning - it fits seamlessly in our pipeline, and the classification or sentiment score ends up being another attribute of the document. This is quite different to how we approach deep learning with Keras, where our purpose was to either generate text or to output probability vectors – it is simply a vector in, vector out method. It is, of course, possible to leverage this information as part of our text analysis pipeline, but the way spaCy does the training under the hood and learns attributes to the documents makes for a very easy way to include the information as part of any text analysis pipeline.

Summary

In the previous chapter we introduced our readers to deep learning for text, and in this chapter, we saw how we can leverage the power of deep learning in our own applications, whether we use Keras or spaCy. Knowing how to assign sentiment scores or classify our documents gives us a huge boost when designing intelligent text systems, and with pretrained models, we don't have to perform heavy computations every time we wish to make such a classification. It is now within our capacity to build a strong and varied text analysis pipeline!

In the next chapter, we will discuss two popular text analysis problems—sentiment analysis and building our own chatbot—and what possible approaches we can take to solve these problems.

References

[1] Keras Sequential Model:
`https://keras.io/getting-started/sequential-model-guide/`

[2] Keras CNN LSTM:
`https://github.com/keras-team/keras/blob/master/examples/imdb_cnn_lstm.py`

[3] Pre-trained Word Embeddings:
`https://blog.keras.io/using-pre-trained-word-embeddings-in-a-keras-model.html`

[4] CNTK:
`https://github.com/Microsoft/CNTK`

[5] Apple CoreML:
`https://developer.apple.com/documentation/coreml`

[6] Keras Text Processing:
`https://keras.io/preprocessing/text/`

[7] Keras Models:
`https://keras.io/models/about-keras-models/`

[8] Keras Layers:
`https://keras.io/layers/about-keras-layers/`

[9] Keras Core Layers:
`https://keras.io/layers/core/`

[10] Keras Datasets:
`https://keras.io/datasets/`

[11] Keras LSTM:
`https://keras.io/layers/recurrent/#lstm`

[12] Keras Convolutional Layers:
`https://keras.io/layers/convolutional/`

[13] Keras examples directory:
`https://github.com/keras-team/keras/tree/master/examples`

[14] Activation function:
`https://en.wikipedia.org/wiki/Activation_function`

[15] Keras Activation functions:
`https://keras.io/activations/`

[16] Pooling layer:
`http://cs231n.github.io/convolutional-networks/#pool`

[17] Sequential Example:
`https://github.com/keras-team/keras/blob/master/examples/imdb_bidirectional_lstm.py`

[18] Convolutional Example:
`https://github.com/keras-team/keras/blob/master/examples/imdb_cnn.py`

[19] Convolutional with embeddings:
`https://github.com/keras-team/keras/blob/master/examples/pretrained_word_embeddings.py`

[20] Deep Learning Keras:
`https://github.com/explosion/spaCy/blob/master/examples/deep_learning_keras.py`

[21] Text Classification Model spaCy:
`https://spacy.io/usage/training#section-textcat`

[22] Text Classification code:
`https://github.com/explosion/spacy/blob/master/examples/training/train_textcat.py`

15
Sentiment Analysis and ChatBots

By now, we are equipped with the skills needed to get started on text analysis projects and to also take a shot at more complicated, meatier projects. Two common text analysis projects that encapsulate a lot of the concepts we have explored throughout the book are sentiment analysis and chatbots. In fact, we've already touched upon all the methods we will be using for these projects, and this chapter will serve as a guide to how one can put up such an application on their own.

In this chapter, we will not be providing the code to how to build a chatbot or sentiment analysis pipeline from the first step to the last, but rather to introduce the reader to a variety of techniques which will help when setting up such a project. Following are the topics we will cover in this chapter:

- Sentiment analysis
- Mining data
- ChatBot

Sentiment analysis

Sentiment analysis is merely another term given to text classification or document classification – where the classifying *feature* happens to be the sentiment of the text. We can understand sentiment as a feeling or opinion about something – if we said *The movie was terrific!*, it means it expresses a positive sentiment or feeling, and if we say *The movie is terrible!*, it would be expressing negative sentiment or feeling. Here, sentiment usually refers to positive or negative sentiment, but this can, of course, be extended to include multiple *sentiments*, such as angry, sad, happy, and maybe even a *thoughtful* sentiment if we so wish. In other words, sentiment analysis tasks are simply classification tasks where each class is a kind of sentiment which we wish to analyze.

In fact, we have seen an example of sentiment analysis in the previous chapter, when we used Keras and spaCy together to build a deep learning pipeline. Sentiment analysis was performed by assigning probability distributions of positive and negative sentiment. In fact, even the examples using only Keras were classifying based on sentiment, but we approached the problem as a simple classification task and not as a sentiment analysis task. The example with spaCy was more explicit, where we assigned scores of sentiments to each document and then did the classification.

Based on what we intend to do with the information of the sentiment, we can approach our problem in different ways – though the core idea that we are simply using probabilities of which class a document will belong in remains the same. It is highly recommended for any sentiment analysis task to end up training your data according to its domain – identifying sentiment in tweets with an algorithm trained on movie reviews will not work as well as one trained on its own domain.

Sometimes it is helpful to prototype your text analysis pipeline or to quickly demo your ideas. In such cases, before working with Keras or spaCy, it might be useful to get a quick gauge of sentiment before actually setting up the heavy machinery. Setting up a quick Naive Bayes classifier can be handy in such a case. We've already come across this classifier in our chapter on clustering and classifying text documents (Chapter 10, *Clustering and Classifying Text*), so we are aware of how to set up our code to do this. Just a note that the following code is a template – we have not defined X or labels.

```
from sklearn.naive_bayes import GaussianNB
gnb = GaussianNB()
gnb.fit(X, labels)
```

We can then use our Naive Bayes machine for predicting a class. Here, the class would be positive or negative sentiment. The Python package TextBlob [1] works on the same principle when classifying or assigning sentiment. It also uses a Naive Bayes classifier under the hood. Again, here, the text variable is a placeholder variable and you are expected to define the text yourself if you wish to see the result of the example.

```
from textblob import TextBlob
analysis = TextBlob(text)
Pos_or_neg = analysis.sentiment.polarity
```

The `Pos_or_neg` variable now contains the sentiment of the text in terms of being positive or negative and is a float. This kind of API allows us to very easily work with the sentiment information, unlike in the case of Keras or scikit-learn where we must predict the class of a document and then assign this to the document. We might have noticed the same API ideology in spaCy as well – after running our document through the pipeline, it tags the documents with different attributes. In the previous chapter (`Chapter 14`, *Keras and spaCy for Deep Learning*), we saw the particular example where we added this attribute to the pipeline. Note that in this example, `nlp` is the trained model we saw in the *Deep Learning with spaCy* section, and we have to finish running that code example to see it work.

```
doc = nlp(text)
sentiment_value = doc.sentiment
```

We can see how TextBlob and spaCy have almost the same way of approaching sentiment analysis from an API point of view. While we can prototype with TextBlob, it is not recommended to be used in any production code, or even in any serious text analysis project - the naive Bayes algorithm is trained on movie reviews, and this context might not always yield the best values. When we use spaCy to assign sentiment scores, we are training our model ourselves, and on data, we want to train on. We can actually build the neural network ourselves, which gives us the opportunity to fine-tune our model for the context in an even finer manner.

A quick google search for `sentiment analysis python` gives us a plethora of results, and most of these involve analysis of tweets for sentiment and tend to use NLTK's built-in sentiment analyzer to perform the analysis. We will be avoiding the use of NLTK's classifier because it also uses a naive Bayes classifier to perform the classification, and unlike TextBlob, does not offer an API that gives documents attributes – like Keras or scikit-learn, it accepts a vector as input and assigns values based on this.

With that being said, it does not hurt to familiarize ourselves with the **Sentiment Analysis** API [2] that NLTK offers, even if only to better follow online tutorials on the matter. If anything, their `SentimentAnalyzer` [3] class offers some use, even if only as a way for us to design our analysis after constructing our own sentiment analyzer.

One useful method which is provided by NLTK is the `show_most_informative_features()` method, which shows us which features are informative (in this case, features are words). For example, if we are classifying spam mail, words such as `winner` or `casino` would be very telling features. The ratios we see in the right most column are the ratios of it being `ok  :  spam`.

```
winner = None ok : spam = 4.5 : 1.0
hello = True ok : spam = 4.5 : 1.0
hello = None spam : ok = 3.3 : 1.0
winner = True spam : ok = 3.3 : 1.0
casino = True spam : ok = 2.0 : 1.0
casino = None ok : spam = 1.5 : 1.0
```

The presence of the words, `winner` and `casino` increases the odds of the mail being marked as spam. But it is possible to extract the same information from a scikit-learn model, for example. Let's write a small method to do this and examine it:

```
def print_top10(vectorizer, clf, class_labels):
    """Prints features with the highest coefficient values, per class"""
# get feature names returns the features used in the classifier,
# and here the words in the vocabulary are the features
    feature_names = vectorizer.get_feature_names()
# We now loop over every class label
    for i, class_label in enumerate(class_labels):
# clf.coef_ contains the coefficients of each class; we extract the
# 10 highest coefficient values, which are a way to measure which
# features (words) are most influencing the probability of a document
# belonging to that class
        top10 = np.argsort(clf.coef_[i])[-10:]
# we finally print the particular class and the top 10 features (words)
# of that class
        print("%s: %s" % (class_label,
            " ".join(feature_names[j] for j in top10)))
```

Here, simply extract the coefficient values for each feature, and sort it before printing it. This particular example is for multi-class classifiers; if we are using a binary classifier, then `clf.coef_[0]` would also do the trick. It's possible with even a little bit of effort to replicate all NLTK functions with spaCy, scikit-learn, and Gensim. As for what kind of machine learning technique best works for sentiment analysis, the state-of-the-art at the moment remains deep learning techniques – in particular, a bidirectional LSTM is particularly good at understanding sentiment in text. We have already seen examples of how to construct such neural networks in the previous chapters. As for why these work the best, it is because this is a form of a recurrent neural network - this means that context is carried in further layers or nodes of the network. LSTM stands for **long short-term memory** – this is precisely the idea that is encapsulated, and memory is essential in understanding context. Bidirectional means that we have a context in either direction. Of course, with a field as rapidly evolving as deep learning, a new architecture might be able to outperform LSTMs soon.

Adding more information or depth to your neural network (such as using word embeddings or stacking up more layers) might further increase our performance, and so can increase the number of training epochs. Of course, like any other problem we intend to solve using deep learning, a lot of fine-tuning is required for high accuracies. For a little more information about why LSTMs work so well for sentiment analysis, the following posts can be useful:

1. LSTMs for sentiment analysis [4]
2. Understanding LSTMs [5]

With more advanced tools at our disposal, we can skip using NLTK to analyze sentiment. It still remains important to be able to mine the internet for useful textual data which we can use to analyze sentiment – we will be discussing two such sources, in particular, Reddit and Twitter.

Reddit for mining data

In the very first chapter we talked about mining the internet for data sources – now, we're going to actually explore how to do this. We've mentioned before how Reddit [6] can be an interesting data source because it includes *real* conversations with mostly grammatically correct sentences – it also has subreddits where we can focus on interest groups. Reddit also happens to have a well-organized API which we can use to mine for data, meaning that a lot of cleaning effort is saved!

To be able to gather data without a problem, one must first sign up for an account on Reddit. This link, `https://www.reddit.com/` will help you sign up, and some browsing of the website yourself will help build context for our experiment.

After getting comfortable with the nature of the website and the data we will be gathering, we should take a look at the API rules, which can be found on the wiki – `https://github.com/reddit-archive/reddit/wiki/API`. Two rules that particularly stand out here are that we can only send 60 requests per minute and that we don't lie about the user agent. A user agent is a software acting on behalf of a user, and in the case of accessing the internet, it is information about which browser or application is accessing the internet. These are not too difficult to adhere to, and if the preceding links have all been read, we can start looking at some code.

```
import requests
import json
```

```
# Add your username below
hdr = {'User-Agent': ':r/news.single.result:v1.0' +
       '(by /u/username)'}
url = 'https://www.reddit.com/r/news/.json'
req = requests.get(url, headers=hdr)
data = json.loads(req.text)
```

In the preceding lines of code, we are mining results from the subreddit r/news [7], which is subreddit largely discussing American and international news and politics. We could mine from any subreddit which we are comfortable with in terms of the content or material on that subreddit. Some things we should be careful about in the code are the user-agent and the Reddit username we have created our account with.

The best part about Reddit data is the format we are receiving our data in – JSON! There are many standard ways to load JSON in Python, and the JSON encoder and decoder [8] helps us do this easily.

The textual data stored in the JSON can be topic modeled, used to train Word2Vec for a particular context, or as we have been discussing – classified for sentiment. The r/news and r/politics subreddits are particularly interesting places to attempt this, as they tend to receive the most polarizing posts. I could personally recommend that you have a look at the following subreddits:

1. r/news
2. r/politics
3. r/The_Donald
4. r/AskReddit
5. r/todayilearned
6. r/worldnews
7. r/explainlikeimfive
8. r/StarWars
9. r/books

And if interested in the more eclectic material, or internet memes, you can look at these:

1. r/prequelmemes
2. r/dankmemes
3. r/memeeconomy

A few things to be careful about is to make sure not to anger the API by making more than 60 requests per minute – this would mean using the `time` [9] library to organize our requests. The fact that Reddit is already organized into many subreddits based on interest groups, hobbies, or subjects means that it is a rich source of textual information *with* appropriate context which we can adjust, something we cannot as easily do with other online data sources.

With all these limitations, we might be tempted to download historical data – in which case, this Reddit `thread` (meta!) has links to about 1.7 billion comments at about 250 GB, after being compressed.

One associated project written in Python which used Reddit for some interesting results is sense2vec [10], where the creators of spaCy used Reddit data to attempt a semantic analysis of Reddit. The best part is that we can find the entire code-base of the project here on Reddit: `https://github.com/explosion/sense2vec`, meaning we are free to play around with it. This means that we can use the sense2vec on other sources of data, or even modify what is considered as *semantics*. Since it is a web app, it is a neat way to look at how to display results online.

Twitter for mining data

While Reddit is a great way to analyze a more structured form of data, we often turn to social media to analyze text – there seem to be more *real-world* implications, and for social scientists, it can serve as a treasure trove of textual data. Indeed, sentiment analysis for tweets is a very popular project for budding data scientists because it allows one to try their hand at both data collection and data analyzing.

In all our examples throughout the book, we have dealt with datasets that are usually loaded from the packages we use, such as the 20 Newsgroup dataset (from scikit-learn), the Lee news corpus (from Gensim), or the IMDB dataset (Keras). While it is important to know how to work with well-documented datasets which are also used as benchmarks in research when working in real-world scenarios things are not so easy, and data has to be collected. We've already dealt with the importance of thoroughly cleaning our textual data, and with Twitter, we need to be doubly careful. We are now suddenly presented with smileys, emoticons, hashtags, abbreviations, slang, and so much more. Handling this means we have to make sure what kind of analysis we wish to perform – in some cases, we might want to use information in hashtags, and in some cases, we might not. It is the same case with smiley faces – for example, including them as a word might heavily influence the result of our sentiment analysis classifier – a ":-)" would likely correlate highly with positive sentiment and a ":-(" with negative sentiment.

If we would just want to classify tweets, a model with smileys would be more efficient – but if we also wish to understand what kind of semantic information might be present in tweets, it might be more prudent to remove anything which is not a word. In the end, how we wish to clean and process our tweet depends on our use case.

With that being said, there is already datasets present which allow us to leverage Twitter data for sentiment analysis. This `link` [11] gives us access to a dataset that has labeled data for sentiment analysis, which is, as we can guess, very important when we are training our data. The majority of this data comes from the University of Michigan Kaggle challenge, which we can read about here - `https://www.kaggle.com/c/si650winter11`. While another popular Twitter dataset is the Sentiment140 dataset, which can be found here – `http://help.sentiment140.com/for-students/`.

We can use these datasets to train our classifier as they are already labeled. As for using this classifier to actively label new tweets, we would need to use a Twitter API to get the data. The official twitter API for Python is **tweepy** [12], and it works well. Much like Reddit, we are required to make an account before we can use it. An account can be made here: `https://apps.twitter.com/`.

Once we have created this account, we would have received information about consumer tokens and access tokens. The authentication tutorial [13] on the tweepy documentation website provides even more information about how to deal with this.

Our first few lines of code to set up our API is as follows:

```
import tweepy

# Authentication and access using keys:
auth = tweepy.OAuthHandler(CONSUMER_KEY, CONSUMER_SECRET)
auth.set_access_token(ACCESS_TOKEN, ACCESS_SECRET)

# Return API with authentication:
api = tweepy.API(auth)
```

We then use the API object to do all of our extraction. Considering the current political climate, a proper twitter query is Donald Trump, and a popular user to analyze is @realDonaldTrump.

```
tweets = api.user_timeline(screen_name="realDonaldTrump", count=20)
For tweet in tweets:
    print(tweet.text)
```

And bam, with just about 7 lines of code, we have access to the 200 most recent Donald Trump tweets. Of course, this is just raw text, so we would still have to clean the text, and more importantly, store it in an alternate data structure that is more amenable to text analysis.

If we wish to, for example, search for Donald Trump on Twitter instead of looking at his personal handle, we would need to run this:

```
tweets = api.get_tweets(query = 'Donald Trump', count = 200)
```

It is worth having a look at tweepy's documentation [14] to see what else it is capable of, especially if we intend to use it extensively.

We've seen the availability of Twitter datasets that are already cleaned and/or labeled – as well as how to mine real-time Twitter data off the internet. Reddit also remains another important source to mine data off, and as social scientists increasingly look toward the internet to understand social behavior better, they must also know how to interact and mine this data. We have just seen how easy it is to do this!

ChatBots

Getting a machine to learn to speak like a human being has been a holy grail for computer scientists as well as linguists – of all the things which machines can mimic human behavior, holding a conversation has been a challenging ordeal. The quest to make such a machine which can chat with us humans (or a chatbot, if you will), has had many different approaches, and while none of them work perfectly, it is important to be aware of them - and pick and choose which kind will be the best for our purpose!

As for why *we* would want to build them – chatbots are increasingly used by businesses; both to help customers to answer basic questions, as well as for building more complex personal assistants. It is also becoming increasingly easier to build such chatbots, and using open source tools.

There are many motivations to study the art of conversation for machines, from both a research perspective and a more practical approach. An ideal artificial intelligence bot should be able to remember context from earlier in the conversation, build on this information when coming up with responses, and possibly have a personality of its own. Of course, it is tough to properly measure how well a conversation is held up, or how much of a personality a bot has. What we can measure is how well a response one can give based on a question or query, and this offers one way to judge how well a bot performs.

The famous **Turing Test** [15] argues that if we cannot differentiate between a chatbot and a human, it is a truly intelligent bot. Our purpose is to however not fool human beings (or debate whether this is truly a measure of intelligence!), but to rather build a bot which can answer human questions with some level of *intelligence*.

We will discuss possible methods to do this, and provide documentation, reading material, and code snippets. There is no one perfect chatbot, as this is a field which is still slowly evolving, and state of the art will take quite a while before it is achieved. It is highly likely that we ourselves have interacted with such chatbots – Siri [16] is arguably the most popular example, and Amazon's Alexa [17] is also a well-known personal digital assistant. Despite a large amount of money pumped into these applications, they are still with many flaws, and customers have complained about Siri's poor understanding of some English accents, as well as the lack of flexibility in coming up with responses.

This post [18] compares the major personal assistants and ranks them on a variety of measures – from smartest to funniest. It is also possible to now use Facebook Messenger to develop businesses using their chatbot API [19] as well. Like we mentioned before, building a chatbot has become increasingly easy.

Traditional chatbots worked largely with logical constructs which helped create responses, where the program would attempt to break the user input into different parts and match it with possible inputs while choosing an appropriate output. One of the first such constructs was **AIML (Artificial Intelligence Markup Language)** [20]. It served as an XML dialect for creating natural language agents. Based on certain *templates*, it would help choose an appropriate response to a query. One can argue that is not true intelligence, as we are directly limited by the number of examples we have, and we do not naturally generate language but merely choose the closest possible response to the question. For a long time though, this was the only way to construct chatbots - while it was helped with advancements in the field of natural language processing, such as better accuracies in POS identification or NER tagging, it was still largely just choosing out the best option.

In fact, in 2010, if one was to build a chatbot using Python, we would not be using machine learning techniques as much as just using a rule-based system with a little bit of fine-tuning. The vert first chatbot, **ELIZA** [21], was built in 1966! While for a *believable* system we might still use this, recent advances in deep learning have led us a lot closer to replicating conversations.

We have already discussed the exact technologies which are doing this – text generation using deep learning. In fact, this was our first exposure to deep learning with text! The sequence to sequence modeling has made our chatbots smarter, and they are not better able to understand the context and not simply choose the most appropriate response.

The first real taste of this is in the landmark paper by Oriol Vinyals and Quoc V. Lee from Google, *A Neural Conversational Model* [22]. In the paper, they describe a sequence to sequence model, where it would predict the next sentence, given the previous one. Trained on an IT Helpdesk dataset, this bot provided very, very *human* responses; arguably, they didn't always make sense, but it is certainly still very impressive. The following is an excerpt from the research paper, where a machine and human discuss VPN connectivity issues.

Conversation 1: VPN issues:

Describe your problem: *I am having issues accessing VPN*

Machine: *hi*

Human: *hello*

Machine: *Could you please let me know what are the operating systems you are using?*

Human: *I am using Linux*

Machine: *ok it was in the SSL VPN on which you stated it was broken*

Machine: *please check if you are logged in to corp network*

Machine: *what is the error that you are running, please*

Human: *I am seeing an error related to VPN*

Machine: *what is the error message that you are getting when connecting to VPN using network connect?*

Human: *connection refused or something like that*

Machine: *may I know the version of network connect you connect?*

Human: *I am not sure I know that*

Machine: *is the network connect prompting for any user certificate*

Machine:*?*

Human: *yes*

Machine: *are you at home or at work at the moment?*

Machine: *office?*

Human: *I am at home*

Machine: *try this*

Machine: *goto <URL> page and enter your name and password*

Human: *done*

Machine: *try logging in with <NAME> and check if its working fine now*

Human: *yes, now it works!*

Machine: *great*

Machine: *anything else that I can help*

Human: *no, that was very useful*

Machine: *you are other than <NAME> :)*

Machine: *have a nice night*

It is indeed quite remarkable to see what looks like a very plausible conversation between two humans! What is especially impressive here is that the questions asked do not have to be seen before in the training dataset – the context here is learned during the training process. There are no rules provided in the preceding example, and all the responses are learned purely with data. It is really worth one's time to explore all the conversations listed out in the paper. We will provide one more examples to illustrate the power of a generative model, again from the research paper:

Conversation 4: Philosophical Q&A:

Human: *what is the purpose of life?*

Machine: *to serve the greater good.*

Human: *what is the purpose of living?*

Machine: *to live forever.*

Human: *what is the purpose of existence?*

Machine: *to find out what happens when we get to the planet earth.*

Human: *where are you now?*

Machine: *I'm in the middle of nowhere.*

Human: *what is the purpose of dying?*

Machine: *to have a life.*

Human: *what is the purpose of being intelligent?*

Machine: *to find out what it is.*

Human: *what is the purpose of emotions?*

Machine: *I don't know.*

We can truly see the power of our generative model here, where it discusses the meaning of life, among other things. There are some drawbacks, though – it is difficult to train such a neural network to have a personality as well as be helpful, which means it is difficult to pass the Turing test, for example. As it is a generative model, it also means it might not give a coherent or relevant solution every time, and rather just responds with what could possibly be the best response. These neural nets are trained with question-answer pairs to understand what a *response* should look like.

Again, we would like to point out that we have already seen this in action before when we trained a text generating neural network – the only difference being in the kind of text we were generating. If we train our neural network on all the works of J.K. Rowling, we will likely have a text generator which will regale us with stories of magic, or at least attempt to. There have been neural networks that attempt to write code as well, so it is not surprising to imagine that a neural network which when trained on conversations would perform fairly well as a chatbot.

Of course, as promising this may look, it is not without its drawbacks – such a generational model on its own is likely not going to be a working chatbot and will still require a lot of supervision. We are also limited by our data; and if we are building this chatbot for a purpose where precision with the tasks to be performed is important, it might not be the best idea. In such a case, choosing templates might be our best bet!

It is also possible to use these generative models in tandem with a logic-based system. What if we would like to aimlessly chat with a bot without a particular task to be performed, or maybe model a friend's personality in a bot? In such a case, there is hardly a better alternative than a well-trained RNN. One example of a project to try out for users: it is possible to mail WhatsApp conversation logs to yourself. We can very easily extract our own texts or a friends texts, and train an RNN on this data. Imagine building a rule-based bot to mimic a person's typing style – it isn't the easiest thing to do!

We've seen then that there are two possible approaches to creating a chatbot - either have an information retrieval system where we choose the most appropriate response based on a set of rules or create a model that generates text based on the response. Both models have their pros and cons, which we have discussed before.

If we are going to use our intended chatbot in production, using an information retrieval-based system or using a standard chatbot API may be more practical. Two examples of such frameworks are **RASA-NLU** [23] and **ChatterBot** [24].

When using such frameworks, we aren't really building an intelligent system ourselves, but using one built by the API we chose. This isn't necessarily a bad thing, especially if it gets the job done. RASA-NLU, for example, uses JSON files to train its models. You can have a look at the sample data `here` [25].

By adding more entities and the intent, the model learns more context, and can better understand the questions we ask the bot. Interestingly, one of the back-end options which power the bot are spaCy and scikit-learn, two libraries we should be comfortable using with text by now!

Under the hood, they use Word2Vec to better understand the intent, spaCy to clean up text, and scikit-learn to build models. For more details into the inside workings of how RASA functions, their blog post [26] on Medium runs us through some of the concepts used, most of which we would be comfortable looking at at this point. One of the ideas of RASA involves being able to write own parts of your bot instead of it being like a traditional third-party bot API. The code is all in Python, so we can really get our hands dirty and play around with it. It also gives us ideas about how to possibly construct our own clever bot, if we would like to be a little more ambitious!

```
{
    "text": "show me a mexican place in the centre",
    "intent": "restaurant_search",
    "entities": [
        {
            "start": 31,
            "end": 37,
            "value": "centre",
            "entity": "location"
        },
        {
            "start": 10,
            "end": 17,
            "value": "mexican",
            "entity": "cuisine"
        }
```

```
        ]
    }
```

This is an example of a JSON entry to train a RASA model. Here, we give example text, the intent which we are attempting to learn, and the entities field describes the exact nature of the entity.

Of course, building a chatbot doesn't just require us to understand how natural language works – we should also be able to construct a functional front end that can actually talk to the user. This means being aware of how we pass information to an online app, and how to set up the pipeline. This is beyond the scope of the book, but luckily for us, using RASA Core to do this is quite straightforward and their documentation [27] does a good job at how to set up a conversational model. We have to be aware of both RASA NLU and RASA Core to be able to get the most out of things. With RASA Core we are able to set-up our domain and stories, and we use RASA NLU as our *mind*, which is to extract entities. Stories are the way we expect our bot to communicate with users, and we have to train our bot the same way we would train it in our domains. The tutorial [28] runs us through how to build a basic bot using RASA Core.

Another possible Python-based option to help build our bot would be ChatterBot [29]. The logic behind ChatterBot is quite similar to how most information-retrieval based chatbots would work – based on the input sentence of the user; it selects a known statement which is similar to the input statement. There are multiple such possible responses which can be selected, and we call each of the machines which create a response as a **logic adapter**. Once we have our collection of logic adapters, we can return the most likely response to the question. We can create and train our own adapters, both with respect to what kind of information to expect (the input), as well as what kind of responses should be created.

Training such a bot is also very straightforward for a quick test:

```
from chatterbot import ChatBot
bot = ChatBot('Stephen')
bot.train([
    'How are you?',
    'I am good.',
    'That is good to hear.',
    'Thank you',
    'You are welcome.',
])
```

Now this will obviously not make for a very mature or powerful bot but is rather an example of how easy it can train a chatbot with such an API.

We've seen examples of how we can use specific libraries aimed at building chatbots - but how would we start building our very own, at least slightly functional chatbot?

We've already discussed the two separate philosophies of doing this, one being simply generating text, and the other a more pipelined approach.

A pipelined approach would start by parsing and cleaning the user's input, and first identifying the *kind* of sentence the user inputted. Is it a question, or a statement? Does it relate to the bots *domain*, and if so, how? One way to attempt to find this is to build a classifier. We are well aware of how to build a classifier, and how well a neural network can perform in choosing between different classes of documents.

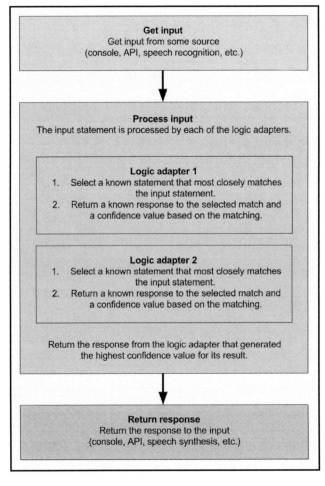

Fig 15.1 The process flow diagram as described on the Chatterbot Documentation website

Now that we have the *type* of user input, let's further analyze the sentence; break it up into different parts of speech, identify named entities, and appropriately construct a sentence as a response. We saw in the RASA example how we added information about Mexican being a kind of cuisine. Using Word2Vec, we can assemble a series of different cuisine options, and suggest alternatives to our user if there doesn't happen to be Mexican food around!

Now how do we choose among the best possible responses to give to the user? Again, a neural network can come in quite handy here, where we can attempt to predict the odds of a particular response based on the input – and choose our most appropriate response. Of course, this means that we still have to construct appropriate **question-response** pairs. Once we choose a question that is similar (for example, *find a place for lunch*, and *find a place for dinner* would be similar questions), we can change the appropriate proper noun in the response with the entity in the question and suggest it as a possible output.

If the kind of chatbot is not built to perform a targeted task in a domain, but just to attempt conversation, we can *generate* a response. This means that we are no longer interested in analyzing the user's input sentence for parts of speech or entities, and we have no use of choosing between sample responses – we want to organically generate a unique (or mostly unique) response to the question. In this case, we will just plug in an RNN and let it work its magic. We then simply spit this back at the user and continue the conversation in the hope that it is interesting. We've seen multiple examples of this when discussing Google's **Neural Conversational model**.

This GitHub repository [30] and blog post [31] discuss an approach not using any machine learning, but just a basic analysis of sentences, and replying with a bot that has access to only a basic set of responses. This kind of way of building a chatbot may not be as powerful, but getting used to the ideas behind the responses are important, and can help us in designing our own pipeline for building a chatbot, if we wish to construct one without the help of an external framework or API.

Of course, this is not a zero-sum game where we have to choose between choosing appropriate responses or generating text. Consider the following pipeline:

1. Accept user input
2. Classify input as a statement, question, or greeting – basically, identify intent
3. If it is a greeting, respond in kind – Hello!
4. If it is a question, look up similar questions in our dataset, perform rudimentary sentence analysis, and choose an appropriate response with the nouns or adjectives replaced

5. If it is a statement or attempt at conversation, let our generative model talk back to the user – at least until the user has a question

6. If the user is saying goodbye, politely wish them goodbye

This is a rough approach – we haven't mentioned how exactly we are going to find a similar document (though going through Chapter 11, *Similarity Queries and Summarization* is a good start!), or how we are going to do our multi-class classification. Based on the context we would want to plug in and play accordingly. At this point, we have all the tools needed to follow this pipeline for our chatbot!

This employs ideas of both generating texts as well as information retrieval. There are multiple machine learning models that can be employed in such a model – a classifier to decide the input type, a topic model for finding similar documents, Word2Vec for identifying intent or certain entities, and a neural network to generate text. All of these models need to be trained appropriately for the kind of task they are expected to perform, with what could be extremely different training data. For example, if we are creating a chatbot with the purpose of helping the user to find the perfect restaurant, we would train the final output to be a restaurant suggestion, and train the conversational bot with data from Reddit/r/food [32]! We can throw in some tweets in there as well for a bot which attempt to replicate *normal* food-related conversation the best possible way.

Of course, building an entire chatbot that can provide both interesting conversations and help find the closest Mexican restaurant is no trivial task – it is why we have entire teams at Google or Apple working on this. But in an attempt to build such a machine, we can learn a lot about the *kind* of things we can do with text along the way. There is no one best way to go about building such a bot and it depends highly on the context and problem we are trying to solve.

A chatbot employs some of the most advanced text analysis techniques – machine learning, computational linguistics, and also basic software engineering sense when deciding our pipeline and serves as an excellent way to exercise the skills picked up throughout this book. Since there is no one *best* chatbot creation method, we have instead in this chapter discussed popular methods currently available in the Python natural language processing world and laid them out in front of you, the reader – it is now up to you to pick up the tools and start building!

Summary

In this chapter, we discussed two important text analysis problems – sentiment analysis and building a chatbot. Sentiment analysis refers to the task of understanding sentiment in the text, and we have seen the various libraries, algorithms, and approaches to perform this task. A crucial part of performing such tasks is gathering data – we then saw how to download data from internet sources such as Twitter or Reddit. The final section of the chapter focused on how to build chatbots. We explored it from both a historical and theoretical point of view and explored Python libraries that help us easily build chatbots. This brings us to the end of the book – you would now be confident in analyzing text the way you see fit, with a variety of techniques, approaches, and settings. We focused on using the most efficient Python open source libraries, with a focus on Gensim, spaCy, Keras, and scikit-learn throughout the book, while still discussing the other Python text analysis libraries available. It is important to know which tool works best in which context, as well as which kind of pipelines and architectures we should explore for a problem. If you have followed the book carefully, with the code examples, Jupyter notebooks, and external links – you should now be able to confidently analyze your text.

References

[1] TextBlob:
http://textblob.readthedocs.io/en/dev/

[2] NLTK Sentiment Analysis:
http://www.nltk.org/howto/sentiment.html

[3] NLTK Sentiment Analyser class:
http://www.nltk.org/_modules/nltk/sentiment/sentiment_analyzer.html

[4] LSTMs for Sentiment Analysis:
http://deeplearning.net/tutorial/lstm.html

[5] Understanding LSTM Networks:
http://colah.github.io/posts/2015-08-Understanding-LSTMs/

[6] Reddit:
https://www.reddit.com/

[7] News subreddit:
https://www.reddit.com/r/news/

[8] JSON:
https://docs.python.org/3.6/library/json.html

[9] Time library:
https://docs.python.org/3.6/library/time.html

[10] sense2vec:
https://explosion.ai/demos/sense2vec

[11] Twitter datasets:
http://thinknook.com/twitter-sentiment-analysis-training-corpus-dataset-2012-09-22/

[12] Tweepy:
http://www.tweepy.org/

[13] Tweepy authentication tutorial:
http://tweepy.readthedocs.io/en/v3.5.0/auth_tutorial.html#auth-tutorial

[14] Tweepy documentation:
http://tweepy.readthedocs.io/en/v3.6.0/getting_started.html

[15] Turing Test:
https://en.wikipedia.org/wiki/Turing_test

[16] Siri:
https://en.wikipedia.org/wiki/Siri

[17] Alexa:
https://en.wikipedia.org/wiki/Amazon_Alexa

[18] Ranking Digital Assistants:
https://www.stonetemple.com/rating-the-smarts-of-the-digital-personal-assistants/

[19] FB messenger bots:
https://messenger.fb.com/

[20] AIML:
https://en.wikipedia.org/wiki/AIML

[21] ELIZA:
https://en.wikipedia.org/wiki/ELIZA

[22] A Neural Conversation Model:
https://arxiv.org/pdf/1506.05869v1.pdf

[23] RASA-NLU:
https://nlu.rasa.com/

[24] Chatterbot:
https://chatterbot.readthedocs.io/en/stable/

[25] RASA sample data:
https://github.com/RASAHQ/rasa_nlu/blob/master/data/examples/rasa/demo-rasa.
json

[26] Do it yourself NLP:
https://medium.com/rasa-blog/do-it-yourself-nlp-for-bot-developers-2e2da2817f3d

[27] RASA Core:
https://core.rasa.com/

[28] Basic bot building:
https://core.rasa.com/tutorial_basics.html

[29] Chatterbot:
https://chatterbot.readthedocs.io/en/stable/

[30] Brobot:
https://github.com/lizadaly/brobot/

[31] Chatbot fundamentals:
https://apps.worldwritable.com/tutorials/chatbot/

[32] reddit food:
https://www.reddit.com/r/food/

Other Books You May Enjoy

If you enjoyed this book, you may be interested in these other books by Packt:

Natural Language Processing with TensorFlow
Thushan Ganegedara

ISBN: 978-1-78847-831-1

- Core concepts of NLP and various approaches to natural language processing
- How to solve NLP tasks by applying TensorFlow functions to create neural networks
- Strategies to process large amounts of data into word representations that can be used by deep learning applications
- Techniques for performing sentence classification and language generation using CNNs and RNNs
- About employing state-of-the art advanced RNNs, like long short-term memory, to solve complex text generation tasks
- How to write automatic translation programs and implement an actual neural machine translator from scratch
- The trends and innovations that are paving the future in NLP

Python Machine Learning, Second Edition

Sebastian Raschka, Vahid Mirjalili

ISBN: 978-1-78712-593-3

- Understand the key frameworks in data science, machine learning, and deep learning
- Harness the power of the latest Python open source libraries in machine learning
- Explore machine learning techniques using challenging real-world data
- Master deep neural network implementation using the TensorFlow library
- Learn the mechanics of classification algorithms to implement the best tool for the job
- Predict continuous target outcomes using regression analysis
- Uncover hidden patterns and structures in data with clustering
- Delve deeper into textual and social media data using sentiment analysis

Leave a review - let other readers know what you think

Please share your thoughts on this book with others by leaving a review on the site that you bought it from. If you purchased the book from Amazon, please leave us an honest review on this book's Amazon page. This is vital so that other potential readers can see and use your unbiased opinion to make purchasing decisions, we can understand what our customers think about our products, and our authors can see your feedback on the title that they have worked with Packt to create. It will only take a few minutes of your time, but is valuable to other potential customers, our authors, and Packt. Thank you!

Index

Printed in Great Britain
by Amazon